How to
WRITE A
BOOK
PROPOSAL

4TH EDITION

How to
WRITE A
BOOK
PROPOSAL

4TH EDITION

WD

WRITER'S DIGEST BOOKS

WritersDigest**.com**
Cincinnati, Ohio

MICHAEL LARSEN, AAR

For more resources for writers, visit www.writersdigest.com/books.

To receive a free weekly e-mail newsletter delivering tips and updates about writing and about Writer's Digest products, register directly at WritersDigest.com/getnewsletter

15 14 13 12 11 5 4 3 2 1

Distributed in Canada by Fraser Direct
100 Armstrong Avenue
Georgetown, Ontario, Canada L7G 5S4
Tel: (905) 877-4411

Distributed in the U.K. and Europe by F+W Media International
Brunel House, Newton Abbot, Devon, TQ12 4PU, England
Tel: (+44) 1626-323200, Fax: (+44) 1626-323319
E-mail: postmaster@davidandcharles.co.uk

Distributed in Australia by Capricorn Link
P.O. Box 704, Windsor, NSW 2756 Australia
Tel: (02) 4577-3555

Edited by: Melissa Wuske
Designed by: Claudean Wheeler
Production coordinated by: Debbie Thomas

ACKNOWLEDGMENTS
FOR THE FOURTH EDITION

To all the writers, editors, and publishing professionals from which I've learned, my thanks for helping to provide the knowledge between these covers.

My great, lasting thanks go to

- our clients, from whom we continue to learn.
- Claire Kavanaugh, for her great eye.
- Stephanie Chandler, for her help and knowledge about marketing and technology.
- Jacob Morgan, for his advice about online marketing.
- David Marshall, for his knowledge of technology.
- my editor, Melissa Wuske, for her help and encouragement.
- the rest of the staff at *Writer's Digest* who worked on the book.
- Kelly Nickell, Jane Friedman, and Chuck Sambuchino—extra thanks for your support.
- Adele Horwitz and Antonia Anderson, for their comments on the manuscript.
- Kathryn Wayne, for helping with the appendix on competitive books.
- Kathryn's husband, Gary Nelson, for all he did to help a house become a home.
- agents Rita Rosenkranz, who read the manuscript, and Robert Shepard, who read part of it, despite moving to Los Angeles—extra, tremendous thanks for your time and insights.
- our authors for letting me add their work for this addition: Ted Allrich, Kathleen Archambeau, Kirk Boyd, Jane Flaherty, Catherine Friend, the late Shivani Goodman, Allan Hamilton, Lawrence Knowles, Jay Conrad Levinson, Adam Najberg, David Perry, Kevin Reifler, Peter Stark, and Nick Vacca.
- Laurie McLean, our agenting colleague, for her passion, intelligence, creativity, marketing savvy, and joie de vivre.
- Denny and Diana Nolan, for their friendship and hospitality.

- my brother Ray, a tower of strength, and his wife, Mary Ann, for their help in keeping a roof over the agency.
- Elizabeth, for all that she is and does.

To one and all, my gratitude!

TABLE OF CONTENTS

PART VII: ENSURING YOUR PROPOSAL IS READY TO SUBMIT

PART VIII: FINDING A HAPPY HOME FOR YOUR BOOK

PART IX: PLOTTING YOUR FUTURE

APPENDICES

PART I:
WHY THE BOOK? WHY YOU?

CHAPTER 1

Why Now Is the Best Time Ever to Write Books:
Twenty Reasons for You to Be a Writer

Now is the most amazing time ever to be alive and the best time ever to be a writer. If luck is ability meeting opportunity, you are one of the luckiest writers who ever lived. Here's why you should commit your life to being a writer:

1. You are the most important person in the publishing process because you make it possible. If it weren't for writers, agents and publishers would have to do something else for a living.

2. You have more options for getting your books published, some of which—e-books, print-on-demand, podcasting, blogs, and websites—cost little or nothing.

3. You can publish or distribute your work as an e-book, podcast, or print-on-demand book for free or a small cost. If your book costs you nothing to write and publish, and only one person buys it, it's making money.

4. There are more ways to profit from your books, including spin-off products, speaking, and subsidiary rights. Books in English, the international language of culture and commerce, and in translation are selling in more countries. E-book sales are an additional revenue stream, and with links to content on the Web that already exists or that you or your

publisher create, they explode the potential for enriching how readers experience your book.

5. You have more models—books and authors—to help guide your writing and your career. You don't have to figure out how to write a how-to book or build a career; you can use your favorite books and authors as models.

6. There are more subjects for you to write about.

7. You can sell your book by writing a proposal. A writer's first novel usually must be completed before she can sell it, but 90 percent of nonfiction is sold with proposals. These proposals usually contain just one chapter or 10 percent of the manuscript, information about the book, an outline, and how you'll promote the book and yourself.

8. Finding an agent is easier. If you have a salable book, it's easy to acquire an agent—and new agencies are springing up all the time.

9. Selling your book yourself is easier. Most writers sell their books themselves—without the help of agents. Chapter thirty-seven tells you how.

10. If you come up with an idea for a series of books you are passionate about writing and promoting, you can create a career out of it. You can practice "niche craft" and build your career book by book.

MASTER OF NICHE CRAFT

Jay Conrad Levinson self-published a book called *Earning Money Without a Job: The Economics of Freedom.* I read a story about Jay in the *San Francisco Chronicle*, called him, and sold the book to Henry Holt. Then Jay wanted to write a book called *Secrets for Making Big Profits From Your Small Business.* But when I read his proposal, I saw the phrase *guerrilla marketing*, and I knew that had to be the title. *Guerrilla Marketing* is now in its fourth edition and has spawned more than forty spin-off books in what has become a virtually endless series. Jay is a master at practicing niche craft.

---

11. You have more ways to test-market your books. You can maximize the value of your book before you sell it by test-marketing it. Chapter twenty-one tells you how.

12. Writing is a forgiving art. You can write as many drafts as you need—only the last one counts. As long as you have knowledgeable readers, and you learn from mistakes, writing salable books is inevitable.

13. You can be an author without being a writer. The two assets authors have are a body of salable information and the ability to promote their work. They can work with an editor or collaborator or hire a ghostwriter.

14. You can advance a cause or belief. A book can change hearts, minds, and the world.

15. You have access to an amazing array of resources—and some of them are free. Finding the books, magazines, events, classes, organizations, publishing professionals, online resources, information, and communities you need is easier and faster than ever.

16. You will do a better job writing and promoting with each book you write. Think of your career as a lifetime endeavor with ten or twenty books in it, each better and more profitable than the previous one.

17. Becoming a successful author is easier than becoming a successful actor, artist, dancer, composer, or musician. Writers have an easier, faster path to success than other kinds of artists. Only 1 percent of actors succeed; *Writer's Digest* reports that 6 percent of writers make a living writing.

18. You don't have to quit your day job. You can keep writing until you're making the income you need to devote your life to your calling.

19. Today's information technology is the greatest tool for writers since the printing press. Technology will help you with every aspect of being a writer.

20. You get to spend your life browsing in bookstores and reading books, and they're tax deductible!

    Apart from these reasons are the pleasures of

    - finding the right words to express your ideas.
    - finishing your books.
    - finding an agent and publisher you love.

- receiving checks.
- seeing your name in print.
- getting good reviews.
- hearing from readers who love your work.
- having a growing community of fans around the world who buy whatever you create.
- watching your craft and career develop and bring you greater recognition and rewards.
- living the life you were born to live.
- leaving a legacy of which you'll be proud.

The goal of this book is to help you get your book published as well and as quickly as you can. The next chapter will give you options for getting the most out of this book in the least amount of time.

CHAPTER 2

McBook: The Fastest, Easiest Way to Use This Book

Time is your most precious asset, and I don't want to waste it. Far more valuable than the money you spent buying this book—for which I am very grateful—will be the time you spend using it. The book has three levels of information:

- how-to information
- key points
- everything else that will entertain or enlighten you

Here are three ways to use this book:

- The fastest, easiest way: Simply focus on the how-to info as you write your proposal.
- Read the key points first and then use the how-to info later as you write your proposal.
- The best way: Read it before writing your proposal and then use the how-to info as you write your proposal.

You can vary the way you read the book, depending on your degree of interest in what you're reading, or you can experiment to find the way the book will work best for you. Agents and editors vary in what they like to see in a proposal, but this book will enable you to give anyone what she needs. If you're writing a proposal for a specific publisher, you can zero in on what the house's website tells you it needs and then find those sections in this book to use as a guide.

You're welcome to write or call me with questions. For a quarter of a century, I have been sustained in part by letters from writers who sold their books because of this book. I hope you will become one of those writers, and I look forward to hearing about your success.

Onward!

CHAPTER 3

What's In It for You?
Reasons to Use This Book

Based on thirty-eight years of experience as an agent, I guarantee this book is worth your time. If you disagree, send the receipt, and I'll refund your money and postage.

- I've shortened chapters to make the book a faster read.

- The book shows you how to make your proposal irresistible from word one, as fast and in as few words as possible.

- The book helps you use technology to write and sell your proposal and to promote your book.

- This books helps you start taking advantage of the tremendous opportunities awaiting you.

- This book provides an up-to-date model for you to follow to become a successful author.

- The book helps you set literary and financial goals that will determine
  - what you write.
  - how you write.
  - how you build your platform.

- your promotion plan.
- the editor, publisher, and deal you get for your book.

- The book has new sample proposals and parts of proposals.

- I've updated the book so you can meet the evolving challenges of writing, selling, and promoting your books. I will continue to update the book at www.larsenpomada.com. If you're an agent or writer who would like to post a proposal or part of one, please e-mail it to me at larsenpoma@aol.com.

- To try to make the book enjoyable to read, I use humor to help the medicine go down.

Following your passion is the subject of the next chapter.

CHAPTER 4

Pushing Your Hot Buttons: Choosing the Right Book for You to Write

An *In the Bleachers* cartoon by Steve Moore shows a jockey sitting at the starting gate, thinking to himself: *Why am I dressed like this? Who are all these people? What am I doing on a horse? Where am I?* The caption says: *Seconds before the start of the race, Filipe suffers a mental lapse commonly known among jockeys as "rider's block."*

Jockeys may have a problem, but writers shouldn't. The world is awash with ideas. There are more subjects to write about and more kinds of books to write than ever: how-tos; memoirs; biographies; histories; reference books; anthologies; exposés; humor, gift, and illustrated books; trivia, game, and puzzle books; books that tie into movies and events; the story of an idea, company, industry, process, product, or service; or a vision of the future.

THIRTEEN WAYS TO KNOW YOU HAVE THE RIGHT IDEA FOR YOUR BOOK

When Michael Pietsch at Little, Brown and Company first read part of David Foster Wallace's novel *Infinite Jest*, he said, "I want to do this book more than I want to breathe." How much do you want to do your book?

Your challenge: finding the best book for you to write because the idea pushes as many of the following hot buttons for you as it can.

1. Your passion for writing it
2. Its potential for generating fame and fortune
3. The timing for it
4. Its originality
5. Your credentials or years of experience in your field
6. Your track record
7. Your ability to write about it
8. Your platform
9. Your ability to test-market it
10. Your ability to promote it
11. Its potential to be a series
12. The size of the markets for it
13. The communities you have online and off to help you

Finding the right focus for your book—neither too broad nor too narrow—is essential. As one wag put it, "Don't start vast projects with half-vast ideas."

If there is a book you really want to read but it hasn't been written yet, then you must write it."

—TONI MORRISON

Nobel Prize–winning author Toni Morrison suggests one criterion for deciding to write a book: Would you buy it?

Here's a scenario for you: Want a million bucks to write a book? You can pick the subject later. Does this sound like a fantasy? It happened to Bob Woodward, coauthor of *All the President's Men*. The catch: It happened after his fourth consecutive book hit the top of the best-seller list. Offering him the money without a subject was a safe bet. Woodward went on to have twelve number-one bestsellers and is still at it.

You can't count on enjoying the spectacular career that Bob Woodward has earned, but writing a successful book can transform your life. If you have an idea for a book that will interest enough people, and if you can prove that you can research, organize, and write a book—and then promote it—you can get published.

But this requires a shift in your thinking from being a writer to being what author Sam Horn calls an *authorpreneur*—a new model for becoming a successful author discussed in chapter forty-one. You must make your proposal irresistible before you submit it. Its fate is sealed with the e-mail or envelope in which you submit it.

What to do when lightning strikes is the subject of the next chapter.

CHAPTER 5

Getting Off the Pin:
The First Three Steps to Take With Your Idea

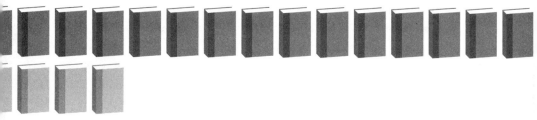

A *New Yorker* cartoon by Mick Stevens shows Adam and Eve sitting together under a tree in Eden, and Adam says, "I can't help thinking that there's a book in this." Someone once said, "Getting an idea should be like sitting on a pin; it should make you jump up and do something." The moment you can't help thinking there's a book in your idea, take the following three steps.

1. Find your models. For any kind of book you want to write, models abound. Make yourself an expert on your subject by reading the most important competing books and browsing through the others. Read between the lines to see what they *don't* do so you can make your book different and better.

Competing books will be models for yours. They will enable you to anticipate editors' and readers' expectations for books like yours. They will help you visualize your book by establishing criteria for style, tone, features, benefits, illustrations, back matter, and the length of your book and chapters. They can also serve as models and help sell *your* book by proving there's a market for such books. Try to find one or two successful books you can use as a model for your book and can mention in your book hook. A publisher of competing or complementary books may buy yours.

2. Test-market the idea on your communities. Practice convincing writers, booksellers, experts, and authors of books on the subject that there will be enough interest in the book two years from now, and after, to justify writing it. Their feedback may help you fine-tune your idea.

3. Write your proposal ASAP without sacrificing quality. Ideas are in the air because the raw material for them is in the media sphere that envelops us. Assume others have your idea.

When a subject is hot, publishers are hit with a deluge of proposals about it. They also mine their backlists for books on the subject. If your book is about a breaking news story or a hot subject, you must write your proposal quickly, and sell it before another writer beats you to it or before interest in the subject wanes.

However, if your topic isn't time sensitive, consider writing your manuscript before you write your proposal. Chapter twenty-nine lists the advantages of writing your manuscript first. Information about how to create an irresistible proposal follows that.

HOT TIP

If you come up with an idea for a book that has never been done, it means one of two things:

- You've created a great opportunity.

- There's a reason it's never been done before.

Taking the three steps explored in this chapter will enable you to figure out which one it is.

PART II:
STARTING YOUR
OVERVIEW RIGHT

CHAPTER 6

Getting Paid to Write Your Book:
The Parts of an Irresistible Proposal

Instant gratification takes too long.

—Carrie Fisher

Some writers find it easier to write the book than the proposal. For others, writing the proposal is the most creative part of doing a book. Why? Because you have the freedom to plan the book in the way that excites you most without

- bearing the responsibility for writing it.
- changing your vision to suit your publisher's needs.
- being pressured by the deadline that comes with a contract and the advance your publisher wants to earn back ASAP.

There are three rules for writing the novel. Unfortunately, no one knows what they are.

—W. Somerset Maugham

There are many ways to write a proposal, just as there many ways to write a book. My approach has evolved over the years, and the transformation of publishing continues to change it.

How to Write a Book Proposal

Most proposals range from thirty-five to fifty pages. A proposal has three parts in a logical sequence:

- overview
- outline
- sample chapter

Each part has to impress agents and editors enough to convince them to keep reading.

THE OVERVIEW

Your overview must prove that you have a marketable, practical idea and that you are the right person to write about it and promote it. The overview gives you the chance to provide as much ammunition about you and your book as you can muster. It should contain these elements:

- The opening hook that will most excite editors about your subject
- The book hook:
    - the title and selling handle (up to fifteen words of selling copy about the book)
    - the books or authors you're using as models for your book
    - the suggested (or actual) length of your manuscript and when you will deliver it
    - the book's benefits (optional)
    - special features (optional)
    - information about a self-published edition (optional)

- (Optional) A foreword by a well-known authority: If getting a foreword isn't possible, include the following sentence: *The author will contact [names of potential authorities and, if needed, their credentials] for a foreword and cover quotes.*
- Markets: The types of readers and retailers, organizations, or institutions who'll be interested in your book. The size of each group and other information to show you know your audience and how to write a book for those readers. Other possible markets: schools, businesses, and subsidiary-rights markets such as film and foreign publishers.

ission statement: One first-person paragraph about your
itment to write and promote your book.

atform: A list of whatever will impress editors about your
ty to your readers. Online, this includes the number of unique
visitors or subscribers to your blog or website, your tangible influence
on social networks, and online articles you've published.

Offline, your platform may include the number of articles you've had
published in print media as well as the number of talks you give each
year, the number of people you give them to, where you give them, and
your media exposure. Editors may not expect authors of quote books to
have a platform; business authors must. For certain kinds of books, an
author's platform is important for big and medium-sized houses.

- Promotion: A plan (listed in descending order of impressiveness)
describing what you will do to promote your book, online and off, during its crucial one-to-three-month launch window and after. Publishers won't expect big plans from memoirists, and the smaller the house
you'll be happy with, the less important your platform and plan.

- Competing books: A list of the ten or so strongest competitors for your
book—not just bestsellers. In addition to basic info about each book (title,
author, publisher, year of publication, page count, format, price, ISBN),
include two phrases—each starting with a verb—about each competitor's
strengths and weaknesses. List the competitors in order of importance.

- Complementary books: A short list of books on the subject that won't
compete with yours but will prove that the subject is marketable.

- About the author: Up to a page about yourself, giving information that
isn't in your platform. Begin with the most important information.

THE OUTLINE

Your outline should have one paragraph of description about every chapter.
For an informational book, you could also use a bulleted list of the information you will provide.

A SAMPLE CHAPTER

You must write one or more chapters that will most excite editors by proving you will fulfill the promise to readers and make your book enjoyable to read. Include about 10 percent of the book, or twenty-five pages—enough to give editors a solid slice of the content.

WHERE AND HOW TO START YOUR PROPOSAL

This list I've just given you is the *what*, not the *how*. It tells you what you need for your proposal, not how to write it. If you could just use the list to write your proposal, the book would end here, and my job as author and agent would be a lot easier!

This book presents the parts of a proposal in a logical order. But you may write your proposal in any order you wish. If you want to start with the easiest parts, try your bio, your mission statement, your platform, the markets for your book, the back matter, and special features. As Henry Ford said, "Nothing is particularly hard if you divide it into small jobs."

In *The Complete Idiot's Guide to Getting Published*, Association of Authors' Representatives (AAR) member Sheree Bykofsky and Jennifer Basye Sander suggest that you type the title page first and put it on your wall to inspire you.

Consider focusing on just one hook, one part of the overview, or one chapter outline at a time, and devote the rest of your time to getting ready to write the next part of your proposal. Make writing your proposal and your book as easy and enjoyable as you can while being rigorous about keeping to a timeline for completing it.

In *Editors on Editing*, Jane von Mehren says, "The best proposals are those that elicit the fewest questions. Why? Because you've anticipated and answered them all."

Let's go step by step through the process of creating a proposal that will get you the editor, publisher, and deal you want. We'll start with your first challenge: creating an enticing first page.

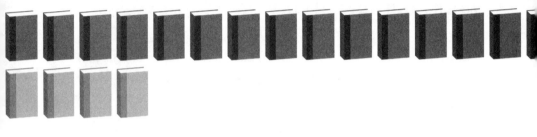

CHAPTER 7

Selling the Sizzle:
Your Opening and Hook

THE GOLDEN RULE FOR CREATING YOUR OPENING HOOK

Excite editors about your subject.

Sell the sizzle, not the steak.

—A MARKETING MAXIM

Your overview is the sizzle in your proposal. If it doesn't sell you and your book, agents and editors won't check the bones (the outline of your book) or try the steak (your sample chapter). Ask yourself: "What will excite editors who have seen thousands of proposals?" You're not selling just your book, you're selling yourself. So, like your proposal, every word must help answer one of these two questions in as few words as possible:

- Why this book?
- Why you?

The opening of your proposal must convince readers your book will have what it takes to succeed in an increasingly competitive marketplace. Your overview sets the standard for the tone, style, and quality of what follows. Your proposal must convince an editor of the following:

- You have a salable idea.
- You can write it.
- You can promote it.

Whether you are selling a proposal with a sample chapter, a complete manuscript, or a self-published or previously published book, you need an overview. The overview provides editors with the information they need to write the proposal they use to help justify buying a book at their weekly editorial board meeting.

YOUR OPENING HOOK

Begin halfway down the page and center the word *Overview*. Then, as briefly as you can, hook editors to your subject with a quote, an event, an idea, a joke, a cartoon, or a statistic—the single most exciting thing you can write about the subject that makes your book sound new, needed, and timely. A hook can also be a compelling anecdote that supports a statistic.

For example, if you are writing a how-to book, consider starting with an anecdote about how someone used your technique to solve a problem or improve his life. Then provide a round, accurate figure for how many people need your book.

For a business how-to book, the story might be about how the Wide-Open-Spaces Company in Wherever, Texas, used your technique and increased its sales by 100 percent in six months. Your next sentence can mention how many other companies can benefit from the same approach. You must convince editors that your subject warrants a book. Try to make your hook grab readers the way the lead paragraph in a magazine story does. If you're writing a narrative book that reads like a novel and has a dynamite opening, start with the first paragraph.

United Press International tells its journalists if they hook readers with the first six words, readers will read the first paragraph. If they read the first paragraph, they will read the first three paragraphs, and if they read the first three paragraphs, they'll finish the story.

Editors vote with their eyes. Everything you write must make them vote to keep reading.

EXAMPLE: *Climbing the Corporate Ladder in High Heels*

Kathleen Archambeau, a speaker, executive, and consultant, nailed the market for the book in her first sentence. She then used other stats and compelling copy to help sell her subject with admirable brevity. Here's her hook:

> There are 63 million working women in America. But only one percent are in the CEO and Chairman ranks in the Fortune 500, and only five percent are top earners. While women comprise nearly 50 percent of the workforce, they perform more than 90 percent of the household and childcare duties.
>
> More than 40 percent of corporate professionals over forty never marry or have children. So they ask themselves: "Has my life become all work and no play? Does having a successful career mean losing out on a happy life?" They *can* have it all, but not all at once.

HOT TIP

People like to read about other people. That's why anecdotes are effective ways to get your points across. Use fictional techniques to make anecdotes read like short stories that pack a wallop by being as humorous, dramatic, inspirational, or startling as possible.

Anecdotes humanize a book by presenting a slice of life readers can relate to. They also make for more enjoyable, memorable reading than abstract ideas. As Jack Canfield says, "Facts tell, stories sell."

EXAMPLE: *The Everyday Advocate:*
How to Stand Up for Your Autistic Child

In *The Everyday Advocate*, Areva Martin created a compelling blend of memoir and advice. Being a frequent guest on *Dr. Phil* helped as an autism expert sell her book, as did the quote Dr. Phil McGraw, also a best-selling author, provided. He hailed the book as *the* book on the subject. No wonder Laney Becker at the Markson Thoma Literary Agency was able to convince New American Library to snap the book up.

OVERVIEW

> I'm no stranger to hardship. You don't go from being a young girl, raised by a disabled grandmother and a night-shift janitor, to being a Harvard law honors graduate who runs a successful law firm in LA, without a lot of sweat and

tears. After coming so far, I assumed the toughest challenges were behind me; I thought I could handle anything. Then I had an autistic child.

Today, one out of every 150 children born in the United States has autism. That's more than a 700 percent increase in the number of children diagnosed in the last twenty years. The Center for Disease Control has declared autism a national health crisis—yet there is no central source of information for this rapidly growing epidemic.

While I searched for ways to help my son, Marty, most of the information I found was conflicting and difficult to understand. Misinformation, ignorance and intolerance abound, even among the caregivers and experts we've all learned to trust. As Marty grew older, I faced new, more complicated battles, including getting him the education and health care services he needed. Even with my legal expertise, learning to be an advocate for my own son was, and remains, the biggest challenge I've ever faced. I found myself thinking: If it's this hard for me, it's got to be impossible for anyone without the benefit of my education, training and legal experience.

In *The Everyday Advocate: How to Stand Up for Your Autistic Child*, I share my hard-won knowledge not only with other parents—but with relatives, caregivers and professionals—making the book a valuable read for everyone who loves or cares for children with autism.

Areva's hook is longer than what's advisable for most books, but her book warranted a more detailed hook. A chapter outline from her book is in chapter twenty-five.

EXAMPLE: *The Compassionate Carnivore: Or, How to Keep Animals Happy, Save Old MacDonald's Farm, Reduce Your Hoofprint, and Still Eat Meat*

Here's how Catherine Friend's authoritative, engaging voice helped sell her book.

Meat is the flesh of a dead animal.

While the people who can't deal with this fact bury their heads in the sand, an ever-growing group of folks is paying attention. They can pronounce *sustainability*. They want to consider humane ways to raise animals. They want to do the right thing. They buy organic vegetables, drink fair-trade coffee, and consider the impact of their purchases on the planet. They are—and here's the key—connecting their purchases to a problem.

These conscious consumers had help making these connections. When environmentalists connected the air, water, and global-warming problems to people's actions, people began to say, "What I do really does make a difference." They began to care and to change.

But when it comes to meat, the connection was severed decades ago when people moved to cities and began eating Swanson's Chicken Pot Pies and Oscar Meyer Hot Dogs. We forgot that a chicken was killed to make the pot pie, that a steer and hog were killed to make the hot dog. A huge gap appeared between us and our meat.

HOT TIPS

- Avoid the words *I*, *we*, *us*, and *our* unless the book is about you. Editors are wary of authors who overuse the word *I* unless it's relevant to the book. Unless you or your experience are part of the book, write about the subject, not yourself. AAR member Robert Shepard thinks it's okay to use the *I* word when discussing oneself as long as it's not overused. I agree, but the surest way to avoid using it too much is not to use it.

- Avoid the words *you* and *your* in your introduction and outline. These first two parts of the proposal are about the book—you are writing these first two parts for the editor, not for the book buyer. If you feel the need to address readers directly, as this sentence does, do it in your sample chapter.

- Use round, accurate numbers in your hook. If a number isn't round, qualify it by writing *nearly*, *almost*, or *more than* (not *over*).

EXAMPLE: *Stooples: Office Tools for Hopeless Fools*

Being desk-bound galley slaves, editors could relate to *Stooples*, and the authors (Kevin Reifler, Adam Najberg, and Nick Vacca) made it easy for them to get a sense of the book's potential.

> American businesses receive millions of catalogs a year from Staples, Office Max, Office Depot and others. They support an office supply market that spends $325 billion a year and grows by 4 percent a year. The leader of the pack is Staples, a juggernaut with more than 500 stores in nine countries and annual sales of more than $3 billion.
>
> But what if a Staples catalogue went off the deep end? What if instead of pens, pencils and computers, it offered Office Massacre Defense Systems, Rubick's Cubicles, Snivel Slacks, Disappointing Revenue Ritalin and Accent Decoders.

What if every product was highlighted by a humorous photo that made good-natured fun of the ineptitude and wackiness of businesses large and small?

Then you'd have *Stooples: Office Supplies for the Rest of Us* by Kevin Reifler, Adam Najberg and Nick Vacca.

Note the final title in the heading.

PUTTING A NUMBER TO IT

Let's say you want to write a book about a new way to stop drinking. Like average readers, editors are aware of the problem in a general way. You need to provide statistics about how many people drink too much and the toll it takes in lives, health costs, and lost work time to convince editors the subject merits another book.

Using numbers—dates, geography, money, size, the number of people, the growth of a trend—will

- give credibility to your facts and to you as an authority on the subject
- put the subject into context for editors
- prove there will be wide national interest in the subject when your book comes out two years from now.

You'll use some of this information again in the section on markets.

EXAMPLE: *9 Steps for Reversing or Preventing Cancer and Other Diseases: Learn to Heal From Within*

An anecdote about a woman who used Shivani Goodman's advice to cure herself preceded this subject hook.

> One in every four deaths in America is from cancer, and half of all Americans, *more than 92 million* people, will get cancer. *Forty percent of those diagnosed with cancer this year will not be alive in five years.* More children under age fifteen die from cancer than any other disease. And the death rate continues to rise as cancer replaces heart disease as the number one killer of adults. In addition, millions are suffering from other diseases that limit or interrupt the quality of life.
>
> The National Cancer Institute estimates that cancer costs Americans $60 billion a year. So not only are the treatments ineffective, but they threaten the financial security of America's families.

EXAMPLE: *Comfort Zone Investing: Build Wealth and Sleep Well at Night*

Ted Allrich wrote *The On-Line Investor*, the first book on the subject, which was discussed in the last edition of this book. Here is the opening hook for Ted's second book, *Comfort Zone Investing*:

> The best time to invest is when you have money.
> —Sir John Templeton, founder, Templeton Funds

> With that great insight, people know when to invest. But how and where are the better questions. People fear that if they invest, especially in stocks and bonds, there's a chance all or most of their money will disappear. *Comfort Zone Investing* will help readers overcome anxieties through understanding and knowledge and guide them to investments in their comfort zones.
>
> Most people don't know enough about investing. Too often, individual investors get a hot tip from a friend or hear about a stock from a talking head on TV. Without any or very little research, or an understanding of the stock market, they buy a stock and hope for the best. But there is no hope in the stock market.

YOUR BOOK HOOK

After you hook editors to your subject, the next challenge is to ensnare them with the essential information about your book:

- The title and the selling handle for your book. Even though the full title is on the title page of your proposal, repeat it here and then use a short version of it.

- The books or authors serving as models for your book.

- The expected (or actual) word count of your manuscript (and the number of illustrations, if you use them) and how many months after receiving your advance you will deliver your manuscript.

- An optional list of your book's major benefits (discussed in chapter ten).

- An optional list of your book's special features: anecdotes, humor, checklists, sidebars, exercises, summaries, boxed copy, icons, and anything else you will do to give you book visual appeal, links to Web content, back matter, and anything else you will do to make your book visually appealing and useful.

- (Optional) If you've self-published your book, tell editors whatever will help sell it. Include

  - sales figures and information about subsidiary-rights sales.
  - a list of changes, if any, you want to make in the new edition.
  - how many manuscript pages of new material you will add, if any.
  - the number of months after signing you will deliver the manuscript.

Include reviews and articles about the book with key passages underlined.

EXAMPLE: *Day of Deceit: The Truth About FDR and Pearl Harbor*

A concise example by Robert Stinnett whose book we sold to Free Press:

> *Day of Deceit: The Truth About FDR and Pearl Harbor* will be the first book to prove that FDR knew in advance about Pearl Harbor and approved it. The manuscript will be X pages with forty-three illustrations, and author will deliver the manuscript nine months after receiving the advance.

The next chapter discusses how to nail your title.

CHAPTER 8

Naming Rites: Finding the Answers You Need to Choose Your Title

> **THE GOLDEN RULES FOR CREATING TITLES FOR YOUR BOOKS AND CHAPTERS**
>
> • Make your titles tell and sell.
>
> • Make your titles appeal to the heart as well as the head.
>
> • Use your models as guides.
>
> • Use your communities to test your titles.

A good title is the title of a successful book.

—RAYMOND CHANDLER

One New York editor said to us, "If the title is good enough, it doesn't matter what's in the book." *Everything Men Know About Women* proves her right. The book has sold more than 750,000 copies. How do I know that the title alone sold the book? Because it's 120 blank pages!

You're in your favorite bookstore just after your book is published. You start walking the aisles, delighted to find your book face up on the new nonfiction table in the front of the store. You pause to look at it and also take in the books around it.

How long do you spend looking at the covers of other books? Two seconds each, if you are the average book buyer. And guess what? That's how long everyone who walks by the table will spend looking at your cover. Two seconds is less time than it took you to read the previous sentence.

Two seconds for the colors, design, artwork, title, and perhaps a quote and the name of the person who did the foreword. A large proportion of books have tombstone covers. Nobody could think of an image that could capture the essence of the book in a way that would help sell it, so words are all browsers have to go on. That's not necessarily a bad thing, but it makes the right title all the more important. Finding the perfect title for your book will be an "Aha!" experience. You will know it the moment you think of it or hear it. It will be love at first sound.

It's been said that business books provide affirmation, not information, and that what it takes to be successful in business hasn't changed much. But authors keep coming up with fresh, timely ways of expressing their ideas in titles that make their books salable to new readers. This works for French cookbooks, too.

Ideally, your book should be new wine in a new bottle. It should contain new information that will face no competition and that will bear a title that separates it from other books. But if, as is true for most books, your book will not be the first one on the subject, it's all the more essential that your "bottle" be new, that you conceptualize your book in a way that makes it seem fresh— give it a title that justifies another book on the subject.

Assume the editors at big houses are experts on the subject, have seen hundreds of proposals about it, and have bought many of them. They will know immediately how well your book will compete with others on the subject.

The perfect title for your book will get them excited about it, in part because they know your title will excite their editorial boards, sales reps, publicists, subsidiary-rights department, and booksellers, as well as the media and book buyers. Your title will help them position your book in relation to competing books.

THE HEAD AND THE HEART: TITLING WITH BOTH SIDES OF YOUR BRAIN

Creating the best title and, if necessary, subtitle for your book involves using both sides of your brain because the best titles appeal to the heart as well as to the head. For your title, you need the right side of your brain. You need to draw on your creativity to capture the essence of your book or to synthesize its benefits in a short, simple, visual, and accurate title that paints a picture and creates an emotional response.

The left side of your brain faces the challenge of coming up with the subtitle: the shortest, simplest, clearest way of expressing what your book will do for your readers to justify their buying and reading it.

THE TELL-AND-SELL FACTOR

In *How to Drive Your Competition Crazy*, Guy Kawasaki tells the story of how nobody at a private boy's school signed up for a course called "Home Economics for Boys," but the class filled up immediately when the school changed the name of the course to "Bachelor Living."

In the same way, the right title for your book unites two realities.

- What you're selling and what people are buying
- What your book says and the most compelling way to conceptualize that body of information so it will appeal to as many potential book buyers as possible and exclude as few as possible

Susan Sontag says that writing is like "making bouillon cubes out of soup." If your book will be the essence of what you want to say, your title will be the essence of that essence.

Titles for self-help books, books on popular culture—in fact, any book aimed at a mass audience—must have a high tell-and-sell factor. Together, your title and subtitle must tell—describe what your book is—and sell—motivate book buyers to pick it up off the shelf. Make your title as clear, concise, compelling, and commercial as your subject allows.

> **HOT TIP**
>
> The longer you make anything in your proposal—words, sentences, titles, paragraphs, chapters, anecdotes, and the book itself—the better it must be to justify its length.

Make your title a big red flag that screams, "Stop and pick me up! You can't live without me! I'm worth twice the price! Take me home now!" An effective how-to title incorporates the notions of a desirable activity or skill to be learned, a systematic approach to learning it, and, perhaps, a time within which the reader will acquire the skill. Good examples include the following.

- *The 90-Second Fitness Solution*
- *How to Make Someone Fall in Love With You in 90 Minutes or Less*
- *The 4-Day Diet*

Benefits that a book or chapter title might convey include speed, quality, economy, or a system or program of steps readers can take to bring about the change they seek. Using numbers, like *10 Steps for Curing Health*, is a simple way to present a systematic approach and describe the structure of your book or chapter.

The following titles (which we sold) tell and sell and combine a catchy title and subtitle to convey each book's benefit:

- *Hit by a Farm: How I Learned to Stop Worrying and Love the Barn* by Catherine Friend
- *Stooples: Office Tools for Hopeless Fools* by Kevin Reifler, Adam Najberg, and Nick Vacca
- *Black Belt Negotiating: Become a Master Negotiator Using Powerful Lessons From the Martial Arts* by Michael Soon Lee

---

HOT TIP

- Try out your title on your networks to study their response to it.
- Don't offer agents or editors a string of titles to choose from; pick the best one. You can share the others later.
- Align your title, your manuscript, your talks, and your promotion with your readers' needs, values, and fears. The more you help your readers, the more they'll help you.

GENERIC VICTORIANS

Shortly after we started our agency, I drove a cab for a while to make up for the royalties we hadn't started earning yet. Driving a taxi gave me the chance to see parts of San Francisco we hadn't explored. It also enabled me to discover the beautifully painted Victorians that were sprouting up like flowers around the city.

I knew there was a book in them, so I took photos of the houses and wrote a proposal for a book. It took a year and a half to sell. Local publishers said the color photos would make the book too costly to produce. New York editors said the book was too "regional," the kiss of death for a New York publisher.

Finally, Cyril Nelson, an editor at Dutton, stopped in San Francisco on his way to visit his printer in Japan. After driving him around the city to see the houses, he became a believer and risked six thousand dollars on the book.

When photographer Morley Baer and I were roaming around San Francisco shooting houses for the book, he suggested we call the book *Painted Ladies*. As soon as he said it, I laughed with delight. It was the perfect title. We knew we needed a subtitle, and *San Francisco's Victorians* was the logical choice, but we were stuck for the right adjective. Cy was right on target with the word *resplendent*.

The first book, published in 1978, started a national trend that led to five more books. The trademarked words *painted ladies* have become generic for multicolored Victorians.

> **HOT TIP**
>
> If you luck into the title of a lifetime that has a word or phrase you can use for your talks and for a series of books, buy the domain name for your website immediately and trademark the word or phrase as soon as your publisher agrees with you.

If you can't think of an ideal title for your book, perhaps your agent or editor will, or maybe you will as you are writing the book. Your title may change in the course of writing and producing your book. If you're lucky, you will settle on a title that you, your editor, and the S&M (that's sales and marketing) crowd agree will create the strongest response on bookstore shelves. Use the titles of successful books like yours to spark your imagination.

GETTING A TITLE PAST THE GATEKEEPERS

Between you and your book thriving on bookstore shelves two years from now are nine gatekeepers who will have a say about the title for your book: you, your communities, your agent, your editor, your publisher's editorial board, your publisher's sales reps, the bookstore chains, the warehouse clubs, and discounters like Walmart. If any one of them doesn't like the title, regardless of the previous responses to it, the title is toast.

Writers are less concerned about titles than they need to be. They assume their publisher will change the title, so they don't spend enough time on it or enlist other writers to help. They are also too close to their work to create the best titles for their books.

Big publishers are working with too many books to pay enough attention to all of them. If they get stuck on a title, they choose the least objectionable one. What percentage of published books have the best titles for them? My guess: fewer than 10 percent. Check out your shelves and bookstores to see if you agree.

The best insurance: Enlist your communities and do whatever it takes to come up with the best title for your book. If you're planning a series of books, the title you choose must serve you well for the series. It will become your brand. As I said before, you'll know it when you hear it; you'll get goose bumps. Finding the right title for your book challenges your publisher either to use it or to find a better one.

The range of nonfiction books and the endless possibilities for creating titles can make the challenge daunting.

FINDING THE ANSWERS YOU NEED
TO CHOOSE YOUR TITLE

When I worked at Bantam, the editors used to talk about a Little, Brown and Company novel called *Five Days*. It didn't sell well, so when Bantam published the mass-market edition of the book, they changed the title to *Five Nights*. *Five Days* tells; *Five Nights* sells. This is a timeless example of what a title should be: evocative, intriguing, enticing, appealing to the emotions more than to the mind. This applies equally to the titles of your chapters.

A *New Yorker* cartoon shows a man, his hand extended, introducing himself to a woman at a party, and he's saying to her, "Hi. I'm, I'm, I'm ... You'll have to forgive me, I'm terrible with names."

Being terrible with names is not an option when it comes to naming your book. A symbol or metaphor that captures the essence of your book can crystallize the meaning and structure of the book. Let your imagination run wild and have fun thinking about all the possibilities. The authors must have had fun coming up with the following titles:

- *How to Pull Strings and Influence Puppets*
- *My Indecision Is Final*
- *Ventriloquism for the Complete Dummy*

Children's-book agent Andrea Brown finds that the right title is especially important for children's books. Humorous titles like *Cloudy With a Chance of Meatballs* or *The Cat Ate My Gymsuit* sell much better than straightforward titles.

You must have a creative distance from your book and be a bit of a visionary or a poet to come up with a title that excites you. You need the distance that astronauts in space have when they behold Spaceship Earth.

TWO WAYS TO SIMPLIFY FINDING YOUR TITLE

Here are two simple ways for finding a title:

- The titles for serious reference works, biographies, or books proposing a scientific or political theory need only tell, not sell. People buy them because they want the information, so you can simply name the information to create the title. As elsewhere, be guided by comparable books you admire. David McCullough didn't need anything fancier than *John Adams* to have a bestseller, a must-read for biographers and memoirists.

- Your book may need only a title. Thanks to the success of the movie *Saturday Night Fever*, Karen Lustgarten's *The Complete Guide to Disco Dancing*—one of our books that came out shortly after the movie debuted—didn't need a subtitle to hit the best-seller list. (The photo of her on the cover made its way onto a postage stamp commemorating the seventies. How's that for finding immortality?) Other books of ours that didn't require subtitles include the following:
  - *Learning to Write Fiction From the Masters* by Barnaby Conrad
  - *Random House Webster's Quotationary* compiled by Leonard Roy Frank
  - *Fun Places to Go With Children in Northern California* by Elizabeth Pomada (now in its ninth edition)

NINETEEN QUESTIONS IN SEARCH OF ONE ANSWER

If the easy ways won't work, here are nineteen questions to ask yourself to help you find the title for your book:

1. Does my title have an impact of an ad or article headline, compelling people to read the copy that follows? Using the word *free* helped Jay Conrad Levinson with *Guerrilla Marketing for Free: Dozens of No-Cost Tactics to Promote Your Business and Energize Your Profits.*

2. Does my title have three words that capture the essence of my book's promise? When one writer was stuck for a title, Oscar Dystel, then the president of Bantam, asked him, "What's the point of the book in three words, no more, no less?" The writer replied, "Quick weight loss," which became the heart of the title for the bestseller *The Doctor's Quick Weight Loss Diet.*

    The title was one of the reasons *If Life Is a Game, These Are the Rules,* by Chérie Carter-Scott, hit the top of the *New York Times* best-seller list. The subtitle—*Ten Rules for Being Human as Introduced in Chicken Soup for the Soul*—also helped, as did the hour Oprah joined her audience watching Chérie's presentation.

3. Does my title make use of a memorable image, symbol, or metaphor that captures the essence of my book in a way that can be the basis for my book's cover art, promotional materials, and future books?

    Allan Hamilton's *The Scalpel and the Soul* combines an intriguing juxtaposition and alliteration that captures the essence of his spiritual memoir. His proposal is in Appendix D.

    Another example of an evocative title that agent Robert Shepard likes to use is *Friday Night Lights,* a bestseller and then a television series.

4. Does my title sell my solution? Don't sell a question; sell an answer. Don't sell a problem; sell a solution. Make your title positive and empowering. Convince book buyers that you're going to solve their problem. An example: Edward Segal's *Getting Your 15 Minutes of Fame and More! A Guide to Guaranteeing Your Business Success.*

5. For a how-to book: Is my title the prescription for the cure my book will provide? Readers want a how-to book to be a magic pill. They want to follow the directions and enjoy the benefit the title prescribes. Harold Lustig did this with his book *4 Steps to Financial Security for Lesbian and Gay Couples*.

6. Does my title make the biggest promise that my book will fulfill? Here is a brilliant title by David J. Lieberman: *Get Anyone to Do Anything: Never Feel Powerless Again—With Psychological Secrets to Control and Influence Every Situation*. That title is so good it was optioned for a movie twice!

7. Does my title broadcast my unique selling proposition (USP)? Create a USP that will make your book stand out from the competition. This is particularly important for a book that will face a lot of competition, like *The Only Negotiating Guide You'll Ever Need: 101 Ways to Win Every Time in Any Situation* by Peter Stark and Jane Flaherty.

HOT TIP

When publishing people refer to a title, they use only one or two words, so do as they do: After you give the full title in your book hook, use a shorthand version of it in the rest of your proposal so editors won't have to keep reading the whole title.

Keep your title short and simple, six words or less, and add an explanatory subtitle if you need to. *1776* did the job for David McCullough's bestseller, but *Dry* is the shortest title I've ever seen. (It's a memoir that involves alcohol and fishing.) Malcolm Gladwell's bestseller *Blink* is also admirably concise. Book designer Karris Ross has found that keeping subtitles to around ten words makes them easier to understand.

You will also help book buyers who are researching books by subject if the first or second word of your title conveys the subject of the book. Ingram, the nation's largest wholesaler, gives only the first sixteen letters of a title in its computerized book list that booksellers use for ordering. Then again, there's always David Reuben's *Everything You Always Wanted to Know About Sex But Were Afraid to Ask*. Thirteen words didn't keep it from becoming a bestseller.

8. Is the title of my book the same title as the talks I will give about the book? The same title for both creates synergy. Whether it's to hear you or read your book, you're asking for people's time. Your title must convince them their time will be time well spent.

9. Does my title use proprietary nomenclature, a way of capturing the essence of my book that makes it mine alone? Jay Conrad Levinson's name has become synonymous with Guerrilla Marketing, the brand he built.

10. Can I use a variation of my title for other books? The *Guerrilla Marketing* series, the *Dummies* books, and the *Chicken Soup* series prove that the right title helps create enduring brands.

11. Does my title broadcast my book's benefit so well that it creates an irresistible urge to buy my book? Another example by David J. Lieberman: *Never Be Lied to Again: How to Get the Truth in 5 Minutes or Less in Any Conversation or Situation.*

12. Does my title offer one or more of the golden oldies that people have always wanted and needed most: sex, love, food, health, laughter, pleasure, peace of mind, work, power, success, making money, and saving money? Also consider the following subjects of national and global interest:
    - Leisure interests such as games, sports, movies, music, and socializing that people enjoy online and off
    - East meeting West in the Asian (if not the Chinese) century as authors draw on eastern traditions in lifestyle books about health, fitness, food, work, gardening, spirituality, and design
    - Universal concerns including work, business, politics, peace, the environment, food, health, fitness, education, sustainability, water, religion, technology, multiculturalism, and aging

13. Does my title capture how my book will affect my readers? Will it inform them, enlighten them, entertain them, persuade them, inspire them, make them laugh, help them lead better lives, or provide any combination

of the above? Here's the title for Francesca De Grandis's book: *Be a Goddess! A Guide to Celtic Spells and Wisdom for Self-Healing, Prosperity and Great Sex.*

14. Does my title use wordplay to help make it memorable? The techniques you can use include

- Rhyme: *Private Lives of Ministers' Wives* by Liz Greenbacker and Sherry Taylor

- Rhythm: *If Life Is a Game, These Are the Rules* by Chérie Carter-Scott

- Alliteration: *Amazeing Art: Wonders of the Ancient World* by Christopher Berg

- Verbal and visual puns: *$ellmates: The Art of Living and Working Together* (one of my favorite ideas that needs a writer)

- Wordplay (changing a letter or a word in a well-known phrase or using its opposite): *Tongue Fu! How to Deflect, Disarm, and Defuse Any Verbal Conflict*, a great title by Sam Horn; *Stuff Happens (And Then You Fix It!): 9 Reality Rules to Steer Your Life Back in the Right Direction* by John Alston and Lloyd Thaxton; and *Winning the Battle of the Exes: How to Make the Last Day of Your Divorce the First Day of a Lifelong Friendship*, another idea that needs a writer.

- Two contrasting or opposing phrases: *Men Are From Mars, Women Are From Venus* by John Gray

- Humorous titles, essential for books with humor: *I'm Not as Old as I Used to Be: Reclaiming Your Life in the Second Half* by Frances Weaver and *How Now Brown Sow: A Fat-Free Guide to Raising Pigs in Your Apartment*, an idea unlikely to find a writer. I can't convince Jack Canfield to do *Chicken Soup for the Shoemaker's Soul* or *Chicken Soup for the Filet of Soul*, but I keep hoping.

15. Does my title use words that sell?

- Words that sell products and services: *sex(y), now, success, first, complete, how to, you, health, balance, transform, original, diet, weight loss, God, soul, spiritual, inspirational, overcome*

How to Write a Book Proposal

- Money words: *free, money (-making/saving), save, profit, risk-free, guarantee, income, tax-free*
- Superlatives: *biggest, largest, best, oldest, youngest, richest, most beautiful, most exciting, most complete, cheapest*
- Time words: *now; today*; a number followed by *seconds, minute(s), hour(s), day(s), week(s), month(s), year(s); speed, quick (-ly) (-er) (-est), fast (-er) (-est), instant(ly), convenient*
- Words that suggest a system or program: a number followed by *secrets, steps, stepping stones, keys, ways, commandments, building blocks*
- Crossover words: *at home and at work, in your personal and professional life, for parents and teachers*
- Combined words: putting two words together to create a new one, like *Negotiauctions: New Dealmaking Strategies for a Competitive Marketplace* by Guhan Subramanian

16. Does my title promise an experience that will be funny, dramatic, inspirational, transforming, moving, amazing, or enlightening? *From Buchenwald to Carnegie Hall* is a Holocaust memoir that captures the essence of pianist Marian Filar's remarkable story that Charles Patterson helped him tell.

17. Does my title make use of the title of a successful book? *Freakonomics* spawned titles that made use of its last three syllables, and authors have been mining Edward Gibbon's *The Decline and Fall of the Roman Empire* for more than two hundred years.

    You can look at all titles to create a variation for your book, but the better known the source, the more impact the title will have.

    One tribute to a book's success is a parody of the book's title. Along with speaker Scott Friedman, I'm waiting for someone to write *The 7 Habits of Highly Effective Nuns.* You know your book is successful when someone does a parody of it.

18. Does my title appeal to the needs, fears, and values of my potential readers? When one of our writers wanted to write a book called *The Health Food Hustlers*, I suggested that it would be more salable if he called it *The*

Insider's Guide to Health Foods, which made the book a service instead of just an exposé, and that was the title Bantam used for the book.

19. Do I have a catchy title that has nothing to do with the subtitle? Two best-selling examples: Harvey Mackay's *Swim With the Sharks Without Being Eaten Alive: Outsell, Outmanage, Outmotivate, and Outnegotiate Your Competition* and Richard Bolles's *What Color Is Your Parachute? A Practical Manual for Job-Hunters and Career-Changers.*

Any of these possibilities may spark the title for your book. Playing around with them will lead you to chapter titles, subheads, and phrases you can use in talks, articles, your blog, your newsletter, your website, and on social networks. The titles of successful books will also inspire your creativity.

The following chapter will show you how to provide your book's markets.

CHAPTER 9

The Instant Sell: Your Selling Handle and the Models for Your Book

THE GOLDEN RULE FOR YOUR SELLING HANDLE

Sell what readers will buy.

You will spend months writing your book, but sales reps, who may be selling hundreds of books at a time, may only spend seconds selling it. So, as a sales rep once remarked in *Publishers Weekly*: "We need an expeditious, concise, sales-oriented handle that says a lot about the book in as few words as possible."

What reps need is an effective one-line selling handle. Broadway producer David Belasco's warning to playwrights also applies to you: "If you can't write your idea on the back of my calling card, you don't have a clear idea." It's the high-concept idea of the log line, the one line of copy in *TV Guide* that must convince viewers to watch the show. Your selling handle will be a one-line statement of your primary goal for your book.

MODELING YOUR BOOK

The Hollywood pitch, the movie version of a selling handle, is what film agents use to pitch ideas. This pitch often combines two successful movies: "It's gonna be colossal! It's *E.T.* meets *Jurassic Park*!" Comparing a book to one or more well-known books or authors gives booksellers and media people an immediate grasp of the models for your book. Kirkus Book Reviews used two nonfiction bestsellers to desribe W. Bruce Cameron's novel, *A Dog's Purpose*: "*Marley and Me* meets *Tuesdays with Morrie*."

Your book's selling handle may be its thematic, structural, or stylistic resemblance to one or two books or authors. The following examples can serve as selling handles because editors will immediately understand what you're selling, and you will both have a model on which to pin your literary and commercial hopes.

- A *Fast Food Nation* about fashion
- A *What to Expect When Your Dog Is Expecting* (not a bad idea, at least for an article)
- A book in the high-energy, freewheeling style of Tom Wolfe

ESTABLISHING YOUR MARKETING POSITION

You can't just think about what you're selling; you must also think about what your potential readers are buying. Isolate what makes your book unique, what sets it apart from your competition. Then create a concise, memorable phrase that conveys your book's content and appeal.

You want to establish your book's "marketing position." Because the best marketing position a product or service can have is to be the first of its kind, write—if you can—that your book "will be the first book to ... " If yours can't be the first book to do something, make it "the only book to ... "

You don't have to use either of these approaches, but you must find a compelling phrase to explain why your book merits publication and why editors should read your proposal.

> **HOT TIP**
>
> Unless you have a complete manuscript or a self-published book, use the word *will* when referring to your book because it doesn't exist yet.

Your selling handle must broadcast the benefit readers will gain from your book. If you have trouble coming up with a strong title or selling handle, try this: List your book's substance and benefits in the form of phrases. Then see if you can abstract from them one enticing phrase that captures the essence of your book. Selling handles vary in length, but as everywhere else in your proposal, the fewer the words the better—fifteen, at most.

Here are some successful selling handles our authors have created.

- **Kathleen Archambeau:** *Climbing the Corporate Ladder in High Heels* will be the first book to tell women how to be successful and happy without becoming just like men.

- **Catherine Friend:** *Meeting My Meat: Adventures of a Tender Carnivore* will be the first book to tell readers about the lives of animals and still support their choice to eat meat.

  The final title for Catherine's book was *The Compassionate Carnivore.* My partner Elizabeth's idea for the title was *Hi, My Name's Fluffy. I'll Be Your Lamb Chop Tonight.*

- **Kevin Reifler, Adam Najberg, and Nick Vacca:** *Stooples* will parody business through the tools of all trades: office products and the catalogues that flog them. It will follow the path laid down by *Dilbert* and *The Onion,* but do it like *Items from Our Catalogue,* the bestselling takeoff on L.L. Bean.

- **Shivani Goodman:** Shivani had finished her manuscript, so she writes about the book in the present tense: *9 Steps for Reversing or Preventing Cancer and All Other Diseases Without Surgery, Drugs or Changing Your Diet* is the first book to present a program with practical, step-by-step techniques and vital tools that have been tested in this country and fourteen others.

HOT TIP

Editors resist what seems self-serving. Let your idea, your supporting facts, your passion, and your writing make your case.

GOING FOR *60 MINUTES*

The more competition your book will face, the more important it is for your selling handle to mention what your book will be the first to have. If you're writing a biography, a history, or an exposé, what your book will add to the record will help determine the value of your book. So after your selling handle, add a paragraph that begins, *The book will reveal for the first time that …* and then have a list of one-liners, with the new information in descending order of its ability to sell books, generate reviews, or get you on *60 Minutes*.

People don't buy books—they buy benefits. Keep going to see when and how you should list the benefits your book will offer your readers.

CHAPTER 10

Bennies for Readers, Royalties for You: Listing Your Book's Benefits (Optional)

THE GOLDEN RULE ABOUT LISTING BENEFITS

Make your book more salable by showing how it will help your readers.

Including a list of your book's benefits will help prove why it's needed. This is even more valuable if you are the first author to provide a benefit, which is worth mentioning. So if your book's benefits warrant more explanation than what you've provided so far, add a list of benefits in descending order of their ability to sell books. Listing benefits may make sense for a how-to book, but it's not necessary for many narrative books such as memoirs.

EXAMPLE: *Guerrilla Trade Show Selling*

Here's how Jay Conrad Levinson, Mark S.A. Smith, and Orvel Ray Wilson listed their book's benefits.

> *Guerrilla Trade Show Selling* will:
>
> - Maximize readers' trade show investment.
> - Enable readers to avoid image-damaging, business-killing show behavior. Some companies will be better off if they don't participate in trade shows.

- Give readers control over their trade show sales results, leaving little to chance. Include ideas to salvage shows with poor exhibit placement, wrong show selection, missing exhibits, and seven other problem situations.

- Enable small companies to compete with larger well-established competitors. Large competitors often don't prepare their exhibit sales staff properly. A small, well-trained exhibit staff will beat a large, unprepared staff every time.

- Save time, money, and energy in creating in-house training programs or researching the scattered information on trade show selling. This will eliminate the need to hire sales trainers—perhaps inexperienced at trade show selling—or expensive consultants.

- Repay the investment in this book thousands of times over.

HOT TIP

Keep in mind the distinction between features and benefits. Features are contained in your book; benefits are what your features do for your readers. Features create benefits; benefits create fans.

The next chapter discusses how and when to include special features in your book.

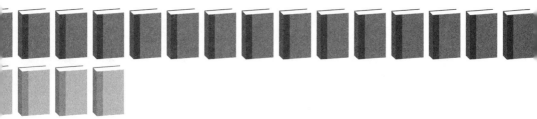

CHAPTER 11

Adding Value to Your Book: Special Features (Optional)

THE GOLDEN RULE FOR HAVING SPECIAL FEATURES

Add special features to make your book more helpful, visually appealing, and pleasurable to read.

Workman is the most creative publisher in Manhattan. You can see this in how they present information and design their books. Editor-in-chief Susan Bolotin says they "layer" information by having subheads, boxed information, illustrations, and graphic elements to draw the eye and invite readers into the text. They also use white space and choose creative formats to give their books eye appeal. When deciding the format in which to publish a book, publisher Peter Workman will pick up different-sized books to help decide which one looks and feels right.

The next part of your overview describes other important features your book will provide. Will the book be humorous, serious, or down-to-earth? Will it contain anecdotes? What kind of personality will it have?

If what you will illustrate is not already clear, explain it. Visual appeal is an essential element in selling products and services, so publishers want to avoid an endless chain of paragraphs—blocks of copy that aren't inviting to the eye. Here are ways to break up your text:

- subheads
- illustrations
- sidebars
- exercises
- checklists
- chapter summaries
- copy in the margins
- boxed and screened information
- quotations

Visual appeal is important in books intended for a wide audience; it's not as vital for serious or academic books. Be a model follower.

EXAMPLE: *Stooples: Office Tools for Hopeless Fools*

The authors had a clear vision of their parody, and they made St. Martin's job easier by doing the design work.

Stooples is envisioned at 128 pages at 8½" × 11", and will contain:

- 200 products with humorous photos
- short pieces of humor that complement the products
- an introductory letter by Stooples' CEO
- humorous attacks on Stooples' competitors OfficeHacks and OfficePeephole, complete with graphics such as a red circle and diagonal stripe with Office-Hacks name in the middle of the circle
- e-mails from the Stooples' CEO on strange challenges the company is facing such as lost shipments, OfficeHacks counter measures, OfficePeephole's strange management practices
- instructions such as how to ship by mail
- a final section with the most humorous stories that have appeared on the book's website

Stooples will follow the format of the Staples catalogue. The book will highlight products in the following categories: office supplies, technology, custom printing, furniture, office machines, and attire and accessories.

Categories that are not in an office-supply catalogue include drugs, people, lunchroom/bathroom, and esoterica.

The authors will keep adding new material to make the book as timely as possible. The authors will provide the design for the book.

When you find humor, see if one of these four ways will enable you to use it.

1. Use it as is.

2. If it isn't about your subject, build a bridge between it and your subject to make it relevant. In *How to Get a Literary Agent*, I tell the story of a man named George Bosque who robbed Brink's of a million dollars, spent it in a year and a half, and was then caught by police.

   When the police asked how he managed to spend the money in a year and a half, he replied, "Well, I spent half of it on gambling, drink, and romance, and I guess I squandered the rest."

   That has nothing to do with publishing, but I tied the two together by writing: *If publishers think they're getting the next Tom Clancy or Danielle Steel, they'll squander a bundle in the best-seller sweepstakes.*

3. Change humor so it's relevant. "Want to know how to make a small fortune from writing? Start with a large fortune and write full time." Elizabeth and I first heard this anecdote when we were writing books about Victorian houses that need a lot of work. In our talks, we changed the punch line: *Start with a large fortune and buy a Victorian.*

4. Use humor you encounter as a springboard for creating new humor. Develop an instinct for comedy by looking for the funny aspects of everything you experience. This is a skill that will help you weather hard times as well as write.

LAUGHING TO LEARN AND EARN: USING HUMOR IN YOUR BOOK

Communication and information are entertainment, and if you don't understand that, you're not going to communicate.

—JOHN NAISBITT, BEST-SELLING AUTHOR OF *MEGATRENDS*

In our entertainment-driven culture, entertainment is the price of attention, so strive to make your book as enjoyable to look at and read as it is informative. Dramatic, revelatory, and inspirational writing make books enjoyable to read.

So does humor. Best-selling author Norman Cousins believed that "laughter is inner jogging," and we all need a good workout. The more you laugh, the more open you are to learning, and the more your readers laugh, the more you earn.

Humor makes books more enjoyable to read, which in turn makes them sell better. If you're writing an exposé or a serious book, humor may be out of place. Otherwise, a book will benefit from adding humor. John Grogan's ability to make readers laugh made the sad ending of his bestseller *Marley & Me* all the more effective. But don't feel you have to become the next Dave Barry. You will find humor in

- Google—the word *humor* has hundreds of millions of links
- magazines with humor in them, including *The New Yorker*
- quote books
- joke books
- books by comedians and humor writers
- books of anecdotes
- biographies
- other books about your subject
- cartoon books, although you'll have to pay for permission if you use the drawing instead of only the caption
- books on popular culture
- books on writing humor
- comedy clubs
- comedy CDs

If money is no object, you can hire a comedy writer to create material for your book. Where there's a wit, there's a way.

HOT TIPS

- If you want to use humor, include it consistently throughout your book.
- Decide on the number of jokes or anecdotes you'd like in your chapters and how best to integrate them. Use humor, drama, compelling insights,

---

How to Write a Book Proposal

or inspirational writing to move your readers and make your book a pleasure to read. Test-market the effect of your work on readers and listeners to make sure it's having the impact you want. Ask readers to grade the impact of each high-impact moment on a scale of one to ten.

- The best hope that books have for being successful is word of mouth and, thanks to computers, word of mouse. The funnier a book is, regardless of who writes or publishes it or how well it's promoted, the better the word of mouth it will generate. It's impossible to make most books too funny or to prevent the success of those that are funny enough. The effective combination of humor and content will also lead to your success on the speaking circuit, and speaking enables you to test-market your humor before you write your book.

YOUR BACK MATTER

In a cartoon by Harley Schwadron, a patient is on a hospital gurney, and a nurse standing over him says, "They're going to take you back to surgery, professor. Dr. Bickel got confused and removed your glossary instead of your appendix."

Add a glossary or appendix if they will help readers. If your models have back matter, include it. List back matter in the order in which it will appear:

- resource directory (may include books, periodicals, organizations, events, blogs, and websites—you may want to add these resources to your site and update them regularly)
- appendices
- footnotes
- glossary
- bibliography
- index

Writers can usually list their back matter in one sentence. However, if you need to describe your appendices, use a separate page at the end of the outline to supplement your mention of them in your overview.

HOT TIPS

- Librarians like back matter because it adds to a book's value as a research tool. Publishers like to please librarians because school, college, and public libraries are major customers.

- Offer to put your back matter on your website if your publisher wishes. This will shorten the book and lower the cover price.

- Avoid footnotes in your proposal—they're distracting and will make your proposal (and your book) look academic. If your book will have footnotes, make them blind footnotes, divided by chapter, that readers can find at the end of your book by page numbers. If you use them in your sample chapter, include them at the end of your proposal.

- Avoid asterisks to indicate information at the bottom of a page. They also interrupt the flow of the text.

- Include nothing that will prevent readers from reading from your first word to your last, ideally without stopping.

SELLING A SELF-PUBLISHED BOOK

Self-publishing in print and as an e-book or podcast is a huge, growing, and positive trend. It empowers authors to find the audience for their books and gives them the chance to test-market their books to prove they will sell. Jossey-Bass executive editor Alan Rinzler reported that publishers pick up 5 percent of self-published books, a higher percentage than books that haven't been self-published. If you sell enough copies of your book, publishers will take an interest.

Here's the information you may want to include about a self-published book:

- the title, if different
- the name of the site or publisher you used
- the year
- the number of copies sold
- subsidiary-rights sales
- quotes from reviews and their sources
- links to information on the Web about the book
- anything else that will help convince editors to buy the book

You'll be sending publishers your overview with a copy of the printed book. For a podcast or e-book, attach it if you e-mail your overview.

HOT TIP

Having an overview of a follow-up book that arouses the publishers' interest will be a further incentive to buy the first book.

Now it's time to zero in on the markets for your book that justify publishing it.

PART III:
YOUR BOOK'S MARKET
AND COMPETITION

CHAPTER 12

Following the Money:
Four Kinds of Markets for Your Book

There's a *New Yorker* cartoon by Victoria Roberts showing a man and a woman at a church altar taking their vows, and the woman says, "I'm delighted to love, honor, and obey, but I'm keeping my electronic rights."

FOUR KINDS OF MARKETS FOR YOUR BOOK

Three of the most important words of the last century were *Follow the money.* Deep Throat, the source of information about the Watergate break-in in 1972 that led to President Richard Nixon's resignation two years later, uttered them in William Goldman's screenplay *All the President's Men.*

Your proposal must enable an editor to show the editorial board the money that will convince the powers that be to let the editor buy your book. You can help the lucky editor who's going to buy your book by showing how your book will make money. How? By describing the markets for your book.

Your book will have four kinds of markets.

1. Consumers
2. Bookstores and other consumer outlets
3. Special Sales
4. Subsidiary rights

CONSUMERS

After you describe your book, tell editors who will buy it and where. Beginning with the largest group of potential readers, describe the buyers for your book. You can present your book's readership by the following characteristics:

- age
- gender
- income—for example, upmarket (*The Truffle Sniffer's Cookbook*) or down-market (*473 Ways to Use Spam to Stuff a Turkey*)
- occupation, including the number of professionals in the field
- ethnicity
- interest in hobbies, sports, or other leisure activities
- location
- religious, political, or other beliefs, such as the fifty million cultural creatives
- memberships in organizations
- statistics on sales of related books, magazines, services, or merchandise
- the number of top-ranked blogs on the subject
- the amount of other online activities
- the growing awareness of your subject because of television, films, advertising, the news, or the Web
- the number of people who have the problem your book addresses
- attendance at events
- rights of passage: birth, education, marriage, parenting, retirement, death

Use up-to-date round figures from reliable sources to show that the audience for your book is large enough to justify publishing it. Google and your reference librarian can point you to the best sources, online and off, for the figures you need.

How to Write a Book Proposal

How can you suggest a large number of potential readers when you can't provide numbers? One way is to state that your book will appeal to readers who are "personally or professionally interested in [your subject]." Women buy—for themselves and others—80 percent of books sold, so a book that caters to them has a head start.

Including a statistic in your subject hook will give editors a sense of the market for your book. Figures lend credibility and authority to your assertions, but you may not need them. This may be the case if you refer to a large enough number of groups of potential readers or if there are obviously enough book buyers in the groups to assure a market for your book.

Example: *9 Steps for Reversing or Preventing Cancer and Other Diseases: Learn to Heal From Within*

Shivani Goodman lets the numbers make her case.

- Everybody four years and older can benefit from the book.
- The cancer market: 120 million people:
  - 20 million patients
  - 100 million loved ones (each patient has at least five loved ones)
- The market of people with other diseases: more than 370 million people with one or more life-threatening and other problems, including: [list of eleven disorders with the number of people suffering from them]
- The caregiver market: more than 50 million people who have neither training nor healing-circle support groups to help
- The volunteer market: more than 6 million people, who work for hospices, social service agencies, self-help groups, and hospitals
- The health-care professionals market: more than 500,000 people such as [list of twenty-three professional titles]
- The adoption market: self-healing courses at alternative health schools, healing centers and hospitals
- The library market: college and public libraries

SUBSIDIARY RIGHTS

- Because the book is simple, easy to use, timeless, and universal, it will have foreign-rights potential in more than twenty countries in which the author teaches or has clients and students.

- The book will have potential for the following clubs: One Spirit, Book-of-the-Month Club, and the Audio Book Club.

- The book will have potential for first- and second-serial rights. The author has written sections of chapters so they can stand alone as articles.

- The author has produced five CDs and two videos of the exercises included in the book.

JUMPING ON BANDWAGONS

Editors like to jump on bandwagons, so mention a pattern of growth if you have one in the numbers you present. For instance, if your book will be about computer games, statistics on the growing number of consumers buying them will give editors ammunition for acquiring your book.

EXAMPLE: *Comfort Zone Investing*

Here is how Ted Allrich described the markets for *Comfort Zone Investing*:

> Books on investing keep appearing because people keep buying them. More than half of American households own stocks or mutual funds. That's more than 80 million adults. Most of them have a strong desire to learn more about how to invest better, what makes the stock market move, how the capital markets work, and how to make sense of economic news. They are searching for a way to get comfortable with investing.
>
> This book will have information that will help 90 percent of investors from the most naïve to the most sophisticated. Through the knowledge in *Comfort Zone Investing*, they will reach new levels of understanding about the markets in general and stocks in particular.
>
> The book will also help newly divorced men and women, recent college graduates, about-to-retire workers, sons and daughters inheriting wealth, and workers who lose their 401(k) plans and must manage their own retirement accounts.
>
> Many stockbrokers need help understanding the markets. They are given research reports but don't usually understand how the economy or the stock market works. There are almost 70,000 stockbrokers.

Editors at large houses know about the markets for their specialties; the other people whose support they need, such as sales and marketing directors, may not. And publishers want to know you can accurately assess the markets for your book.

EXAMPLE: *Stooples: Office Tools for Hopeless Fools*

The authors created a fine example of how to use popular culture to build a case for a book.

These three success stories show the market for *Stooples*:

- The success of the NBC hit series *The Office*, adapted from the successful BBC series

- Scott Adams' *Dilbert* appears in 2,000 papers in sixty-five countries in almost twenty languages and online. The *Dilbert* site has almost 1.5 million unique visitors a week. The cartoon appears on office walls and corkboards. More than 10 million *Dilbert* books have been sold, as well as 10 million calendars. One reason for *Dilbert's* enduring popularity is its timeliness. Adams is so tuned into what's going on that loyal readers expect to hear *Dilbert's* response to the latest fads and trends. It's *Doonesbury* in a corporate context.

- More than 1.5 million people read *The Onion* online or off. Paid circulation is 250,000, but readership is double that. Crown has published three compilations. Onion Radio News, sixty-second fake reports, air daily on more than eighty stations. A screenplay to be produced by David Zucker and Gil Netter is in the works.

Stooples will appeal to employees at all levels in businesses of all sizes in all fields, from wage slaves who sit in no-privacy cubicles to executives tethered to BlackBerries, and to sales reps who are more intimate with their BlackBerries than their mates.

The news parodies will give the book immediacy and appeal to the people who enjoy the news segments on *Saturday Night Live* and in *The Onion*.

BOOKSTORES AND OTHER CONSUMER OUTLETS

Trade paperbacks and hardcover books are sold through bookstores and other consumer outlets. Bookstores, drugstores, airports, and supermarkets are among the 50,000 outlets that sell mass-market books.

If your book will have crossover potential—the potential to sell on more than one shelf in a bookstore by appealing to more than one group of consumers—mention that. On the back of trade paperback covers publishers often list the categories where they recommend books be stocked. The following books are examples:

- *The Compassionate Carnivore: Or, How to Keep Animals Happy, Save Old MacDonald's Farm, Reduce Your Hoofprint, and Still Eat Meat*: food/nature
- *Copyediting & Proofreading for Dummies*: reference/writing
- *The Worrywart's Companion: Twenty-One Ways to Soothe Yourself and Worry Smart*: psychology/self-help

Other consumer outlets include:

- stores other than bookstores
- online booksellers
- television shopping channels, such as QVC
- warehouse clubs
- conventions
- catalogs

CHICKEN SOUP FOR THE SALE

One of the ways that has enabled Jack Canfield and Mark Victor Hansen to sell more than 100 million books is to bypass marketing: getting stores other than bookstores to sell their books. Beauty parlors, gas stations, and other outlets that don't sell books have sold *Chicken Soup* books. It's a win-win-win deal: The stores and the authors profit, and so does the charity each book supports.

In your proposal, list specialty stores such as music, sporting goods, hardware, stationery, or gourmet cooking that sell similar books. Check with stores to see if they will sell your book. If they will, ask them how many such stores there are in the country and how they buy their books. You may not find a large selection of books in specialty stores, but if your book has that potential, use the information.

Say you want to write a book called *Snore Your Way to Total Fitness: 101 Exercises You Can Do While You Sleep*. Mentioning in your proposal that fitness centers will sell your book is good, but it's not the heart of the markets for your book. Assume that publishers don't sell books to fitness centers and don't know how to. So if you can, add value to the idea by explaining how you will sell to the fitness centers. Find out if whoever sells to fitness centers will carry your book. If you can, help make the sale in advance by telling the publisher how it can be done or, better still, by including a written commitment for an order.

HOT TIP

Bringing publishers written commitments for enough book orders or one big one will guarantee the sale of your book. How far into four figures orders need to be will depend on the book and the size of the publisher you want. Mention any commitments you have in your promotion plan, and if they're big enough, in your cover letter.

EXAMPLE: *Guerrilla Marketing for Job Hunters 2.0*

The given is that job hunters will look for books on the career shelves in bookstores. But here is how David Perry and Jay Conrad Levinson described the markets for *Guerrilla Marketing for Job Hunters 2.0: 1,001 Unconventional Tips, Tricks, and Tactics for Landing Your Dream Job*. The list symbolizes how much job hunting now takes place online, which also affected the promotion plan you'll find in chapter nineteen.

Here are nine of the affinity groups for *Guerrilla Marketing for Job Hunters 2.0*:

1. **Top 185 employment blogs.** The top 185 blogs on employment are already linked to David's *Guerrilla Job Hunting* blog, http://guerrillajobhunting. typepad.com. About 20,000 employment blogs exist.

2. **42,000 online job boards.** Monster.com with all its presence only accounts for three-quarters of 1 percent of the market share. The smaller boards are clamoring for content to post on their sites. Nearly all job boards have affiliate links to Amazon.com and Barnes & Noble, allowing them to recommend books and receive royalties though on-line purchases.

3. **158,000 headhunters.** The vast majority of headhunters prep their candidates for interviews before they send them to a client. The book will appeal to both the headhunters and their candidates.

4. **20,000 temp agencies.** According to *Staffing Today,* American staffing firms hire more than 11 million temporary and contract employees a year. *Guerrilla Marketing* is an ally for employment counselors who need to prep their temps to avoid humiliation.

5. **College and university guidance counselors.** Nearly 1,200 community colleges and more than 1,700 universities have about 20 million full- and part-time students. The authors will reach them through CollegeRecruiter. com and other job boards. CollegeRecruiter.com, the most used job board for college students, has agreed to post a Guerrilla Marketing Fast Fact once a week for the first year.

6. **Career counselors** at 62,000 elementary and high schools.

7. **Outplacement professionals** across America.

8. **Subscribers to trade magazines** in human resources, technology, healthcare, manufacturing, finance, natural resources, public service, counseling, and career management. According to Burrelles, there are almost eighty publications covering HR and personnel. There are hundreds more for industries like engineering, healthcare, and government, which all strive to keep their readers up to date with articles and advice on career matters.

9. **E-zines,** such as *Executive Recruiters Exchange, Recruiters On-line,* and *Recruiters Network,* all of which send daily bulletins to their subscribers.

SPECIAL SALES

Special sales are bulk and premium sales to corporations or institutions that buy large quantities of books for internal use or to give away or sell. A corporation might buy a book on business writing for its employees.

This kind of sale is more likely with a mass-market book than a more expensive trade paperback, more likely with a paperback than a hardcover, and more likely when a company can see the book.

Noting which kinds of companies use books and discussing this possibility with friends who know marketing will help you decide if your book can generate special sales. Only a tiny percentage of books are used this way, so don't spend much time investigating it unless you can deliver a sale yourself.

Major publishers have special sales departments, and if a business or organization buys enough books, publishers customize the cover and text to suit the buyer's needs.

Institutional Markets: Course Adoptions

If your book will have adoption potential in schools or other institutions, identify the courses and academic levels for which it will be suitable. To make this market valuable instead of just an idea that may or may not come to pass, name the teachers and their schools—ideally, both well known— who will adopt your book and the courses they will use it for; the more courses and schools, the better.

Libraries

School, college, public, and corporate libraries are collectively a large potential market for books. If your book will have special appeal to any of these libraries, double-check this with librarians and mention it in your proposal.

SUBSIDIARY RIGHTS

The fourth kind of market for your book, subsidiary rights, provides an ever-growing number of ways your book can keep earning you income long after publication. Every book has primary and subsidiary rights. Publishers acquire the primary rights to a book and try to keep as many subsidiary rights as they can.

Primary Rights

Publishers expect to acquire a book's primary rights, enabling them to sell the book as is or in adapted and condensed form. These rights include:

- publishing and selling the book in hardcover, trade paperback, and as a mass-market paperback
- selling permission to excerpt part of a book within another work
- book-club rights

- second-serial rights to excerpt the book, condense it, or serialize the whole book in a periodical after publication
- reproducing the text in a large-type and a royalty-free braille edition
- reproducing the text in other forms and media, including electronic media like e-books
- publishing and selling the book in unbound sheets—outside the United States, for example
- selling school editions of the book, adapting it as needed
- photocopying rights to all or part of the book for internal use by a school or business
- selling the book through direct-response marketing channels such as direct mail, television ads, and infomercials
- selling the book as a premium to businesses or nonprofits as a promotional tool
- selling the book in bulk quantities to customers outside the book industry
- granting the right to use part of the text to promote the book—for example, in a review

SUBSIDIARY RIGHTS

The following list will show you why your book may generate income long after publication. Subsidiary rights include:

- first-serial rights to excerpt the book (in a periodical/magazine) before publication
- British and translation rights
- rights to produce abridged, unabridged, and dramatized audio versions of the book
- performance rights for feature films, television movies, DVDs, CDs, plays, and radio broadcasts
- electronic rights for items including software, multimedia applications, and mobile applications
- merchandising rights for items such as T-shirts, coffee mugs, note cards, toys, and calendars

We create technology faster than we can make a business model for it, and these new technologies create opportunities and challenges. The model for who should own these rights and how authors should be compensated continues to evolve. The tension between information that wants to be free and writers who wants to be paid will not end soon, but the opportunities they offer for generating cash and connecting with your readers will continue to grow.

CHAPTER 13

Sizing Up the Comps:
Competing and Complementary Books

THE GOLDEN RULE FOR ANALYZING COMPETING BOOKS

Dig the hole your book will fill.

We get calls about books that face competition, and one of the first questions I ask is, "How many books are out there on the subject?" Sometimes the writers have no idea what books will surround theirs on bookstore shelves, a response that proves those writers are not ready to begin their proposals, let alone contact agents.

Editors must prove to their editorial board that a book can stand up to the heat of competing books without burning out. Perigee editor Meg Leder spends more time with the competing-books section of a proposal than any other part of it. Your ability to place your book in the context of competing books is essential to selling it.

COMPETING TITLES

The more books that exist on a subject, the larger the market must be to justify another book on the subject, and the harder it may be to find the gap your book will fill. Your proposal must prove you and your book can survive and thrive despite the past and future competition.

Fortunately, memoirs and books about charmed subjects like pets, the Civil War, and readers' needs, values, and fears have timeless appeal. Enterprising writers are always coming up with new ideas for successful books. A new angle, a fresh face, a well-written book, the right timing, a platform, and enough promotion can make a book sell despite competition.

Editors and their colleagues in sales and marketing will want you to help do the market research. Once you've told them everything they need to know about your book, make use of the data you gathered when you researched competing books to ease their fears about the competition.

You must convince publishers that

- you're an expert on the subject who knows about the competing books.
- you're being professional in the way you are approaching the project.
- your ability to assess the competition helps prove you can judge your own book accurately.
- you have used your knowledge to come up with a new slant that justifies another book on your subject.
- you know that editors need this information for their colleagues, if not for themselves.

Assume editors will check the information with BookScan and online booksellers. BookScan tracks book sales through major retail outlets, which amounts to about 70 percent of total sales. If competing books have sold poorly, you may have difficulty convincing an editor that your book will beat the trend. (Unfortunately, BookScan is not available for the public to access: generally only publishers and other industry insiders can afford it.)

At large publishing houses, editors usually work on a range of subjects, but they also have specialties. An editor who is known for a particular category will understand the competition and the audience, and will be impressed if your proposal shows a level of knowledge about the market that approaches her own. One way to show your expertise is a stellar section on competing titles that reflects an in-depth understanding of how the market is being served, and who the key authors are.

List competing books in order of importance, beginning the description of each book on a new line and supplying the following for each:

- full title
- author
- publisher, without the house's location
- year of publication
- number of pages
- format (hardcover, trade paperback, or mass-market)
- trim size, if you're proposing an art or photography book
- price
- ISBN

FINDING COMPETING BOOKS

Editors will expect you to size up competing books. These nine sources will help you provide information editors need to buy your book.

- Online booksellers: Let your fingertips do the browsing at the following.

- Amazon.com enables you to see bestsellers by subject and which consumers are preordering, as well as other links.

- BookFinder.com lists more than 150 million new and used books.

- Booksellers: Before trying out your title and idea on editors, try them out on early customers for your book—booksellers. Two of the joys of the literary life are browsing in bookstores and buying books. Become friends with local booksellers who love books. Support the people you want to support you. Buying books and discussing your favorites are all you have to do.

  Ask your local or online bookseller to notify you about new books in your field. Online booksellers take advance orders as soon as they receive publishers' catalogs—months ahead of publication. Publishers use these orders to determine how many copies to print.

  Booksellers thrive on their passion for books, and they light up when they find a kindred spirit with whom they can share their latest discovery. Someday they will stock your books and have book-signing parties for you.

- Librarians: Whether you reach them by phone or in person, reference librarians are excellent sources of information about finding books.

- A book's copyright page has an ascending line of numbers with the highest to the left. The lowest number to the right is the number of the latest printing—the higher the number, the greater the sales. There may also be a line of numbers for the year of the printing that will tell you the date of the latest printing.

- *Books in Print (BIP)*: This is an annual publication that lists all books in print in three ways: by title, author, and subject. The subject guide in *BIP* will tell you what's available on the subject you're writing about. For children's books, check www.childrensbooksinprint.com. Search the *BIP* database at www.booksinprint.com.

- *Publishers Weekly*: The industry's weekly trade journal reviews upcoming books and publishes summer, fall, and winter announcement issues in which publishers list their new titles. For more information, visit www.publishersweekly.com.

- Bibliographies of competing books: These are sources of information about the sources that competing books use. They will be models for you.

Avoid beginning descriptions with "This book," "It," or the title. Write two sentence fragments, starting each with a verb, explaining what competing books do and what they fail to do. Writing too much about competing books is a common problem. Keep your descriptions as short as possible.

End the list with a statement about why your book will be different and better than the competition. You may use a list of reasons that begins *[Your title] will be better than the competition because it ... .* Then list the reasons, beginning each reason with a verb. You may repeat what you wrote in your book hook, but change the wording.

If you're writing about dieting, parenting, relationships, or psychological self-help—subjects about which there are hundreds of competing books—describe only about six of the most competitive.

Keep this section brief, about two pages. The proposal is about your book, not the competition. You must, however, convince editors that you have an accurate perspective about what's out there and that you have done justice to the competition.

EXAMPLE: *Tongue Fu!*

Here's how Sam Horn described competing books in her proposal for *Tongue Fu! How to Deflect, Disarm, and Defuse Any Verbal Conflict*:

Tongue Fu! has only three major competitors:

- *Verbal Judo: The Gentle Art of Persuasion*, George J. Thompson (William Morrow, 1994, 222 pages). Claims to help readers control the outcome of every dispute in the home, classroom, and boardroom. By a former policeman who created his methods for fellow officers. Focuses primarily on what to do when faced with volatile and potentially violent situations.

- *The Magic of Conflict: Turning a Life of Work Into a Work of Art*, Thomas Crum (Touchstone, 1987, 254 pages). Shows how to apply the martial art of aikido to daily conflicts. Emphasizes the importance of being centered and outlines how to use this "New Age stress-reduction strategy" to turn struggle into success.

- *The Gentle Art of Verbal Self-Defense*, Suzette Haden Elgin (Dorset Press, 1980, 310 pages). Contains useful information, but difficult to read. Small type and academic jargon. Published in eight languages with four follow-up books.

Tongue Fu! will be the first book to present a gentle, easy-to-read, comprehensive approach to avoiding verbal aggression and using communication to improve relationships.

large house. You must supply strong enough evidence to the contrary if you're seeking a major publisher.

COMPLEMENTARY BOOKS

Even if no competitive books on your topic exist, every book will have complementary books. The success of books on the same subject or that are the same kind as yours but won't compete with yours will help convince editors of the value of your book. If the books aren't well known, indicate what they cover. Give the full title, author, publisher, and publication year for six books or fewer, along with one sentence fragment about it.

If you are preparing your proposal for a specific publisher, mention books on that publisher's list that complement yours. Close with a statement about how the existence of these books proves the salability of yours.

EXAMPLE: *9 Steps for Reversing or Preventing Cancer and Other Diseases: Learn to Heal From Within*

In Shivani Goodman's proposal, she discusses only classics in her field but concludes by reiterating the justification for her book.

9 Steps complements these groundbreaking bestsellers:

- *Love, Medicine & Miracles: Lessons Learned About Self-Healing From a Surgeon's Experience With Exceptional Patients* by Bernie S. Siegel. Demonstrates how unconditional love is the most powerful stimulant of the immune system, influencing patients' recovery.

- *Quantum Healing: Exploring the Frontiers of Mind/Body Medicine* by Deepak Chopra. Shows how the intelligence of the body has the potential to defeat cancer and heart disease, and cure other serious illnesses.

- *Getting Well Again* by O. Carl Simonton, James Creighton, Stephanie Matthew Simonton, and Stephanie Matthews. Introduces scientific basis of stress and other emotional factors contributing to the onset and progress of cancer as well as self-help techniques for survival.

- *You Can Heal Your Life* by Louise L. Hay. Covers the mental causes behind disease and includes affirmations for healing.

These perennials prove the salability of the subject. *9 Steps* builds on and expands these complementary books by

- offering a complete, comprehensive self-healing program to reverse or prevent disease while enhancing creativity and intuition.

- providing an emotional support system, with a manual to form and facilitate healing circles to reverse or prevent disease.

- featuring simple, practical, nurturing advice and exercises that can be understood by people of all ages and levels of experience.

- giving personal and professional examples that will make the book relevant for readers whether they are patients, parents, loved ones, caregivers, health-care professionals, support group members, or people wanting to improve their health and all areas of their life.

PART IV:
REACHING READERS:
YOUR PLATFORM
AND PROMOTION PLAN

CHAPTER 14

The Base of Your Golden Triangle: Creating the Communities You Need

THE GOLDEN RULE FOR BUILDING COMMUNITIES

Make building your communities a lifelong effort because the more people you know, the further you'll go.

One of the most hopeful signs for our future is that, because of desire, necessity, and technology, people are creating more kinds of communities in more ways and places. The potential for understanding and collaboration is bringing the world together. If we fulfill this potential, our future will be glorious.

Publishing is a people business built and sustained by relationships. Because it's not a path to wealth, people are in publishing because they want to be. Despite the competition for bestsellers, publishing is a community of people who love books and telling people about them. This shared passion gives the business a special quality that makes it the best business to be in.

As a writer, you forge a community of readers who yearn to share books they love. One community of readers alone can make your book a bestseller: the country's 800,000 book clubs—many of which communicate online.

BUILDING THE GOLDEN TRIANGLE

Nothing in life is more important than relationships. Whether they're communicating across a table or across the globe, people's relationships give life meaning and value. As a writer, you need to create communities to help you achieve your goals.

The three sides of the Golden Triangle of a successful writing career are Writing, Promoting, and Building Communities. At the apex of the triangle is your vision of success. The two sides are Writing and Promoting. The base of the triangle is Building Communities because people are essential to your success.

You can't reach the top without writing and promoting books that deliver. But the people who want to help you are crucial for getting you from where you are to where you want to go. To become a successful author, you need to build communities online and off. These communities include:

- Your family, relatives, and neighbors
- Your friends from home, school, and work
- Other people who will
  - give you feedback on your work
  - help you find an agent and publisher
  - share what they know about your subject, writing, agents, publishers, promotion, booksellers, and getting publicity
  - write about you and your book
  - do talks, books, and tours with you
  - give you quotes and a foreword for your book
  - forward your e-mails about your book and your needs to their networks
  - exchange links, blog posts, videos, and e-mail lists
  - write for each other's blogs and e-zines
  - trade ads on websites and in e-zines

- give you information you can offer as e-bonuses when you sell your book online
- link to your sites, blogs, e-zines, videos, and events
- sell your book at their presentations
- have your promotional info at their talks
- Opinion makers in the media, academia, government, and related organizations
- Your publishing community of editors, organizations, teachers, booksellers, librarians, reviewers, and sales reps
- A promotion network of people who will give you feedback on your media kit, website, and other online activities, and help you promote your work
- Your invisible chain of booksellers who will welcome you when you tour
- Big mouths who adore you and your work, and champion you and your book every chance they get
- If you're a speaker, speakers who can give you leads and recommend you for speaking engagements, audiences, clients, bureaus, and meeting planners
- People around the country who can tell you about local media, booksellers, and people in your field and give you a place to lay your head while researching and promoting your book
- Your mastermind group: five to nine people who meet every two weeks, in person or on the phone, who serve as the board of directors for each other by generating and refining ideas and holding each other accountable for actions they commit to taking before the next meeting
- Your techie network: people who help you with technology
- Your growing community of fans who read everything you write, buy everything you sell, attend every event you do online and off, and tell people to buy your book

HOT TIP

It will take four steps for your book to succeed.

1. People have to buy your book.

2. However, if they buy your book and don't read it or don't like it, it will have a short life. People must read your book.

3. People have to love your book. But even that isn't enough.

4. Your readers must tell all the people they know that they *have* to read your book.

Word of mouth and mouse are the most potent forms of promotion for books, just as they are for movies. What a book's first group of readers tell other readers determines a book's fate. Now that technology has collapsed time and distance, word of mouse can make your book succeed faster than ever.

Publishers spend millions of dollars a year buying and promoting potential bestsellers that fail, while even a self-published book like William Young's novel, *The Shack*, can become a bestseller. Word of mouth will make any book succeed, regardless of who publishes it or how, so the challenge for your book is to generate enough word of mouth that its sales build their own momentum.

BUILDING YOUR COMMUNITIES OFF-LINE

Build your communities as you build your platform.

- Read books, write to the authors, and build relationships.
- Track the careers of authors in your field and get to know them.
- Join organizations for writers and those in your field.
- Go to book events and events in your field. Face-to-face networking is still essential.
- Ask everyone you know to tell you about everyone they know who will help you.
- Collect business cards.

FANS FOR LIFE: WILL YOUR BOOK CREATE A CIRCLE OR A STRAIGHT LINE?

Jay Conrad Levinson, author of *Guerrilla Marketing*, believes that when people buy a copy of your book, they start a path on a straight line or a circle.

- If they don't read your book, don't finish it, or don't like it, they're on a straight line out of your life.

- If they do like your book, they're fans at the start of an endless circle. Your fans will buy your other books and the products they generate, visit your website, come to your events, and become unofficial sales reps when they tell their communities about you and your book.

The Web makes it easier than ever for you to have fans for life by maintaining the communities you need and that need you. They will remain essential allies who will help you build your career, so make serving them a lifelong passion. They will repay your efforts many times over. But as important as building communities is, balance it with your other personal and professional priorities.

The next chapter discusses the foundation for your promotion campaign: your platform.

CHAPTER 15

Eyes Are the Prize:
Building the Platform Your Book Needs

> **THE GOLDEN RULE OF WRITING ABOUT YOUR PLATFORM**
>
> Show you are continually visible to the markets for your book.

It's all about ears and eyeballs—the more of them you have reading, watching, and listening regularly, the more books you'll sell. All you need to do to see how dependent sales are on visibility is to look at a nonfiction best-seller list.

Authors have written promotion plans committing themselves to do all kinds of things to promote their books, but then didn't do them. If authors renege, publishers have no recourse, so they won't believe authors who say they'll give fifty talks per year around the country when they've given only five locally.

Publishers protect themselves by signing authors who are already using as many ways as they can to keep themselves in front of potential book buyers. Building your platform gives you the chance to test-market your book, an essential step for proving it will sell, which you will read about later.

YOUR PLATFORM

Your platform is a list, in descending order of importance, of what you have done and are doing to make potential book buyers aware of you and your work. You build your platform by developing and maintaining your *continuing* presence around the country and in print, broadcast, electronic trade, and consumer media. The word *continuing* is an essential aspect of a platform—it's not scattered one-shot appearances, which is why social media have become hugely important.

Large houses want writers ready to break out as successful authors. For books that depend on author promotion, the level of an author's visibility around the country is an essential factor in determining whether to acquire a book and how big a bet to place on it. Your promotion plan must be a believable expansion of what you are already doing.

Publishers won't expect every author to go around the country giving talks unless they can get paid enough to justify the effort, but thanks to the Web, all authors can and must have an online platform. Smaller houses are less concerned about platform because they don't have to sell as many copies of a book as big houses do. However, if you're writing a book you want to sell to a large or midsize New York publisher, and its success will depend on your promotion, you need a platform before selling it. For most new writers, this means choosing between a small- or mid-sized house outside Manhattan or taking the time to build a platform before selling the book.

If you're a speaker or want to be one, a book will enable you to increase your speaking fees and sell books at your talks. Publishers will know you'll have all the incentive you need to stay on the road, and you will have still more incentive if your book is the first in a series.

Publishers also want authors who will make building the readership for their books a permanent part of their career. If you do this, your publisher will have the confidence to keep buying your books; they will know that enough readers will buy your books to justify publishing them.

Your publisher will hope that the first printing of each new book will be bigger than that of your previous book because of your growing readership; new readers will buy your previous books, making them evergreens—backlist books that continue to sell.

When a book by an unknown writer is published, the challenge of reviews and promotion is to create a critical mass of passionate readers who will convince enough other readers to buy the book. If you and your publisher can achieve this level of momentum, your book will be a bestseller. The speed—

publishers call it *velocity*—with which your book flies out of stores will help determine whether it makes the bestseller lists.

It's said that it takes five mentions of a product to convince people to try it. So, the cumulative impact of readers hearing about a book from a variety of sources can also get your book to the cash register. So make your goal to become and remain as visible as you can in as many ways as you can. Your sales will reflect your visibility.

Example: *Stooples: Office Tools for Hopeless Fools*

Here's an example of how to build a platform and a market for a book online while writing it. The number of visits a site is already getting for a book will affect an editor's commitment to a book.

> The author's website, www.stooples.com, introduces four products and adds three news stories a week. In a buzz-building campaign, Kevin Reifler is sending press releases to hundreds of journalists every week, announcing a special price on a new product. He tracks the number of journalists who open the e-mail and hit the link to the site.
>
> Kevin also submits the site weekly to search engines and humor compilation sites. It's listed on humor-related search engines like HumorLinks.com, which will help generate awareness for the book.
>
> Kevin Reifler is president of two public relations and marketing firms: LegalVoice, www.legalvoice.com, and BusinessTech PR, www.businesstechpr.com. A former vice president with the public relations giant Hill & Knowlton, Kevin is an expert in promotion through aggressive publicity and will use his agencies and his skill and experience to promote the book.
>
> Adam Najberg is the Dow Jones Money Editor for Europe, Africa and the Middle East, which will give him credibility with the media. He has an extensive network of journalists who helped him promote his business humor project, BusinessTwaddle.com, and who will help him generate press for the book.

YOUR TRADE PLATFORM

If you are a doctor, lawyer, historian, psychologist, or other professional whose colleagues are a market for your book, large and midsize houses will want you to have a platform in your field.

They will expect you to be wired to what's going on in your field. A trade-off: The smaller the field, the fewer the sales, but the easier book buyers are to reach. Publishers will want you to have published articles in trade journals and to have spoken at trade shows or conferences. They will expect you to be a member of professional organizations. Being in a leadership position, locally or nationally, will impress editors more.

NAILING DOWN YOUR PLATFORM

To translate your platform into prose, use the header "The Author's Platform," and list (in descending order of importance) what you have done and are doing to promote your work and yourself. Include the following information in whichever order will best help editors say yes:

- The books you've written with sales figures, quotes from reviews, and links to the websites for them

- The number of talks you have done on the subject, the number you do in a year, and the number of people you speak to in a year. Include a link to a video of your speaking

- The names of major corporations/nonprofits for which you have spoken

- Your speaking fee, if impressive

- If you are selling anything, explain how many you sell and how much you average in sales at a talk or in a year's time

- The name of a newspaper or magazine in which you have a column, plus its circulation, if large, with links to samples of your work

- National radio or television shows on which you appear and how often, or how much media you get per year; include links to audio and video clips

- The online social networks in which you're active and the number of people you're connected to on each, if it's impressive

- The number of articles on the subject (and on other subjects) you've had published, and where, with links to the strongest of them

         How to Write a Book Proposal

- How long you've been writing your blog and how many people read it

- How many people visit your website per month

- The size of your e-newsletter subscriber list and a link to the newsletter

- The size of your e-mail list

- Anything else that will impress editors

Include a link to your online media or speaker's kit. Editors will check you out online and run a Google search to see what turns up. Ideally, your site should turn up first in search engine results. This is an indicator of how visible you are and how powerful your platform is.

The goal of including your platform is to convince editors that

- your visibility will make your book failproof.

- with your publisher's help, you will make your book as successful as you and they want it to be.

EXAMPLE: *9 Steps for Reversing or Preventing Cancer and Other Diseases: Learn to Heal From Within*

Although an online platform is now essential for a book like Shivani Goodman's, her paragraph proves she's ready to be published.

> Shivani has lectured, taught, and conducted seminars worldwide for 50,000 people for more than twenty-five years and has been interviewed hundreds of times on radio and television in this country and abroad. Since 1977, Goodman has presented forty seminars a year in the United States, England and Israel.
>
> Her audiences include individuals, physicians and therapists. She has taught royalty, celebrities, professionals, businesspeople, and housewives.
>
> Shivani has presented with O. Carl Simonton, M.D., bestselling coauthor of *Getting Well Again*, to physicians, psychologists, nurses, and social workers at hospitals. The author is a frequent speaker on stress management and self-healing at conventions, including: [list]
>
> Goodman has been the featured speaker for groups as diverse as: [list]
>
> She has also conducted seminars for organizations in cities including: [list]
>
> Articles about the author, and her television and radio appearances, draw people to her presentations.

Shivani self-published *Babaji: Meeting With Truth*, now in its fourth printing, which has sold more than 22,000 copies and been translated into six languages. More than 200 people came to her talks about it at the Bodhi Tree bookstore in Los Angeles, breaking previous attendance records, and the book sold out. She sells it on her website.

Next comes the key to promotion for all authors: an online platform.

CHAPTER 16

The Web as Synergy Machine: Building Your Online Platform

THE GOLDEN RULES FOR BUILDING YOUR ONLINE PLATFORM

Serve, don't sell.

IN SEARCH OF E-BUZZ: JOINING THE GREAT CONVERSATION

Social media is simply a combination of publicity, networking, and entertainment.

—JEN SINGER, AUTHOR OF THE *STOP SECOND-GUESSING YOURSELF* GUIDES TO PARENTING

In the Internet marketing classic, *The Cluetrain Manifesto* by Rick Levine, Christopher Locke, Doc Searls, and David Weinberger, the authors wrote that the Internet is "the great conversation," which offers a perpetually open invitation to anyone with access to the Internet. The book also says "markets are a conversation."

Joining the conversation is a tremendous opportunity and is essential to your future. The Internet does not mean money in the moment, but it will enable people to know, like, and trust you. Once they do, commerce will follow.

EIGHTEEN WAYS TO BUILD YOUR ONLINE PLATFORM

The following information adapts and expands Stephanie Chandler's excellent list in *The Author's Guide to Building an Online Platform: Leverage the Internet to Sell More Books*. First, see how other authors are using these tools and then adapt them for yourself. The Resource Directory (Appendix A) lists websites to help you, but these sites are a tiny part of continuing stream of tools and opportunities. Also, online tools will continue to change, even if the strategies don't.

1. **E-mail signature.** It may include:
   - your name and professional or academic degree
   - the title of your book, pub date (if it's in the future), and publisher, if the name will impress readers
   - contact info, including website, blog, social media addresses, audio and video links, phone number, and mailing address
   - upcoming events
   - products and services you offer
   - organizations you're a member of

   Balance keeping your signature brief and maximizing the promotional opportunity it provides. Keep it updated.

HOT TIP

Help people who want to e-mail you: Use your name in your e-mail address and make that address as short, clear, simple, and easy to remember as you can. As obvious as this advice is, every day I see addresses that don't follow it.

---

2. **Links.** Penny C. Sansevieri, author of *Red Hot Internet Publicity: An Insider's Guide to Marketing Your Book on the Internet*, says, "The biggest and best push with online marketing is the link building." Your links to your blog, other blogs, articles, profile, videos, audios, online posts, communities, directories, and whatever else you want to share (that promotes you and your book) are an essential part of the power of the Web. Continue to add reciprocal links to your site, which will keep increasing its value.

How to Write a Book Proposal

3. **Website.** Your homepage is the front door to your living room in cyber-space, and it has only seconds to give visitors a compelling reason to stay. Your content and presentation must capture interest immediately.

It's possible to start a free blog (on sites such as Wordpress and Blogger) rather than commit to a full-fledged site—just keep in mind that free blogs have ads and limited functionality. Authors should invest in a first-rate site. Visiting authors' sites will enable you do decide what will work best for you and may lead you to the designer who can help you.

Here is a list of common content and functionality you'll find on authors' sites (adapted from the second edition of *Guerrilla Marketing for Writers: 100 Weapons for Selling Your Work*):

- contact information
- media kit and speaker's kit, if you have one
- upcoming appearances
- blog
- a description of books, products, and services
- links to other helpful sites, video and audio files, and anything else that adds value to your site
- links to your articles
- newsletter sign-up or other free information to capture e-mail addresses
- a sample chapter or a new chapter every month or annotated table of contents
- updates to published books; mention in the back of your book that it's being updated online.
- a forum so visitors can

  - ask questions
  - add stories or information or links to them
  - provide links to other sites worth visiting
  - discuss what's going on in your field and their experiences with your books, products, and services
  - suggest how to improve your site and anything on it; reward those who offer ideas you use

- New material you test-market by asking for feedback

- reviews of your books or quotes from them
- testimonials about your books, classes, and talks
- photos of your book and illustrations
- surveys, questionnaires, and contests
- a teacher's guide, if your book has adoption potential
- a reading guide, if your book will interest book clubs
- an evaluation form for your talks and your site
- answers to frequently asked questions
- an annotated recommended reading list of books in your field, books about writing and publishing, and other books you love
- one or more ways to buy your books, products, and services. Linking to booksellers might earn you a commission. If you sell copies, be creative about what value you alone can add to the book, such as:
  - a link to free information with the confirmation of a purchase
  - personalized, autographed, and gift-wrapped copies
  - multiple-copy discounts
  - a discount on other products or services, based on date of purchase, or the first ten responses to a blog post (or any other reason you can think of)
  - a free book if the customer buys other products or services, or responds to a blog post quickly
- a resource directory for your topic—the one from your book or one created for the website that you keep up to date
- paid advertising or ads you trade for; keep these focused on products and services that will interest your readers.
- a professional-looking but endearing photo of yourself
- the name of your site, along with contact information and links to all the pages on your site, at the top and bottom of every site page
- as many other reasons as you can devise to convince visitors to stay, return often, and tell others to visit your site
- a way for visitors to subscribe to your blog, newsletter, or site updates, all of which are important for maintaining the relationship

4. **Social communities.** Twitter, Facebook, YouTube, LinkedIn, and other social networks are dynamic ways to connect with your communities.

Social networks give you the chance to build relationships with potential readers, but it is not a channel for direct selling. As Christopher Locke said in *Gonzo Marketing*, "The fundamental message of marketing must change from 'we want your money' to 'we share your interests.'"

Online communities can

- help you find people who share your passions.
- enable you to help people by giving them information, advice, and encouragement.
- build traffic for your site, blog, videos, and events.
- promote what you do and sell.
- help you add addresses to your e-mail list.
- add subscribers to your e-newsletter.

- create opportunities for starting affiliate programs.
- increase your value to others by enabling you to share what you learn.
- create and test new information, handouts, and booklets.
- start virtual relationships that develop into real-world friendships.
- raise your search-engine rankings because your posts can be added automatically to your home page.

Build social profiles that reflect your goals. Let your personality and distinctive voice shine through. Although you want people to get to know you, focus less on sharing personal information and more on being a source of helpful information and an authority on your subject.

Be active by providing quotes, insights, news about people and your subject, blog posts, articles, books, events, videos, websites, recommendations, resources, tech tips, reminders, and products and services. Bookmark your favorite sites on Digg, Delicious, and StumbleUpon so you can share them.

Social networks also give you the chance to meet and learn from top authors and key people in your field. Friend them on Facebook, follow them on Twitter, link to them on LinkedIn, and participate on other sites that are right for your book. The big expense here is time, so focus on the best opportunities to reach your potential readers (Where do your readers congregate? Go there!), and spend your hours online productively.

5. **Participation in discussion groups, forums, and chat rooms.** Find communities of interest in your subject. Contribute to them and, when you're ready, start your own group.

6. **Community of bloggers.** Search blog directories to locate blogs that cover subjects related to yours. Ask top-ranked bloggers for guest posts, a column, links, and—when the time comes—reviews and interviews (and to be a stop on your blog tour, which I discuss in chapter nineteen).

HOT TIP FROM STEPHANIE CHANDLER
....

Visit www.allexperts.com and, if you are one, start imparting your wisdom.

7. **Articles.** Take advantage of the abundant opportunities to write short articles or top-ten lists for industry publications and related websites. Aim for one or two articles a month; include links and your bio at the end of them. Make a list of sites in your field that accept articles and use one of the syndicates listed in the Resource Directory (see Appendix B).

8. **Blog.** A blog allows you to post brief entries about your subject and yourself that will interest or help readers. Make it a goal to become a spokesperson in your field. To help build your readership, think visually. Find ways to use photos and graphics to give your blog visual appeal.

   With growing frequency, blogs are becoming books, and "blooks" are becoming bestsellers, among them *The 4-Hour Workweek* by Timothy Ferriss, *I Hope They Serve Beer in Hell* by Tucker Max, and *Julie & Julia: My Year of Cooking Dangerously* by Julie Powell.

   But before you try to publish your blog as a book or use it as a sample of your manuscript, make sure it's your best work.

HOT TIPS

If the prospect of writing a blog seems daunting, these ideas will reassure you.

- You can try out material in your book as you write your blog, or you can adapt your book into a blog after the book is published.
- Readers stay with a blog post an average of ninety-six seconds, so entries can be a short as one to three paragraphs.
- How often you blog is less important than doing it consistently. But the more often you blog, the more potent its value.
- You can write posts in advance—perhaps a week's worth at a time.
- You can exchange posts with other bloggers.
- You can use new information you discover and recycle it in articles, talks, and books.
- You can enlist others to help answer questions.
- You can use an RSS feed that enables readers to subscribe to your blog.
- You may be able to contribute to popular blogs like the Huffington Post or its equivalent in your field.

> • You can take a break and let readers know when you'll be back. Better still, find someone to fill in for you.
>
> One of the ways Timothy Feriss promoted *The 4-Hour Workweek* was to build relationships with bloggers so they would write about the book. It worked.

9. **Teleseminars and webinars.** Teaching classes

- is a source of income.
- creates customers for your book.
- leads people to what else you're doing online.
- publicizes you and the book, especially if the title of the class is the title of your book.
- enables you to test-market your book.
- generates testimonials you can use on your site and in your press kit.
- gives you the chance to create partnerships by bringing in guest teachers.

On teleseminars, you're just talking, although you can direct students to handouts they can download. On webinars, students see information on their screens as they listen to you speak.

Teach live classes first so you become confident as an instructor. Take teleseminars so you can see how they're organized and presented, and when you're ready to share your work online, begin teaching.

PROMOTING YOUR BLOG

There are more than 100 million blogs, but few are read by enough people to impress editors. If you're writing to be read, here are some ways to promote your blog:

- Announce it to your communities.
- Share links to new posts on your social media networks.
- Comment meaningfully on others' blogs, which usually allows you to include a link back to your own blog.
- Ask for reciprocal links from other blogs.
- Include the address in your e-mail signature, online profile, business card, stationery, and bio.
- Host it on your website.
- Mention it in your books, talks, articles, and conversations.

---

10. **Videos**. YouTube is one of the most popular sites in the world. Creating vlog posts (video blog posts) or book trailers is another way you can share information, teach, and spread the word about you and your book. It doesn't require much Internet savvy to create videos if you already have a Flip cam or a webcam built into your computer. Uploading videos to YouTube and other video-sharing sites (or your own blog) is as simple as uploading a photo or creating an e-mail attachment.

A simple, beautiful example of video that has had more than 400,000 views—www.bkconnection.com/thefivesecrets—was created for John Izzo's *The Five Secrets You Must Discover Before You Die*. Have someone edit and label videos if you can't so they look professional.

So many people watch online video on their computers and television sets that, even if all you can do is be a talking head, find a way to make at least one short, lively book trailer or video. The more visual your book, the greater the potential for using video to sell it. Use what other authors are doing as a guide.

Why do videos?

- They enable potential readers to connect with you in a way words can't.

- You can link to them in your proposal, and they can help sell your book.

- Your book can benefit from viral marketing as viewers share the videos with friends, creating visibility and sales.

- Your personality can help generate sales by showing how enjoyable your book will be to read.

- Videos are a way of test-marketing your book and yourself. The response to your videos will give you and editors an idea of the possible response to your book.

- Editors, media people, and potential speaking clients use videos to judge how well writers communicate.

- Videos raise your rankings on search engines.

If you're not sure where to start, think about the these possible functions for book trailers:

- Demonstrate something in your book

- Show illustrations from your book
- Dramatize scenes from a memoir
- Show excerpts from talks, classes, or TV interviews
- Create a visual diary by showing the places you go to research your book
- Interview people you quote in your book or speakers at an event
- Provide testimonials from readers or people who have used your advice

To see an example of an author who has used videos (posted on YouTube) to build his platform and fan base, visit John Green at www.johngreen books.com.

11. **Podcasts.** Like YouTube, iTunes is another popular site that gives writers an opportunity to reach a very large audience, at no cost. iTunes allows anyone to make podcasts available through their store at regular intervals as a series. You can make your work available as a complete audiobook, in chapters or segments, or in one-minute snippets that help build the audience for your work. People can subscribe to your podcasts through services like iTunes, which will automatically notify subscribers when a new segment is available. Audio-recording software is built into computers and mobile devices.

   Online marketer Penny Sansevieri, at Author Marketing Experts (www.amarketingexpert.com), syndicates podcasts to directories, has them transcribed, and then syndicates those podcasts as articles with links. At Yaktivate.com, Denise Bach teaches clients how to make and use podcasts. Length to aim for: fifteen minutes or less.

12. **Newsletter or e-zine.** Build loyal fans by publishing an e-zine or newsletter with the same kinds of information you use on your blog or find in other newsletters and magazines. Include a sign-up box on every page of your site.

13. **Partnerships.** As suggested in the chapter on building communities, create a community of people who reach a similar audience and look for ways to team up and promote each other. You can publish articles on each other's websites or newsletters, host an event or contest together, or even share a blog. Be creative and pool your resources.

How to Write a Book Proposal

14. **Radio and television shows.** Interview shows provide an opportunity for exposure. Unlike traditional media, in which you might be interviewed for ten minutes, online interviewers welcome guests for up to an hour, and the interviews are archived and available worldwide. Look at BlogTalkRadio as one possible avenue for starting your own online radio show.

15. **Book reviews.** Review books, especially those in your field, that you want to read. Reviewing enables you to

    - get free books.
    - add to your knowledge of the subject.
    - add to your credibility.
    - create relationships with readers, authors, and review services.
    - give search engines another reason to link to you.
    - promote yourself in your signature.

    To maintain your credibility, only write reviews, online or off, that are honest and balanced. But because you want to make friends, not enemies, also only review books you can write about favorably. The authors may review *your* book! You can find broad, lively communities of reviewers at Amazon, GoodReads, and LibraryThing.

16. **Contributions to wikis.** Write for wiki sites in your field and about you and your subject. When the time comes, write about your book on Wikipedia. Include links to your website and blog.

17. **Profile updates.** Many networking sites allow you to post a bio with your public profile. Make sure you have several versions of your bio available in short, medium, and long formats. This will keep you from having to re-create your bio many times and will ensure your message is consistent. Showcase your expertise in your subject, mention your book(s), and include a link to your site or blog. Because of links, search engines, and your communities, everything you do creates synergy with everything else.

18. **Mobile applications.** It's an emerging and exciting medium, but mobile apps for smartphones and the iPad are already becoming a popular

avenue for authors, publishers, and all media/content creators to promote their ideas and products. You can either create and promote a free app (to get the widest possible adoption) or a paid app. You'll probably need technical assistance to create the app and to help identify how to turn your book idea into an engaging interactive experience; read this article to start generating ideas: http://blog.writersdigest.com/norules/2009/10/23/TurnYourBookIntoAnIPhoneApp.aspx.

HOT TIPS

- David Marshall, Berrett-Koehler's director of digital communities, recommends devoting 10 percent of your workweek to social networking.

- Don't worry too much about how good you are when you begin your online efforts. You'll have models to draw on, and you can ask your community to critique your efforts before and after you post. The prevailing wisdom is that you jump in and get better as you go. Start with what you find easiest and enjoy the process!

THE BIG BONUS

The more active you are online, the higher your ranking will be on search engines. This makes it easier for people seeking information to find you and increases the number of hits your name generates. The more links your name generates, and the higher your rankings, the more impressed editors will be.

Whatever you want editors to know about you that's not in your platform will be in your bio, the subject of the next chapter.

CHAPTER 17

Laying Your Life on the Lines: Your Bio

THE GOLDEN RULE OF WRITING YOUR BIO

Include everything about you that's not in your platform and that will help convince an editor to say yes.

After your section on platform, include a section called "About the Author." Describe, in descending order of relevance and importance, everything about you that will prove you can write and promote your book. Don't repeat what's in your platform.

TEN SLICES OF LIFE

Here are ten aspects of your life to cover in the most effective order. Most are optional.

1. If you have had a book on another subject published, give the title, publisher, and publication year. Include sales figures, if they're impressive, and subsidiary rights sales.

2. Editors won't take the time to read complete reviews unless your books have received raves in major periodicals, so, after your bio, under the heading "From the Reviews of [title of book]," include up to a page of

quotes—in order of their value because of the quote or the source. If editors are not likely to be familiar with the source, describe the periodical and note its circulation, if impressive.

3. If your previous book received favorable reviews in important magazines or newspapers, include a link to them, or underline the good parts and enclose the reviews at the end of the proposal or in the left pocket of the paper folder in which you submit your proposal. Don't staple the pages if you or your agent will photocopy them.

4. If your book was blessed with a half page or more of quotes from opinion makers, include quotes in descending order of the words' or the source's impressiveness.

5. If you plan to write books on other subjects, list up to three ideas or titles in the order of their commercial potential. As noted earlier, agents and publishers are eager to discover authors who can be counted on to turn out a book a year, and every idea that editors like is another reason for them to work with you. You might wind up selling another book you plan to write instead of the one you propose. Editors may have their own book ideas, and if they're impressed enough with your proposal, they may give you a writing assignment.

6. Include every facet of your professional experience that adds to your stature as a person and a writer.
   - education
   - awards
   - special skills
   - writers conferences you've attended
   - writing contests you won or in which you received honorable mentions
   - memberships in writers organizations

7. If you've received letters, comments, or publicity about you or your work that will impress editors, include up to a page of quotes from them after your bio. If you're mailing your proposal, you may prefer to include the letters at the end of your proposal.

8. If you own a business, mention it and anything else worth mentioning about it. Include a link to the website for it.

9. If you have a family, mention it along with where you live. If you wish, mention community service, travel, hobbies, other activities you enjoy, and anything else that may create a personal connection between you and an editor.

10. If there's anything else about you that you want editors to know, include it.

COMMON MISTAKES TO AVOID

- Avoid the extremes of hype or false humility, even if you have a lot to be modest about.
- Don't be cute or overly creative. Let your personality shine through in your bio—especially if it will help you sell the proposal or promote your book.
- Don't offer sympathy for agents and editors: *I know that many books pass your desk, but ...*
- Avoid the words *currently* or *at present.* Using the present tense suffices.

HOT TIPS

- Avoid using a résumé instead of a bio. Résumés are formal and contain information editors don't need. You may be applying for work, but you're not applying for a job. If you are an artist or professor, and you think your résumé is also necessary to prove your qualifications, make it an appendix.
- If you are writing a humorous book, be funny.

PICTURE YOURSELF PUBLISHED

Include a photo that will help sell you as a media-genic professional. If you can, make the photo relate to your book. For example, if you are writing a book about fly-fishing, aim for a photo of you standing in your waders and casting into a stream.

If you are sharing authorship with a writer, photographer, or illustrator, include a bio and a photo of each of you. If you're just using someone on a work-for-hire basis and paying her a fee for all rights to her work, include a bio but not a photo.

Writing the promotion plan that will get you published is next.

CHAPTER 18

Ushering Your Baby Into the World: Putting Your Promotion Plan on Paper

THE GOLDEN RULE FOR WRITING YOUR PROMOTION PLAN

Exaggerate nothing.

THE GOLDEN RULE FOR CARRYING OUT YOUR PLAN

Deliver more than you commit to.

Writing is 10 percent, marketing is 90 percent.

—JACK CANFIELD

Your book is your baby. You give birth to it twice: once when you conceive and write it, and again when you and your publisher bring it into the world and nurture its success. Writing your promotion plan is part of that process. It shows your commitment to put your pride and passion to work on behalf of your newborn.

Begin your promotion explanation by telling editors the most impressive thing you will do and then working your way down the list of whatever will convince the editor about your ability to promote your book. When it makes sense, use numbers to indicate how many or how much of something you will do. I've started plans with the traditional off-line activities that publishers like to see, but your online promotion campaign may be more impressive. If it is, start with that (which we'll discuss in the next chapter). Present your plan in whichever order will most excite editors. Feedback from other writers will help ensure your plan is at maximum strength.

Under the subhead "Promotion," begin your plan by writing *To promote the book, the author will ... .* Then begin a bulleted list, starting each new item with a verb.

If you will have a promotion budget, write: *Carry out the following campaign at his/her expense ... .* This indicates that you will cover whatever expenses your plan requires except for copies of your book that your publisher supplies for promotion.

Or you could write: *Match the publisher's out-of-pocket consumer promotion budget up to $X upon signing to carry out the campaign.*

If you have access to a publicist or you will hire one, write *Hire X to* [list whatever your publicist will do online and/or off, that will most effectively and economically get books to the cash register].

INTERESTS VS. AGENDAS

Because tours aren't cost-effective in terms of the publicity or sales they generate, publishers are touring authors less and doing more with them online. However, large houses are promoting hundreds of books a year; you're promoting only one.

If your goal is to become a successful author, you need to build communities of all the people who can and want to help you. You can accomplish a lot online, but meeting people is also essential. Partly because of the isolating effects of technology and working at home, people want more of a relationship with authors than words in a book. This is one reason politicians shake as many hands as they can and authors give talks and do signings.

If you can get yourself around the country without a publicist, write: *Give talks [that you or your publicist will arrange] in the following X major markets and their metropolitan areas, and do signings and media interviews that the publisher arranges [if you're not using a publicist] ... .* Then list, in paragraph form, the cities and metropolitan areas you will go to once your book has been published. If you can get paid enough to speak to justify your time and expenses, or you can afford to spring for the costs and you enjoy speaking, take your act on the road. Give yourself a national tour, but make sure that everyone—your staff and freelance publicist and the publisher's publicist—agree that between talks, doing media, speaking to book clubs, and doing signings, it will be worth your time, energy, and expenses to do a tour.

If you are already giving presentations, you may be able to choose the best places to give them. If not, don't worry—you don't have to know where you will speak in each city. Once your manuscript is accepted, you will have at least nine months to set up places to speak. If you won't have a publicist, try to get a commitment from your publisher when you sell your book to have your staff publicist pitch the media in the cities you will visit. Publishers sometimes use freelance publicists to supplement their efforts. If you haven't chosen a publicist when you sell your book, your publisher may have a recommendation. Appendix B is about hiring a publicist.

If you can get paid to speak, the publication of your book is an opportunity for you to make money. Between speaking fees and back-of-the-room sales, set a goal of at least breaking even with the relationships you create, the publicity and speaking offers you generate, and the new fans and clients you find as bonuses.

HAVE EVENT, WILL TRAVEL

Your publisher will tell you if it's worth doing book signings. Most signings result in fewer than ten sales. What can be more productive is a creative event: a talk, a discussion, a demonstration, a party (perhaps with prizes), hosting an event that ties in with the topic of your book, or a fund-raiser at a bookstore or with an organization. Maybe you can tie it into a holiday or local event. Try to involve your communities in planning as well as attending.

Providing food and drink will give people a reason to come. For her memoir, *Harlot's Sauce*, Patricia Volonakis Davis fed people who came to readings with wine and pasta doused in harlot's sauce—salsa puttanesca. You can see a video of it at www.patriciavdavis.com.

Giving a portion of the proceeds to a worthy cause will be incentive for people to buy books, and you will feel good about giving back to the community.

CLUBBING IT

If you will visit book clubs, you can use bookstores, the website www.meetup.com, Craigslist, and your communities to line up clubs and indicate how many clubs you will speak to. Although clubs may be small, they may post their activities, so you'll be reaching the people they know.

You can also seek out opportunities to be involved in conferences related to the topic of your book. Write: *Give talks at the following conferences/conventions during the year of publication ... .* List trade and consumer conferences and conventions you know you will be able to speak at during the year after publication and those you can speak at every year. If the events are large, indicate how many attendees they have or the combined attendance at all of them.

Conferences don't usually pay expenses for speakers. They rely on attendees who are coming to the conference. But they may provide admission. Don't mention speaking at BookExpo America (BEA), the annual publishing convention. Your publisher will arrange this, if it's possible.

Then, if it makes sense for your book and justifies your time and expense, write *Continue to give X talks to X people a year.* Like giving talks on a tour, this must be a believable extension of your platform. Writers often tell me they're "willing to give as many talks as it takes." This is no help to publishers.

SELLING YOUR BOOK YOURSELF

Publishers always want the biggest buyback—the number of books authors will buy to resell or give away—that authors will commit to in their contract. A John Wiley editor noted that business authors sell books to 25 to 30 percent of their audiences. That stat isn't true for all kinds of books, but 25 percent seems a reasonable goal for other books as well.

If you give a talk that inspires and excites your audience, they will want to take your book home with them, if only, as marketing guru Seth Godin says, as a souvenir. Corporations understand this, which is why they sometimes buy copies for everyone in the audience. If you can sell a four-figure quantity of your book a year, give a round number. Assume that your publisher will include the number in your contract, so commit only to the largest round number you know you can sell.

Base this quantity on the number of talks you give and the average attendance at your talks. A large or midsize house will want that number to have four digits and won't be impressed by a number smaller than three thousand. Small houses will be satisfied with whatever number you provide or, if you can't specify a quantity, just knowing you will sell books.

You may prefer to say: *Sell X books the first X year and X books after that.* Or you may feel more comfortable saying: *Sell X books for X years and continue to sell books after that.*

If you will sell books but don't have enough information to commit to a number, write: *Sell books at my talks.*

Talk to speakers in your field to see what they sell. Commit only to what you are absolutely sure you can deliver. Underpromise and overdeliver. Test-marketing your book will enable you to choose the right number.

You can integrate your online campaign in this section by writing the following outline.

- Do a virtual book tour of
  - X blogs with a readership of X people.
  - X radio and TV shows.
  - X forums, chat rooms, and message boards.
  - X book clubs.

- Use the book's website to …
- Use the following social media in the following ways …
- Promote the book on my blog by …
- Produce a book trailer and post it on …
- Use my newsletter to …
- Use a coupon to offer …
- E-mail X sites with which I have reciprocal links about the book
- Provide a mailing list of online review services

  - Generate online reviews by …

- Use Amazon to …
- Use Google to …
- Teach X teleseminars per year …

THREE OTHER OFF-LINE COMMITMENTS

I. Developing a media kit

Editors are always looking for a combination of three things: an author with an established platform, a book with a solid media hook that virtually guarantees lots of publicity opportunities, and solid writing.

—GREG DANIEL, DANIEL LITERARY GROUP

For your media kit, include anything that will excite the media about you and your book. Keep in mind that authors post their media kits on their websites and don't mail them. There are no hard costs associated with printing and mailing a kit, and there are models galore online. Plan to create one for your book that may include:

- a one-page release (updated periodically)
- a list of ten to fifteen questions that reads like an interview
- your bio
- a photo of you
- a photo of the book cover
- illustrations from the book
- reviews
- a bulleted list of tips
- a bulleted fact sheet on the subject
- a list of appearances
- articles about you, your book, and your subject
- links to a book trailer, audio or video clips of you speaking or being interviewed Because links may not function well, editor Alan Rinzler recommends you also include a link to a video you speaking in a separate file with your proposal
- a list of media coverage you receive

- endorsements and testimonials about the book or yourself
- an excerpt or sample chapter
- information about how to buy your book
- a list of resources about the subject with links to them

If you're contacting the media, write a pitch letter with an irresistible one-line hook explaining why readers, viewers, or listeners will benefit from learning about your book, and a bulleted list of seven to twelve points that expand on your hook. Include a link to your kit.

2. Sending promotional copies

If you plan to mail promotional copies of the book to opinion makers or important publications and organizations in your field yourself, give a round number of copies you will mail with a cover letter and the groups of professionals who will receive them.

If you would like your publisher to mail them, your list has to convince your publisher that mailing these copies will be justified by their potential for promoting your book by generating talks, publicity, and sales. Your publisher may be willing to mail copies to at least part of your list, provide mailing envelopes and postage, or reimburse you for the costs to mail them.

HOT TIP

Staff publicists train on the job, are overworked and underpaid, usually have no compelling incentive to promote a book, and face no consequences if their efforts fail. When you sell your book, find out what your publisher's plans are for promoting it. If you can, meet with your publicist and set up a way for you to follow up so you can keep track of what's going on with your book. Keep in mind that plans may change and publicists may change jobs by pub date.

3. Securing interviews

If you have appeared on shows that have invited you back, and if their names or stations will impress potential publishers, mention them. If you've only had contacts with media people, you can mention them at the end of your plan.

Contacts alone are not ammunition; who knows whether they will be there (or will come through for you) when your book comes out.

Follow these power points by listing whatever else you will do that will excite editors, including the name of a promotional partner who will help you and in what ways (the subject of Appendix C).

If you have big goals—but not the promotion plan to achieve them—consider these alternatives.

- Try small presses or midsize houses outside of New York.
- Build your platform before selling your book.
- Self-publish your book to test-market it and build its value and yours before selling it.

AFTERGLOW: THE MEAT IN MEDIA

Whether you have a publicist or you do your own publicity, print and broadcast media are worth pursuing for five reasons.

- Publicity can be cost-effective and sell books.
- Media people are copycats. Having media exposure gives other media people permission to invite you on.
- You can have links to clips and broadcast interviews on your site and in your publicity materials.
- Being able to say you've been quoted or appeared in major media adds to your credibility.
- Media exposure can lead to speaking and writing opportunities.

EXAMPLE: *9 Steps for Reversing or Preventing Cancer and Other Diseases: Learn to Heal From Within*

Shivani Goodman's proposal included two promotional techniques for her book, plus a lifetime plan. If she were writing this now, she would be doing more online.

> To promote the book, the author will
>
> - match publisher's consumer promotion budget up to $X0,000 on signing to carry out the campaign

- hire X to:
  - set up a publicity tour to the following 10 cities: [list]
  - set up a twenty-city radio satellite tour
  - arrange for talks
  - place newspaper articles and send a story about the book to 10,000 newspapers
  - produce and distribute press kits
  - contact the following twelve kinds of magazines about running an excerpt: [list]
- make fifty presentations a year to [list of thirteen kinds of organizations]. The author will arrange for healthcare professionals to receive obligatory continuing education credits for attending. The author will set up healing circles, using the book as a manual, and conduct seven-day trainings for Healing Circle Facilitators.
- sell X,000 copies of the book a year.
- use the Web to offer a free CD of self-healing exercises, including "The Five-Minute Cancer Cure" for people who buy the book from Amazon on pub date and from www.barnesandnoble.com one week later.
- partner with colleagues that have large e-mail lists to drive buyers to her website.
- write a teacher's guide for the website for those who wish to teach the book's techniques.
- do one teleseminar a month the year of publication.
- send 250 promotional copies to key people in the alternative medical field, medical-related non-profits, media, academia and government, supplying the copies the publisher can't.
- with your approval, submit one excerpt a month to the fifty largest health and other consumer magazines; health or lifestyle editors at the fifty largest newspapers; and seventy-five newsletters for healthcare organizations.
- offer a free seminar on Maui with the purchase of the book that the author will videotape for an infomercial. She will use her connections with the QVC Home Shopping Network to schedule appearances.
- try to sell audios to airlines.

LIFETIME MARKETING PLAN

The author will continue to promote the books by having an annual promotion budget of $20,000 to:

- schedule forty radio telephone interviews a month.
- deliver four presentations a month to healthcare workers and groups, hospitals, healthcare agencies, colleges, civic groups, companies and conferences.
- have X scheduled radio and television interviews in X major markets during national cancer month in October.

TWO BUILT-IN PLANS

9 Steps also had two built-in promotion plans, as follows.

- The book recommends using the book to form healing circles and provides a manual to help patients, parents, caregivers, loved ones, those wanting to prevent disease, and healthcare professionals form and facilitate these groups.
- The book shows readers that they can erase pain, suffering and disease by sharing the book's exercises, and encourages readers to tell two people about it, who will also be encouraged to tell two people about it.

DIY DEPARTMENT: PUBLICIZING YOUR BOOK YOURSELF

Out of necessity, most authors publicize their books themselves. If you will do your publicity, you face the challenge of proving to editors that you can. Having already done it successfully, perhaps in your city, will help.

Even with limited funds, you can

- analyze the nature, size, and location of the markets for your book, and figure out how to reach them effectively and inexpensively.
- contact the media yourself. They have time and space to fill, and they need you. Prepare your website, publicity material, and yourself, and go for it!
- reach thousands of readers through radio shows—and you can do them in your pajamas.
- join writers organizations and go to writers events. Ask people in your writing community to share the techniques they find effective and help you figure out how to apply them to your book.

- do an online search and read writing magazines, *Publishers Weekly*, and books on publishing and promotion.

- consider finding a publicist who will consult with you about what to do and how, and then let you do it yourself, perhaps with the help of an intern, friend, or significant other.

- have a promotion potluck. Invite writers and have a brainstorming session on one another's books.

EXAMPLE: *Stooples: Office Tools for Hopeless Fools*

If Kevin Reifler were writing the plan for *Stooples* now, he would take advantage of social media. But as it is, his plan reflected that Kevin owns two PR agencies.

Kevin and Adam will carry out the following campaign:

- A promotional tour: On publication, the authors will do a tour of the following twenty cities: [list of cities] In each city, the authors will:
    - arrange for a bulk sale or sell books
    - give media interviews
    - speak to at least one business organization
    - develop one-page "ads" for a product that relates to the group they are speaking to and give the product to attendees
    - develop a PowerPoint presentation with a dozen products that the authors will build into a talk about what attendees will see in their offices in the coming year
    - create a product to use as a prop during their talks
    - arrange two phoners a day for the first ninety days after publication.

- Contacting the media: Kevin will contact the following media:
    - wire services including Dow Jones, Associated Press, Reuters, Bloomberg and UPI
    - news/feature services including King Features, Cox, Gannett and Knight Ridder
    - newspapers in the top 200 markets
    - business magazines including *BusinessWeek* and *Forbes*
    - major radio shows across the country that interview authors
    - television shows: if major morning shows book the authors, they will create products to show on the air, like the holiday toy segments
    - entertainment magazines including *People* and *Entertainment Weekly*

- E-mail releases: Kevin will continue to promote the website through press releases to business media, and will expand the campaign to book, entertainment and lifestyle editors. They will also send releases to the writers they know.
  - Prepare a press kit on their site will make use of the book's humor. It will contain:
    - an updated press release
    - author bios and photos
    - a humorous Q&A on the state of the office-supply industry
    - the Stooples company history
    - the copy and photos of three products
- Arrange for reciprocal links from such Web forums as:
  - Fu***edCompany.com, one of the most well-known business frustration websites
  - IHateMyJob.com
  - WorstJob.com
- Conduct two online surveys by asking a series of silly office-related questions such as: Where would you like your boss to stick the pencil sharpener? or Do you miss licking stamps, and what are you licking instead? The results of these surveys will be the focus of additional publicity efforts and will appear on the website. The authors will contact business or anti-business websites to partner on the surveys.
- Run contests on their website to see if readers can come up with wacky office products. They will publicize the winning entries and use them in future books.
- Contact Staples to see if they want to help. If not, they will contact OfficeMax and Office Depot. If one shows interest, they will offer to change the book's name so it's similar to the store's name: OfficeHacks or OfficeDeepHole.

FIVE KEYS TO EFFECTIVE PLANS

Here are five ways to meet publishers' expectations in your plan.

1. Exaggerate nothing. Assume your publisher will insert into their contract your budget and the number of copies you will sell per year.

2. Publishers respond well only to the word *will*. They want to know what you *will* do, not what you are *eager*, *willing*, or *available* to do.

3. Avoid saying *at least* or *a minimum of*. Use round but accurate numbers. If you write *Give talks*, publishers won't know whether you will do two or two

hundred. Provide a number, not a range of numbers. Wrong: *Give forty to sixty talks per year.* Right: *Give fifty talks per year.* Pick a number that's based on what you're already doing. By building your platform before you sell your book, you will know how many compelling talks you can give every year. Including numbers makes your commitments definite.

4. Use the active voice. Passive: *Bloggers in the field will be e-mailed.* Active: *The author will e-mail bloggers.* Tell publishers what *you* will do rather than what will happen to *others.*

5. If it's not obvious, tell publishers how you will do what you promise. To further improve upon the sentence in number four, explain how you will promote the book to bloggers: *E-mail the fifty most important bloggers in the field about the book and offer them: … .*

CHILDREN'S BOOKS

Publishers won't expect the same platform or promotion plan for middle-grade or young-adult books as they do for adult books. Follow this book's advice as closely as you can, adapt it as needed, and join the Society of Children's Book Writers & Illustrators.

FROM VERTICAL TO HORIZONTAL: YOUR PROMOTION TIMELINE

Because your proposal is a selling tool, your promotion plan is a top-down vertical plan that gives editors the information in order of its ability to sell your book. But you will also need a horizontal plan, a timeline so you know what to do when. Editors don't need it and don't want to see it, but you'll need it once your book goes into production. Your promotion network and your publicist will help you create it.

PROMOTION CODA

Don't let yourself be overwhelmed by the challenge of promoting your book. Adapt this advice to suit your book and where you are in your career. Writing a promotion plan works for self-help, how-to, consumer reference, and inspirational books. It also works for books about people whose fame, infamy, or achievements will interest the media and book buyers. If this model isn't right for you or your book, do what works best for you and your book, but make your plan as potent as you can.

Pursue your dreams and take the long view. You will continue to improve in your ability to write and promote your books. Persevere!

The following chapter is about the greatest opportunity writers have ever had to promote their books: online promotion.

CHAPTER 19

Making Your Desk Promotion Central: Your Online Campaign

> **THE GOLDEN RULES FOR ONLINE PROMOTION**
>
> • Find your potential readers and the gatekeepers to them.
>
> • Serve your potential readers as effectively as you can.

Never before has there ever been a better time to market your book.
— Penny Sansevieri, *Red Hot Internet Publicity: An Insider's Guide to Marketing Your Book on the Internet*

This is the best time ever for promoting your book online. Technology is unleashing an endless, accelerating torrent of new possibilities for promoting your book. No book can keep up with them. This chapter focuses on basics. For the latest ideas,

- read the marketing blogs listed in the Resource Directory (Appendix A).
- ask your online community.
- track what competing authors are doing.

Few new writers have the offline promotion plans that Big Apple houses like to see. But all authors can promote their books online. As Jeff Jarvis explains in *What Would Google Do?*, "[The Internet] enables every creator to find a public, the public he or she merits." You will use your online platform and what you learn from what other authors are doing to create a steady flow of helpful information, based on your book and your activities.

- Website: Keep updating your site with news about your book and adding links to and from blogs, videos, and other sites.

- Virtual book tour: It can include anything you do to maximize your visibility, including the following:

  - Blog tour: You can use your relationships with key bloggers in your field by asking them to interview you, write about you and your book, post an excerpt, or review your book. Visit one blog a day and ask bloggers to cross-promote your appearances, an incentive for them to help you.
  - Radio and TV shows: Contact them in advance so you can do one per day, beginning on your pub date.
  - Book clubs: You can talk to book clubs in person, by phone, or Skype.
  - Posting: Social networks, a fan page, groups in your field, forums, chat rooms, and message boards all welcome useful information.
  - E-mail list: One benefit of being active online is that it gives you the opportunity to build an e-mail list to use for your blog, newsletter, classes, and other events, and for doing an e-blast (see the section "The Money's in the E-Mail").
  - Teleseminars: If your book or your knowledge or experience make teaching possible, let your students help spread the word about your book.
  - Events: You can use Amazon's Author Central and other sites.
  - Contests on your site or blog: Ask for free promotional copies as prizes.

THE MONEY'S IN THE E-MAIL

Here, among endless possibilities, are other ways to connect with potential readers.

- An e-mail blast (e-blast): Publicity maven Steve Harrison found that the greatest asset rich writers have is their e-mailing list, so keep gathering addresses—your list will invest in you. You can announce the publication of your book to your e-mail list, which, ideally, is combined with other authors' lists, and offer free, instantly downloadable information as a bonus to recipients who buy your book on the pub date from an online bookseller. Have your customers e-mail you the confirmation of their purchase, at which point you e-mail them a thank-you note with a link to the downloadable information.

Try to get access to the e-mail lists of other writers in your field. Also, ask them to supply e-books, white papers, articles, MP3 files, special reports, or chapters of books you can offer. If you succeed, you're on your way to making your book an online bestseller.

The more sales your list generates, the higher your book will be on the bookseller's best-seller list. *Guerrilla Publicity* coauthor Jill Lublin found it takes fewer copies to hit the top of the list on www.barnesand-noble.com than it does on Amazon.

Renting a list from an author in your field may be possible. However, even if this idea works, it's a short-term phenomenon. Go for the cumulative impact of all your efforts over time.

- Blog and newsletter: Their ability to help you sell books will depend on
  - how many readers you have.
  - the value of what you have to say, whether you draw on your book or provide new information, and the quality of your contributors.
  - how often you communicate.
  - the value and timeliness of your responses to readers.
  - how well you promote your blog and newsletter.
  - the value of what your guest bloggers contribute.

- Articles: Submit articles on a regular basis to both sites in your field and a syndicate. See the Resource Directory (Appendix A).

- Video: Produce and post one or more book trailers, or create a series of video blog posts.

GOING WITH THE FLOW: MAKING THE MOST OF AMAZON

Amazon keeps coming up with new ways for writers to use Author Central to promote themselves and their books. Among the things you can do are

- post a profile of yourself.
- create a blog.
- add to the Book Detail Page.
- use the Tell-a-Friend link to notify your e-mailing list about your book's appearance on Amazon.
- send messages to your readers.
- create a list of your favorite related books, including yours, at Listmania.
- write a guide that relates to your book at "So You'd Like To ... "—a search tool that pulls together all the items and information a person might need for a given topic
- manage your search suggestions.
- add information about your book to the Editorial Reviews section.
- ask people to write reviews, and to start and join discussions about the book.
- write reviews for related books to help readers find your book and build relationships with the authors.
- start an Amazon Friends group.
- add keywords for the help-others-find-this-item link.
- write articles for Askville (askville.amazon.com)—a Q&A forum where people can ask questions and get answers from real people.
- tag your book with relevant terms to add to its searchable keywords.
- join the Associates program so you can earn a commission on whatever people buy when they link to Amazon from your site.

> **HOT TIP**
>
> In *Sell Your Book on Amazon: Top-Secret Tips Guaranteed to Increase Sales for Print-on-Demand and Self-Publishing Writers*, Brent Sampson advises writers to spend five minutes per day on six tactics rather than thirty minutes on one tactic.

THE OTHER ELEPHANT IN THE ROOM: GOOGLE

These are ways that Google can help you promote your book.

- Google Alerts will notify you when anyone posts something about you, your book, or your subject, giving you opportunities to monitor what's on the Web and to then join those conversations.

- One reason to maximize your online presence is to raise your rankings on Google. Using search-engine optimization (SEO) will help.
- Google's Blogger service offers you a free blogging platform.
- Google Groups provides opportunities to join or start communicating about your subject.
- Check out the Google Partner Program for authors.
- And, of course, searching on Google can connect you to the media and any person, product, service, business, organization, or subject you need to promote your book.
- Depending on your book and your promotion budget, you may want to consider using AdWords, Google's online advertising program.

MEETING THE CHALLENGES OF ONLINE PROMOTION

The challenges you face with online promotion are:

- integrating online promotion tools into the most effective plan for your book
- balancing online and offline promotion
- ensuring your time is productive

You will learn from other authors and experience how to do it.

EXAMPLE: *Guerrilla Marketing for Job Hunters 2.0*

David and Jay divided the plan for the second edition of their book into two parts: online and off-line. If they were writing the plan as I was writing this, they would have included more about social media.

> Googling "David Perry guerrilla marketing" generates 160,000 page views; "Jay Levinson guerrilla marketing" yields another 280,000. When bloggers and social networks can quickly debunk unfounded claims by *experts*, the trust that David has built up online since 1996 about job hunting is crucial for promoting the book.
>
> When you combine our online visibility, the trust we've earned, and the lessons the authors learned promoting the first edition, you will understand why most of the promotion will be online.
>
> David watched the book's ranking on Amazon whenever there was any press on the first edition. Blogging and online articles were the most effective

ways to raise the ranking. The only newspaper that affected sales was *The Wall Street Journal*.

So David and Jay are going to leverage the Web using the viral marketing techniques that MySpace, Facebook and Hotmail use.

ONLINE MARKETING

- E-mailing lists: Jay has a network of XX,000 opt-in newsletter subscribers to www.gmarketing.com and 100 online newspapers a month publish his articles, all of whom will receive news about the book.

- Website: David will promote the book on his websites www.perrymartel.com and www.gm4jh.com, which average X0,000 hits a month

- Blog tour: David will do a virtual book tour [which would now include social media; related blogs, forums, and chat rooms; and online radio and TV shows]

- E-mail newsletter: David has a newsletter that he e-mails to recruiters who post jobs and to media people. http://guerrillajobhunting.typepad.com.

- Typepad-Guerrilla Job Hunting blog: http://guerrillajobhunting.typepad.com

- YouTube will host a dozen market-making videos like this: http://youtube.com/watch?v=TlnmPU-T898.

- Webinars to deliver mini-courses and promote the Boot Camp: This one for the mortgage industry sold out days ahead of time: www.perrymartel.com/Video/3mf.wmv

- Guerrilla Marketing Job Board at www.gm4jh.com: The board is an aggregator like www.simplyhired.com and does not compete with major boards, so there is no conflict with boards that carry our articles.

- Job-alert tool: The book's website will integrate spider technology which surfs, sorts and categorizes jobs from individual newsgroups and aggregates them for easy selection. There are 1,000 newsgroups with jobs on them. The site aggregates more than 5,000 new jobs a week from more than 1,000 newsgroups.

- Recruiter tools: The book's website will offer a multi-site job-posting tool that allows recruiters to post a job to hundreds of newsgroups at once through a single window, and each post will carry an ad for the book—automated, viral marketing.

- Job boards: David will syndicate articles to the top 100 boards, and link to the top 200, so they can promote and sell the book to their visitors.

- www.TotalPicture.com: a podcasting site with 30,000 weekly subscribers. Will broadcast weekly a "Guerrilla Job Hunting Minute" podcast. There were three "Minutes" in this podcast: http://media.totalpicture.com/_qt/praill.mp3. This was the first of three podcasts.

- http://ExecuNet.com: the oldest and largest online community of executives in transition. Will host an exclusive monthly "Executive Guerrilla Job Search Webinar." Participants will get a copy of the book. The authors will record the webinars and sell them through the network.

- www.CollegeRecruiter.com: the largest job board for college grads in America, with almost 9 million registered candidates. Will publish a weekly "Guerrilla Job Hunting Tactic."

- http://RecruitingBloggers.com: daily digests of 400 blogs for job hunters and recruiters. Will promote daily blog postings from www.guerrillajob-hunting.typepad.com.

- www.LinkedIn.com: Will distribute "Job Hunting with LinkedIn," a digital supplement with links to a workbook on Amazon.

- www.Job.com: the fourth most visited career destination in the Career Services category. Will run two columns a month in addition to weekly "Guerrilla Job Hunting Tactics."

- http://NetTemps.com: the leading job board for temporary, temp-to-perm and full-time employment through the staffing industry. Will run two columns a month and weekly "Guerrilla Job Hunting Tactics."

- www.JobDig.com: a leading employment site that publishes local weekly newspapers covering eight states, will run two columns a month and weekly "Guerrilla Job Hunting Tactics."

- www.BlogTalkRadio.com: a one-hour weekly podcast for recruiters by recruiters, with an international audience in the thousands. Will host a bi-weekly five-minute phone-in show called "Ask the Guerrilla Headhunter" as part of the show. http://recruitinganimal.typepad.com did podcasts for the first edition: http://recruitinganimal.typepad.com/recruitinganimal/2006/05/review_guerrill.html

- http://JobJournal.com: a popular resource for job seekers, career changers and employment professionals, with one of the Web's largest libraries of career profiles and job-search advice, will run regular "Guerrilla Job Hunting Tactics."

TRADITIONAL MARKETING

- David and his partner, Kevin Donlin, will do thirty keynotes a year and sell books.

- Guerrilla Job Search Boot Camp: a job-search and training organization that David and Kevin own that supplements or replaces outplacement packages for downsized employees. The plan: Train thirty-two instructors who will train 3,000 people.

- Job Fair/Seminar Series: David and Kevin will sell the book at job fairs, bundling it with CDS:
  - Book + CD of job-search tips for $20
  - Book + 2 CDs of job-search tips for $40

  (20–25 percent of audiences buy today-only bundles; the $20 and $40 figures work because attendees have $20 bills.)

- Phoners: Using a database of more than 1,000 radio stations, David will arrange for two phone interviews a week for the first six months and one a week for the next six.

- Articles: David will submit articles to newspapers like *The Wall Street Journal* and the e-zines that covered the first edition.

CATCHING AN EXPLOSION IN PROGRESS

The Web enables you to create a whirlwind of electronic synergy without moving from your chair. When you read these words, the opportunities to use the Web to promote your book will be greater than when I wrote this. So add anything to this list that will make use of the continually exploding possibilities for promotion in cyberspace that will help sell your book.

If you can invest in your promotion, the next chapter has suggestions on how to do it.

CHAPTER 20

Throwing Something in the Pot: Your Promotion Budget (Optional)

> **THE GOLDEN RULES FOR COMMITTING TO A PROMOTION BUDGET**
>
> - To help extract the biggest commitment from your publisher, make the biggest commitment you can.
>
> - Assume that what you spend on publicity won't be justified by the media exposure you get or the sales it generates. Regard it as an investment in your career that will pay off as your career develops.
>
> - Commit only to what you can afford without creating a financial problem for yourself.

TURNING ON THE SPIGOT: GETTING PROMOTION MONEY TO FLOW

Here are six ways to get large publishers to turn on the spigot and let promotional money flow.

1. Have a successful book.
2. Be famous.
3. Convince them to spend a fortune to buy your book.

4. Make a publisher fall in love with your book, so no matter what your advance is, they will do whatever they can to promote it.

5. Convince them your book is a potential bestseller so they will stay with the book as long as sales warrant it—even if they start with a small budget.

6. If you aren't blessed with one of these five situations, make the biggest promotional commitment you can.

Publishers will be more likely to take a chance on your book if they see how professional you and your proposal are, and how committed you are to your book's success. Your proposal is a business plan in which you want a publisher to invest. The given is that you have a salable idea and you can write about it. But these virtues won't prevent your book from failing. Your promotion plan must convince a big or midsize house that its investment will pay off.

SIX PAYOFFS FOR HAVING A PROMOTION BUDGET

When you're deciding whether to invest in promotion, keep your eye on the doughnut, not the hole the expenses will make in your wallet. Here are six payoffs for having a budget:

1. If your publisher will match your budget, you have a good case for requesting an advance at least the size of your combined war chest. A buck for promotion should justify a buck in advance.

2. Your combined budget will affect
   - how your publisher positions your book on its list.
   - how many copies bookstores order and the quantity of the first printing.
   - how the media, book buyers, and subsidiary-rights buyers view and evaluate your book.

3. The more promotion your book receives, the better the chance it will have of selling. The better your first book does, the more your second book will be worth, and the more your publisher will promote it.

4. The more visible you and your book are, the more writing and speaking opportunities will come your way.

5. If a goal in writing and promoting your book is to build your business, visibility will help, as will the authority that comes from being an author.

6. Having a budget will also increase your ability to build your communities of fans, booksellers, authors, and media interviewers, all of whom will be a continuing source of support throughout your career.

If you are one of the tiny percentage of writers who can afford to spend money on promotion and can use the tax deduction, keep reading. If not, skip to the next chapter.

Having a budget is helpful, but equally important is showing you know how to get the biggest bang for the littlest buck. Your budget must make sense in relation to how you will use it. An exaggerated example: You can't say that you will have a promotion budget of $1,000 and that you will mail one thousand books to corporate CEOs. Editors know what that costs, and your plan will lose credibility.

TWO WAYS TO DECIDE ON YOUR BUDGET

- If you know how much you can afford to spend, figure out the most effective way to spend that sum.

- Use the following four steps to determine the budget for your book and the best way to spend it.
  1. Decide how many copies of your book you want to sell in the first six months.
  2. Figure out which promotional tools and techniques you need to use to sell that many books.
  3. Get costs for the materials and services you will need.
  4. If the costs are more than you can afford, scale back your plan until it fits your budget.

Publishers won't buy your book because you have a budget or reject it because you don't. We represented an author committed to spending $70,000 to promote her book, but we couldn't sell it to a publisher.

The lowest budget that will be meaningful to a large house is $25,000. The lowest budget worth mentioning is $15,000. Offer a budget only to large and midsize houses, although there is no certainty they will match it. It may become leverage for you if there are competing bidders for your book.

We once had two publishers who wouldn't bid more than $30,000 for a book, but one of them was willing to match the author's $20,000 promotion budget. That publisher got the deal, and the book benefited from a $40,000 promotion campaign. If your publisher matches your promotion budget, the house will decide how to spend its half, but ask about their plans.

If you can use all or part of your advance for promotion, you're fortunate. But don't write *Use x percent [or all] of the advance for promotion.* You won't know what your advance will be. If you're counting on using your advance for your budget, but the advance isn't big enough for the budget you envision, revise the plan and the budget so it works, and discuss the revision with your publisher.

Your platform or your profession should prove you are making enough money to carry out your plan. Estimate costs with a cushion because, like remodeling, it will cost more than the estimate. If your publisher doesn't match your budget in your contract, you're free to spend whatever you wish.

Maximizing the value of your book before you sell it is up next.

CHAPTER 21

Taking the Guesswork Out of Publishing: Fourteen Ways to Test-Market Your Book to Guarantee Its Success

THE GOLDEN RULE FOR TEST-MARKETING YOUR BOOK

To get the best editor, publisher, and deal for your book, maximize its value by test-marketing it.

AVOIDING THE CURSE OF THE FATAL FIRST PRINTING

My brother Ray, who's in the toy business, says, "Business doesn't go; you have to push it." Building momentum for a book has been compared to getting a 747 off the ground. It takes a lot of gas and runway, but once you achieve liftoff, the sky's the limit.

In *Get Known Before the Book Deal: Use Your Personal Strengths to Grow an Author Platform*, Christina Katz quotes author, blogger, and marketing guru Seth Godin: "The best time to start promoting your book is three years before it comes out." It can take that long to build your platform and ability to promote your book so it can achieve liftoff during its two-week to three-month launch window.

One reason 80 percent of books don't make money is that publishers test-market a book with the first printing. If you're coming from out of nowhere with your book, and the public doesn't know your name, here's how to prevent your book from being a victim of the Curse of the Fatal First Printing: Maximize the value of your book before you sell it by test-marketing it at every stage of its creation. Proving it works will make it easier for you to find an agent, sell it, and make it succeed.

Here's how to guarantee the success of your book by test-marketing it.

1. Test-market your idea. Try it out on your communities of writers, booksellers, and potential buyers to gauge its effectiveness against past and future competition.

2. Test-market your content with a blog. As soon as you feel ready to begin sharing information from your book with potential book buyers, begin contributing to blogs and then start your own. How much it helps will depend on

   - the quality of the information you and your guest bloggers provide.
   - how often you blog.
   - how you respond to readers.
   - how well you promote your blog.

3. Test-market your content with articles. Getting one or more articles published online and off helps prove you can write your book. It also helps prove interest in your idea. Here are the benefits you gain by writing articles:

   - Like your blog, your articles can be the embryo from which your book concept evolves.
   - Having an article published about the subject of your book helps establish your credibility as a writer and authority.
   - One or more articles that are long enough and strong enough in a respected periodical may substitute for a sample chapter.
   - Like your blog, an article may sell your book. Agents and editors spend their lives reading in hopes of discovering writers and ideas. If your article attracts an editor, you may only need a short proposal.

- You may be able to gauge whether your idea is a winner by who publishes your article, the price you receive for it, and the reactions from agents, editors, and readers.

- Researching an article will help you to prove to yourself there's a book in the subject.

- Writing articles will give you a feeling for how well you handle the subject, how you can solve the problems involved in writing the book, how long it will take, and how much you will enjoy writing it.

- The experience will help you decide if you are a sprinter (an article writer) or a marathoner (a book writer) able to go the distance.

- If you need to interview hard-to-reach people, they may be more agreeable to talk if you're on assignment for a newspaper or magazine than if you're doing research for an unsold book.

- Because your proposal may not sell, placing an article will help offset the cost of your time and research. If your article is popular enough, it may lead to additional articles on the subject, which will aid your research and increase the chances of selling your book.

- If your advance won't cover your expenses, selling articles based on the book or serializing it in a magazine will help make up the difference. If you can include a commitment from a major publication, it will be a powerful piece of ammunition for your promotion plan.

- Responses from readers may correct mistakes and provide new facts, sources, and lines of inquiry.

- Instead of, or in addition to, getting your articles published, you can post them on your website where they will promote your book, generate feedback, and enable editors to see more of your work.

- Writing articles after publication will continue to publicize the book. You can adapt your book or write new articles to test-market your next book.

- Articles may generate speaking opportunities.

4. Test-market your content and title with talks or readings. The parts of your presentation will become chapters. A book is a great calling card or

brochure—it will give you instant credibility with anyone on the planet. Books generate talks, but talks generate books.

HOT TIP

Because you can use even an iPhone as a projector, using PowerPoint or video is easier than ever.

As suggested earlier, see if the title of your talk will also serve as the title of your book. Maybe it could also be your brand, domain name, and trademark. Let all of them create synergy by selling each other.

If you're writing a memoir, give readings of parts of it.

HOT TIP

I'm a great believer in handouts: They give your presentation lasting value, add to your credibility, promote you and your book, and contain your contact information. One-page tip sheets (or booklets, bookmarks, or business cards) containing helpful info that comes from your book or site will reinforce your talk and make it more valuable.

For example, writers want to know how to find agents. Chapter thirty-eight in this book has a list of nine ways to do so, but when Elizabeth and I give talks, we've found that this information is more easily relayed by handing out a list than by speaking about all nine ways and then asking listeners to write down the names of books and websites. This way, they'll have the information ready to use, and can focus on our talk. Handouts we use are at www.larsenpomada.com.

Here are other reasons to use handouts:

- They make you and your talk more memorable and helpful.
- You can use them to test new information.
- They can spark questions that wouldn't otherwise be asked and enable you to make your handouts more helpful.
- You can update them easily.
- You can use them on your site as articles and blog posts.

- Listeners can hang them on their wall and refer to them when they need the information, can fax them to friends, and can refer friends to your site to find them.
- You can have a handout promoting your book, yourself, or an event.
- If there are extra copies, organizations may want them for members who couldn't attend your talk.
- You can use an auto-responder to send the handouts to people who buy something from you.
- If your talk is being recorded, you can suggest that listeners e-mail you if they would like the handouts, which may start productive relationships.
- Organizations that invite you to speak may print them for you.

5. Test-market your proposal with early readers. Do this in two or more stages if you can so you can integrate feedback from one set of readers into the version you send to the next set of readers. The more specific you are about the feedback you want, the more helpful your readers will be.

6. Test-market your manuscript. Have your readers grade your manuscript on a scale of one to ten, both as a reading experience and, if applicable, its impact on their lives or thinking. As I mentioned, if it makes sense for your book, ask them to grade what you want to be funny, moving, insightful, or inspirational.

7. Test-market your book by self-publishing it. New technologies have spurred a surge in self-publishing, a venerable tradition in American letters. The ease of publishing books is empowering hundreds of thousands of writers a year to publish their books—the ultimate way to test-market a book. If you have the luxury of writing your book before you sell it, and you have ways to sell it, you may want to prove it will sell by self-publishing it.

To gain momentum for his bestseller *Free: The Future of a Radical Price*, editor Chris Anderson made his book a "freemium" on www.scribd.com by allowing people to read it online for a month without being able to download or print it.

8. Test-market your ability to obtain a foreword and endorsements. You can use your proposal or manuscript to ask for quotes and a foreword from people whose names or affiliations will give your book credibility and salability with your potential readers.

9. Test-market your website. Your site will be so important to your future you will want to make sure it's up and running as soon as you can. A great site can help you promote your book and make a living. Use the sites of authors and professionals in your field as models, and do the same things, but better. Hire or barter for help if you're not tech-savvy enough to go it alone or can't enlist a teenager to help.

   Encourage your communities to visit the site and make suggestions. Also, forge as many links as you can with other sites. The goal is for your site to have maximum impact when your book is published.

10. Test-market your promotion plan. Here are ways to do it:

    - Share your promotion plan with your networks to ensure it will enable you to achieve your goals for the book.

    - Once your book is in stores, test your campaign in your city or in the nearest major market to see if it generates publicity and sales.

    - Integrate what you learn from your first city into your promotion plan and your promotion materials.

    - Or, start by promoting your book to its core audience. If you've written a self-help book that will interest psychologists as well as the general public, consider trying to get psychologists excited about it first. This will prove the book delivers, and they may recommend the book to their clients.

    - Use what you learn from your first city to do a regional campaign and then go national with it.

    - Create a timeline for carrying out your promotion plan and get feedback on it.

11. Test-market the first book in a series. If you are proposing a series of books, whether you sell the second one depends on the fate of the first. The bigger

the series you envision, the more important it is that the first book do well enough to justify your efforts, as well as those of your publisher.

12. Test-market your identity. How you think, write, speak, dress, act, communicate, and relate to people are aspects of your identity as a writer and a person. You need an identity that is

- durable.
- flexible enough to encompass what you want to do.
- commercial enough to achieve your financial goals.
- authentic.
- original.

13. Test-market your goals. One way to evaluate your actions is by answering this question: Do they help you achieve your short- and long-term literary and financial goals? Trust your instincts and common sense in setting your goals, and change them whenever and however you wish. To help you stay focused on your goals, you can

- write down the advance you want for your book—we're talking desire here, not necessity or realism.
- name the ideal publisher(s) for your book.
- take a *New York Times* best-seller list, enlarge it, and paste the title of your book over the book at the top of the list. This worked for Jack Canfield and Mark Victor Hansen.
- design the perfect full-page ad for your book in *The New York Times Sunday Book Review* or *USA Today* that includes copy about the book and quotes from the best people.
- write a dream review for your book for the newspaper or magazine in which you'd most like to see it by the ultimate reviewer.

THE IDEAL REVIEW OF *HOW TO WRITE A BOOK PROPOSAL* BY E.B. WHITE IN *WRITER'S DIGEST*

Literary agent Michael Larsen makes his living by helping his clients use *How to Write a Book Proposal* to sell their work. The book does an excellent job of show-

---

ing writers how they can make their living by following its advice. He has taken *The Elements of Style* to heart, and the book is an impeccable example of the writing he hopes to inspire.

Larsen keeps the structure of a proposal admirably simple. He divides a proposal into three parts: an introduction with information about the book and the author, an outline, and a sample chapter. Examples illustrate his points, and the book includes four annotated proposals he has sold.

The author maintains an engaging balance between a realistic, proven, state-of-the-art approach to writing and selling proposals and an inspirational tone that will keep aspiring writers turning the pages. The Hot Tips alone (which he scatters generously throughout the book) are worth far more than the cover price.

Larsen believes the right book will change the world. His book contributes to that noble cause by helping writers obtain the best possible editor, publisher, and deal for their books. The proposal book is part of a synergistic trilogy of helpful, enjoyable books on agents and promotion, the latter coauthored, that will help writers get the most out of this book.

A member of the Association of Authors' Representatives, Larsen has been a literary agent in San Francisco for almost four decades. During this time, he and his partner, Elizabeth Pomada, have sold books to more than one hundred publishers, as well as written or coauthored fourteen books themselves.

How to Write a Book Proposal was the first book on the subject and remains the best. Larsen is sure enough of his approach that he includes a money-back guarantee, which only one reader in twenty-five years has taken him up on. I guess you just can't please everyone. But, then, 100,000-to-1 suggests a degree of satisfaction that justifies the risk.

His upbeat, can-do approach will leave readers inspired and eager to begin their books. The only problem I had with the book is that when I finished reading it, I couldn't resist starting one of my own!

14. Test-market your commitment to your book, your writing, and your career. If you're reading these words, you can do this. But it will take more than ability—it will take *will-ability*, the unstoppable will to make

it happen. All these opportunities for test-marketing your book also test your commitment.

Writing your proposal should give you a growing sense of excitement about

- how much fun and satisfaction you will have writing the book.
- how good your book will be.
- how great an adventure promoting it will be.
- how gratified you will be about its impact on your readers.
- how you will build a career out of doing a series of books on the subject.

The greater your goals, the more committed you must be to do whatever it takes to reach them. Everything you do for your book helps everything else you do. You are creating seamless synergy between writing, speaking, and promotion that will catapult you toward achieving your goals.

But if, like most new writers, you're starting at square one, you may feel overwhelmed. Don't be! Your goals, your passion for your work, your communities of friends and writers, and a long-term perspective will keep you going. I'm not just writing about your book, I'm writing about the greatest gift you've got: your life. If writing and sharing *your* gifts with the world is what you were born to do, go for it!

PART V:
ADDING AMMUNITION:
THE OTHER PARTS
OF YOUR OVERVIEW

CHAPTER 22

Using Niche Craft to Create a Career Out of Your Idea: Spin-Offs (Optional)

> **THE HOTTEST TIP IN THIS BOOK**
>
> Agents and editors don't want literary one-night stands. They want to discover writers, not just books. Writers who turn out a book a year, each book better and more profitable than the last, are the foundation of successful agents and publishers. If your books ascend to publishing nirvana and become bestsellers, you will be one of your publisher's most prized authors, a *repeater* who produces at least one bestseller a year.

If you're writing a one-of-a-kind book like an autobiography, you get only one shot at it. Otherwise, practice niche craft: Look at your ideas in the broadest perspective. If your book has the potential to be a series, it will make you and your book more important to your publisher. Although it's unusual for first-time authors, you may even be on your way to a multibook deal, which will increase the house's commitment to you and your book.

If you can find an idea for a series of books you are passionate about writing and promoting, you can build a franchise and create a career out of your idea book by book, talk by talk, city by city, country by country. With the right idea, audiobooks, foreign sales, and other subsidiary rights will be a continuing, ever-growing source of income. It's working for Jay Conrad Levinson,

Suze Orman, Robert Kiyosaki, Deepak Chopra, and the Chicken Soupermen. Why not you?

Books often lend themselves to other books on the same subject or with the same structure. If you can develop your book into such a series, begin the spin-off section of your proposal with this statement: *[Your book's title] will be the first in a series of x books, including A, B, and C.* Don't overwhelm publishers with the scope of your idea—list up to three books, beginning with the most commercial idea.

Will your book lend itself to sequels? It depends on how you answer the following questions.

- If you're writing a book for men, are variations for women, children, or young adults possible? (Writing for children is an art unto itself, but your agent or publisher may be able to find a collaborator if you need one.)
- If it's an introductory book, can you write additional books for intermediate and advanced levels?
- If your book is directed at corporate types, would it also be useful to entrepreneurs and nonprofit groups? Would it help people with their private lives?
- If you're planning a book that can be adopted for a college course, can you write other versions that can be used in elementary school, high school, graduate school, English as a Second Language classes, or the burgeoning field of continuing education?

HOT TIP

Want a two-book deal? Make the last two pages of your proposal a single-spaced proposal for your next book.

- Make the first page a Proposal on a Page.
- On the second page, list your chapter titles, with a one-line description of each.

You may even find a publisher who wants to do your second book first.

A series of books is enticing, but a publisher may hesitate to commit to more than one book—especially by a writer without a track record—unless the series promises to be a surefire success. Your publisher may prefer to wait to see a complete manuscript or to see how the first book fares before committing to more books. And publishers don't want authors who seem more concerned about a series than their first book. But if your idea lends itself to being extended into other books, mention them. They will help justify publishing your book.

Should you succeed in publishing a first book, you will have continuing opportunities to generate ideas and copy for future books.

- You can use the last page of your book to ask for readers' reactions or experiences.
- Your blog, videos, website, and social networks will yield helpful information.
- You can ask for feedback when you give talks and interviews.
- Your fans will be eager to share their responses to your book and give you ideas for your next one.
- Your readers and audiences will ask you questions that may lead to ideas.

HOT TIP

You may be able to expand a chapter of your book into another book. In *Guerrilla Marketing Attack*, Jay Conrad Levinson wrote a chapter containing one hundred marketing weapons and a two-line description of each one. For *Guerrilla Marketing Weapons*, he wrote two pages about each one. Once you finish your outline, ask yourself if any chapters are overviews of other books. If so, it will increase the salability of your book. Jay let me use the weapons book as the basis for *Guerrilla Marketing for Writers*. The fourth edition of *Guerrilla Marketing* has a list of two hundred weapons. Think big.

The next chapter discusses the value of finding people whose names on the cover of your book will convince browsers to pick it up.

CHAPTER 23

Star Power:
Your Foreword and Cover Quotes

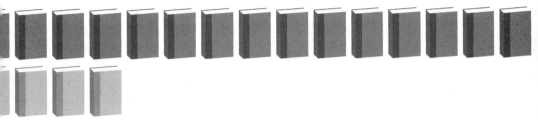

When you buy a nonfiction book, you want the author to be an authority on the subject, to have enough experience in the field and as a writer to write the book. As an author, you become an expert, which is why the word *author* is the first six letters in the word *authority*. How do you acquire authority before you write your first book? Here are three ways:

1. Establish yourself as an expert. What will give you credibility in editors' eyes?

   - A degree in your field
   - The number of years you've worked in the field or done research on the subject
   - The blog, books, and articles you've written, especially on the subject
   - The number of talks you've given on the subject
   - Your visibility online

2. Collaborate with an expert. Finding an authority on a subject or a professional who wants to write a book can be an easy way to break into publishing. Choose a person who is promotable and with whom you will enjoy a happy working marriage.

3. Find experts to write a foreword and give cover quotes. Though the least effective, this is the easiest and most common way to gain authority.

   Because Elizabeth and I knew Ray Bradbury, we were able to get him to write a foreword for Stan Augarten's *State of the Art: A Photographic History of the Integrated Circuit*. Like the rest of Ray's writing, his foreword was poetic, passionate, and visionary—and, at a dollar a word, it was light-years away from the penny-a-word stories Ray used to write for science-fiction magazines. The irony is that Ray was not a fan of computers. When he signed a guest book at the Los Angeles Public Library after Bill Gates had spoken there, Ray wrote *I don't do Windows!*

   According to speaker and author Sam Horn, best-selling authors receive between fifty and one hundred requests a week to read manuscripts. That's another reason to start cultivating relationships with opinion makers in your field.

   The less qualified you are to write your book, the more you need experts to vouch for you. If you want to write a book about health, psychology, or another subject requiring an academic imprimatur, and you don't have an M.D. or a Ph.D., find someone who does to give your book a professional seal of approval, and mention it in your proposal. The person doesn't have to be widely known.

THE FORTUNATE 500

The CEO of a Fortune 500 company, a professor at Harvard, or a member of the cabinet will give a book instant credibility. But if the expert you find is not well known, give his or her credentials, and indicate how long the foreword will be. Five hundred words will do. An expert's name can have value either because book buyers know it or because the person is affiliated with a well-known business or institution.

The time to approach opinion makers for a foreword and quotes is after you've written your proposal and received feedback from your network but before you share it with agents or editors. Your proposal must prove to the opinion maker that you both will benefit from the endorsement.

The two reasons to ask someone to do a foreword are equally important.

1. The person's stature in the field should lend authority to you and your book.
2. The person's fame should help convince browsers who see the name on the jacket to buy the book.

A book buyer who notices the endorsements by people or institutions they know or respect is more likely to buy a book by someone whose name they don't know because it feels like less of a risk.

People usually write quotes and forewords after they have read the manuscript. If the person feels strongly enough about the project or you, he or she may do the foreword in exchange for just the publicity and an autographed book. On the other hand, a well-known authority may ask for and deserve a dollar or more per word.

Your editor may think a foreword isn't necessary or may have a better suggestion for who should write it. The editor may be able to obtain a foreword from someone the house already publishes, which might save you money.

FINDING THE "WRITE" NAMES

Ideally, you'd like endorsements from instantly recognizable names. Depending on the kind of book you're writing, they may include:

- celebrities
- best-selling authors
- nationally known people in print, broadcast, and electronic media
- well-known politicians, government officials, and people in the military
- the top authorities in your field
- CEOs and entrepreneurs
- academicians
- heads of nonprofit organizations

- bloggers or others with large online followings

Even if the person isn't well known, the essential criterion remains: Will the person's name or credentials help sell your book?

How do you approach such people? Your first step should be to contact your networks; they can help you make a list of prospects and figure out how to best approach them. Then you face three challenges.

- They may not be receptive if you contact them without a referral from someone they know.
- The more well-known people are, the more besieged they are with such requests.
- They may prefer to wait until you have a publisher or a manuscript before they commit to giving you a quote.

Because potential readers won't recognize your name, commitments for a foreword and quotes from key people in your field will be powerful ammunition. They will also attest to your credibility and your ability to get help for your book. The most valuable people are those who don't usually give quotes.

Use your proposal to obtain quotes or the commitment to give them before submitting it. When you get a positive response, thank them and say you would appreciate any suggestions they may have about possible editors and other people to ask and, "if possible," their contact information.

Once you decide to write your book, start prospecting by

- Googling candidates.
- consuming media, especially those in your field.
- going to events.
- writing to people to praise their work.

If you can, mention to prospects that you will be quoting them in your book. Be creative and resourceful in meeting this challenge. If you are writing about the environment, consider Robert Redford as well as Al Gore.

If you cannot approach prospects with your proposal, list the ones whom you will approach after your manuscript is finished or accepted. If they're not well known, identify the people you will contact and list them in descending order of their value to your book. This indicates you at least know the people to ask.

EXAMPLE: *Marketing Your Services*

When we sold Rick Crandall's self-published book, *Marketing Your Services: For People Who Hate to Sell*, editors were impressed with the names he had on the cover of his book as well as the sheer quantity of testimonials he had collected for it. Here's what Rick's proposal said about the testimonials. (Note also the money-back guarantee—the author's way of expressing confidence in his work.)

> The three stars featured on the cover—Harvey Mackay, Ken Blanchard, and Tom Peters—will impress buyers. The colors and size of the book were chosen so that it stands out on the shelf. And the 100 percent money-back guarantee is unusual, encouraging browsers to buy.
>
> The book also has strong testimonials from Jay Conrad Levinson and Don Peppers, the hottest name in high-tech marketing *(The One to One Future: Building Relationships One Customer at a Time)*.
>
> The book opens with twenty-four different testimonials from service providers, in alphabetical order, from accounting, advertising, and architecture to stock brokerage, surveying, and window washing. Following these are fifteen more testimonials from experts. More comments are coming in all the time, so a new edition will have even stronger testimonials.

If you have a sense of mission about your book, the following chapter will enable you to use it to help sell your book.

CHAPTER 24

Your Call to Arms: A Mission Statement (Optional)

> **THE GOLDEN RULE FOR WRITING YOUR MISSION STATEMENT**
>
> Make editors feel your commitment to writing and promoting your book so they will share your passion for making it a success.

Your mission statement helps lay the groundwork for your promotion plan and will help ensure your proposal excites editors. It's optional because if, for example, you're writing an A-to-Z reference book, editors won't expect a mission statement; they will judge your book on your ability to research and write the information, and on your book's potential for backlist sales. If your book doesn't need a mission statement, please skip to the next chapter.

Having a mission statement wasn't my idea. I learned it from writers. I gave them the chance to write about their commitment to their book at the end of their bio, but writers felt compelled to place it at the beginning of their promotion plans. Your promotion plan is an expression of your commitment to your book. The kicker: The more passionate you are, the more your plan must reflect your passion.

Money doesn't rule publishing; passion does. It's contagious, but it starts with you. Expressing your enthusiasm and commitment to your book will affect how agents and editors respond to it. Your ideas, style, and promotion plan have to excite them, but your passion for your book must help inspire them to do their best to help make your book succeed and inspire the next link in the publishing chain.

Writing, researching, and promoting your books will take so much time, energy, and commitment that, for most books, your passion for doing it will be essential to your success. If you feel a sense of mission about your book, write one first-person paragraph about it.

EXAMPLE: *9 Steps for Reversing or Preventing Cancer and Other Diseases: Learn to Heal From Within*
Shivani Goodman included why she is passionate about her book.

> When I was dying of cancer I made a vow that if I lived, I would devote my life to help erase sickness, pain and suffering from the world. The book and my talks are helping to fulfill that vow.

EXAMPLE: *Climbing the Corporate Ladder in High Heels*
Kathleen Archambeau explained her mission.

> *Climbing the Corporate Ladder in High Heels* builds on a lifetime of work helping women transform their lives from victims to victors, from pink ghetto girls to highly paid professionals, from corporate clones to self-actualized women. The author is committed to elevating women through her writing, teaching, and lecturing.

MY MISSION WITH THIS BOOK

Helping writers shape their ideas and develop their proposals are two of the pleasures of being a literary agent. So I must make this book as effective as I can to do my job.

My desire to make each edition of the book more helpful is also fueled by letters from writers thanking me because the book enabled them to sell their proposals. They inspire me to keep making the book better.

It's been said that if you love what you do, you'll never have to work again in your life. Having a sense of mission about your book is wonderful, but proving you can promote it is essential. Everything in your proposal is an expression of your commitment to your book.

CHIN UP: SURVIVING THE EXERCISE

Sometimes writers must feel like the guy in the cartoon who asks a bookstore clerk for a book on suicide, and the clerk says, "Why don't you try self-help?"

It may sound like you must know everything about your book before you have fully researched it. But what you do have to do is convince editors that

- you know your subject.
- your idea won't require too much time or money to write and publish.
- you will do a superb job writing and promoting your book.
- you're giving them an opportunity to latch on to a winner.

Editors understand you are presenting your book only on the basis of what you know now. Once the project is sold, you and your editor will have an identical interest in producing the best possible book, and you will be free to improve on what you propose in any way you and your editor agree will help the book. Despite this opportunity, a well-thought-out proposal may save you grief later by ensuring you write the same book the editor bought.

You don't have to be an expert on your subject when you begin researching it. Beginning a proposal with an open mind and a passionate, insatiable curiosity is better than setting out with misconceptions or prejudices. One joy of the writing life is the opportunity to learn new things that enable you to grow both as a person and as a professional. Another is getting paid for the opportunity.

If editors are still reading by the time they get to the end of your overview, they'll finish your proposal. The next part of the book will describe how to write an outline that add to their sense of anticipation. Onward!

PART VI:
PUTTING MEAT ON THE BONES:
YOUR OUTLINE
AND SAMPLE CHAPTER

CHAPTER 25

Chapter Choices:
Finding the Best Way to Write Your Outline

> **THE GOLDEN RULE FOR CHOOSING TITLES**
> **FOR YOUR CHAPTERS**
>
> Give each chapter a title as clear, compact, and compelling as the title of your book.

No good book is ever too long, and no bad book is ever too short.

—Anonymous

The German poet Rainer Maria Rilke believed "prose needs to be built like a cathedral." When you set out to construct an enduring edifice of prose, give yourself a solid foundation on which to build. A sturdy, cohesive foundation will help convince an editor to back your proposal.

You can also think of the outline of your book as the blueprint of the cottage or castle your prose will build. Just as you would not leave a room out of your blueprint, your outline must provide an overview of what your book will cover. And just as you want your new home to be as beautiful as the design you've created for it, your blueprint must reflect the unity and harmony you want in your home.

How closely your finished manuscript matches your blueprint will depend on

How to Write a Book Proposal

- how well you write your outline.
- the need to explore new avenues of investigation.
- suggestions your editor may make.
- how cut-and-dried or open-ended your subject is.

Your book may change unexpectedly because of new ideas or information or an unpredictable turn of events. But, properly done, your outline will be a huge help in writing your book.

PROVE THE WORTH OF YOUR BOOK IDEA

"It's not a book, it's an article." This part of the book will prevent you from hearing this fatal complaint from editors. After you have marshaled the ammunition for your book, the next challenge is to convince editors you have researched the subject well enough to prove there's more than enough information in your idea to fill a book.

Your outline is the skeleton of your book—the parts of your body of information. The goal of your outline is to show how these parts fit together to form a harmonious structure that enables you and your editor to envision the finished book. Your outline must prove that you have come up with the most effective way to present your information, and it must make editors want to read the sample chapter.

Writing your outline also gives you the opportunity to help prove that:

- The quantity and quality of information you uncover will merit the publication of one book and perhaps a series.
- The book will be commercial enough to justify writing and publishing it.
- You will enjoy writing and promoting it.

TENTATIVE TABLE OF CONTENTS

Make the first page of your outline a double-spaced list of chapters (the best time for editors to see the list is just before they read your outline). Along the left margin, type the number of the chapter, followed by the title.

Chapter 1: Title [and subtitle if you use one]   11

If you wish, use subtitles to tell and sell: Tell readers why chapters exist and what they will get out of them to justify their time. If your subtitle will spill over to the next line, type the whole subtitle on the next line. Include the number of the page on which the outline begins and place it flush right on the line the title or subtitle ends.

Make your titles flow naturally, creating a sense of continuity in time, tone, and structure. Whet the editor's appetite for the outline that follows. Make your titles read like headlines that compel people to read the copy that follows. If you're writing a humorous book, make your titles funny.

Consider giving your book a superstructure by dividing it into parts. Give each part a title and use Roman numerals to number them. Deciding to divide your book into parts and creating chapter titles are two more opportunities for you to emulate successful books.

Your list of chapters is not the complete table of contents of your book, so don't include your book's front or back matter. Instead include just the titles of the chapters that editors will read about in your outline.

At the bottom of your list of chapters, include up to three pieces of information: the length of your book, when you'll deliver it, and whether you'll be updating it.

THE LENGTH OF YOUR BOOK

Unless you have a complete manuscript, editors know you are estimating the length of your book. In the proposal and development process, you'll inevitably make changes that you and your editor agree will help your book. But a proposal that presents a clear vision of every aspect of the book makes you look like the professional you aspire to be.

Writing your sample chapter will give you a sense of the relationship between outline and manuscript and how long it will take you to write the book. As you write your sample chapter, you will get a sense of how an outline corresponds to a finished chapter. At the bottom of your list of chapters (or table of contents), state the anticipated word count of your book. If your chapters will average x pages, indicate it. Use your models as guides.

Estimate the length of your book like this: *The manuscript will contain X words, including X words of back matter [if you'll have back matter], X photographs, X line drawings, X maps, and X charts [if you'll have illustrations].* Unless you indicate otherwise, editors assume illustrations are black and white.

Most manuscripts run between 50,000 and 100,000 words. That's 200 to 400 double-spaced, 250-word manuscript pages with 25 lines on a page. The word count you and your editor agree on will be in the contract with your publisher.

YOUR DELIVERY DATE

Here are alternatives for telling editors when you will deliver your manuscript:

- The author will deliver the manuscript X months after receiving the advance.
- The author has finished a draft of the manuscript/X chapters of the book and will deliver the manuscript X months after receiving the advance.

The more time you need to spend earning the income to live on while writing, the longer it will take to deliver your manuscript. When you know what your advance will be, you can fine-tune the delivery date.

When estimating the number of words or the number of months it will take you to finish your manuscript, don't give a range, such as 60,000–80,000 or six to nine months. Avoid the words *about, tentatively, estimated,* or *approximately.* Unless you have a finished manuscript, editors know you are guesstimating. Be specific, even though you can't be sure. This adds authority and credibility to your numbers.

UPDATING YOUR BOOK

Publishers want to publish a book and have it sell forever without needing to be changed. They're reluctant to publish books that need to be updated, unless—as with almanacs, consumer guides, or tax guides—a large enough readership needs the information.

If your book holds the promise of continuing sales but will require updating, write *The author will update the book every X years.* Try to avoid including information that will become dated before you revise it. To be considered an updated and revised edition, at least 10 percent of a book must be new. For a new edition, 30 percent of the book must be new.

A new edition is treated like a new book. It appears in your publisher's catalog again, the reps resell it, and you have another reason to promote it. Meanwhile, you can update your book on your blog or website. You can also update the e-book edition.

NEED HELP ASSEMBLING THE BONES?

If you need help creating your outline or creating a structure for your book, one of these two techniques will help you.

- Use index cards for the parts of chapters. You can shuffle them until they fall into the right order.

- Do what author Sam Horn recommends: mind-mapping.
  - Draw a circle that symbolizes the book and then draw gently curving lines going off from the edge of the circle like strands of hair waving in the breeze.
  - Along one side of each line, write a word or phrase describing the idea for each of your chapters.
  - Draw perpendicular lines off those lines to list words or phrases for the parts of each chapter.

You'll be surprised at how this stimulates your creativity. You can also use mind-mapping to create the title of your book by listing phrases that capture the benefits of your book. Then extract the essence of your book into the one title that belongs inside the circle.

THROW UP AND CLEAN UP: OUTLINING FROM INSIDE OR OUTSIDE

Ray Bradbury condenses the writing process into two verbs: "throw up and clean up." There are two basic ways you can ease your way into writing your outline—from the outside in or the inside out.

- From the outside in: Use the left side of your brain to burrow your way in. List your chapters and the bare bones or subheads of each chapter. Then flesh out the bare bones with connective tissue.

- From the inside out: Use the right side of your brain to create a body of information for you to draw on. Let at least one draft of your manuscript pour out and then create a new file of it, divide it into chapters, and whittle away until you have an outline for each chapter.

How to Write a Book Proposal

The second approach is more likely for a memoir than a biography you've researched enough to know what each chapter will cover. Other books, by their very nature, suggest a structure. A biography is structured chronologically; a how-to book starts with the simplest elements of a skill and guides readers from there.

DISCOVERING WHAT YOUR BOOK WANTS TO BE

Michelangelo believed his statues were waiting for him inside the blocks of marble he carved with hammer and chisel. Imagine you are a sculptor and that your idea is an enormous block of marble, inside of which is a magnificent edifice, the perfect embodiment of your idea. Your job is to use your craft and vision to chip away the superfluous until only an effective, organic structure remains. One sign of great art is that the artist's technique is so effective it disappears into the work.

Your outlines are not showcases meant to dazzle editors with your style—they are an opportunity for you to show how well you can research, organize, and outline your book. In your introduction and outline, content will count more than style.

But even though an outline cannot be a stylistic triumph, every word still counts. Providing a sound structure for your chapters and the book as a whole demonstrates your knowledge of the subject and your ability to transform your idea into a book of which you and your publisher will be proud.

A thin outline also invites unexpected problems. By not thoroughly investigating what's involved in writing your book, you are more likely to encounter more research to do, places to go, people to interview, or more illustrations or permissions to obtain than you thought. A comprehensive outline is the best way to prevent costly, time-consuming surprises.

THE GOLDEN RULES FOR WRITING YOUR OUTLINE

- Write to editors about the chapter.
- Write in the present tense.
- Use outline verbs such as discuss, describe, explain, and examine, varying them and how you use them.

> • Balance keeping your outline short and proving there's a book in your idea.

SIX ALTERNATIVES TO OUTLINING YOUR BOOK

1. Certain kinds of books, such as cartoon books or picture books, may not lend themselves to an outline. But, like readers, editors expect books to have a structure. When I wrote the proposal for *Painted Ladies*, instead of just proposing a book of photographs of houses, I gave the book a structure by dividing it into four sections covering parts of the city. Later, we added another element to the structure of the book by arranging the photographs in the order of an architectural tour.

2. If you are planning a compilation of information such as an almanac, a dictionary, or an encyclopedia, list the topics the book will cover.

3. If your book will consist of a series of chapters, each with the same structure and each presenting the same kind of information, you don't have to prepare an in-depth outline. Just list the chapters and then—in the section on special features—describe what each will contain. For example, if you were going to write a guide to Europe's ten greatest cities, you would list—in order—the cities the book will cover. Then—also in order—you would list what you will cover in each city.

4. Outlining your chapters with a series of bulleted one-line topics can work if you can do justice to the information in your book with only lists and one-line summaries of anecdotes. Using letters or numbers to structure the lists looks academic. Ideas or jargon that editors won't understand will raise questions lists can't answer. They may not explain enough about your chapters. Ask your readers to make sure they understand everything in your outlines.

EXAMPLE: *Timing Is Everything: A Guide to the Best Time to Buy This, Do That and Go There*

Kudos to Mark Di Vincenzo for compiling the advice in *Timing Is Everything*, an idea as brilliant as it is simple. Mark spent twenty-four years as a journalist before starting a public relations agency. Both skills enabled him to promote the book and helped Michelle Wolfson at the Wolfson Literary Agency sell the book to Harper Perennial. The parts of the chapter are short enough that Mark wrote them in paragraph form. Mark mentioned that in the course of researching the book, he would find more examples. His efforts paid off: with the title *Buy Ketchup in May and Fly at Noon*, the book had a five-week run on the *New York Times* best-seller list.

Chapter 5
Health and Wellness

The chapter on health includes answers to questions about the best time to exercise, burn fat, walk and run, stretch, wean a baby, have a pap smear, weigh yourself, do a cardio workout, go to the doctor, take a multivitamin, have a heart attack, call 911, get a massage, have surgery, get a physical.

5. If your book will provide information or instruction, and it will have short chapters, don't use complete sentences for your outlines. Use a bulleted list of phrases, beginning with verbs, the same way you describe competing books. For example: *Describes the three reasons to explain a decision before taking action.* Vary verbs as much as you can.

6. For other kinds of books, describe the contents of the chapter: the instructions in a how-to book, the characters and events in a history or biography, the development of a book's thesis.

   Write one or two paragraphs about each chapter. You may need more, depending on:

   - the kind of book you're writing.
   - how much information you have.
   - how long your chapters will be, based on your models.
   - the guidelines of the agents or publishers you plan to submit your book to.

But for most books, one or two paragraphs for each chapter is enough. Use as few words as possible. If you're not including a sample chapter, consider compensating by writing two-page outlines.

A CONTRARY APPROACH

EXAMPLE: *The Probiotics Revolution: Using Beneficial Bacteria to Fight Inflammation and Chronic Disease—and Live a Longer, Healthier Life*

If a book is going to have distinctive voice and authors with excellent credentials who won't be including a sample chapter, another approach to writing a summary is possible.

Gary B. Huffnagle, Ph.D., and Mairi C. Noverr, Ph.D., at the University of Michigan Medical Center used Sarah Wernick, a successful ghostwriter, so publishers knew the book would be well written. Sarah wrote an abridgement of the book with long summaries using the words *I* and *you*. It enabled ace agent Ted Weinstein to get them a six-figure deal.

CHAPTER 10
FOOD SOURCES OF PROBIOTICS

Most of us—unless we do something about it—have probiotic levels too low to improve health. Because probiotics have difficulty competing with other microbes, they need our help to thrive. We can influence our microbial balance by altering our diet.

As the importance of probiotics becomes clearer, food manufacturers are beginning to feature them on product labels. To understand these labels, you must learn relevant microbe names (which are, of course, in Latin). *The Probiotics Revolution* will describe more than two dozen probiotics found in food.

YOGURT AND OTHER DAIRY PRODUCTS

Élie Metchnikoff, the Nobel Prize-winning microbiologist, studied Bulgarian peasants one hundred years ago. These impoverished peasants lived longer than any other Europeans, and Metchnikoff wondered why. He concluded that their unusually long lives resulted from a diet that featured yogurt and other fermented foods—all of which contain probiotic bacteria.

SELECTING A YOGURT

Look for yogurt whose label says "contains live bacterial cultures" or "active cultures" on the label. The label should list specific probiotic bacteria. Since they work in somewhat different ways, look for a diverse mixture. No yogurt is sugar-free, since all contain a small amount of sugar from the milk. But try

How to Write a Book Proposal

to avoid yogurts that add sugar in the form of sweetened fruit or jam. That's because sugar favors growth of harmful bacteria in the gut, countering the yogurt's benefits. Because of other health concerns, I don't recommend artificially sweetened yogurt except to people with diabetes.

PRACTICAL SUGGESTIONS

The Probiotics Revolution isn't a cookbook, but it will explain how to make your own yogurt and will offer about fifteen recipes. The list doesn't include muffins or cooked sauces, because heating yogurt above 100 degrees kills probiotic bacteria. Most commercial frozen yogurt is cooked during processing, so I'll offer at least one recipe for frozen yogurt, which is easily made in an ice cream maker.

Probiotics are found in dairy products that are aged (cheeses, for example) or cultured (kefir). I'll describe these foods, some of which may be unfamilar, and provide practical information about using them.

WHAT IF I'M LACTOSE INTOLERANT?

Lactose intolerance—an inability to digest the lactose (sugar) in dairy products— is a common problem. But it doesn't have to prevent you from consuming yogurt and other dairy products. The probiotics in yogurt actually break down lactose, so many lactose-intolerant individuals are able to eat it. If you experience gastrointestinal distress from a full cup of yogurt, try four quarter-cup servings consumed at intervals throughout the day. Or take Lactaid, a supplement with enzymes that help digest lactose. In parts of the world such as Asia where lactose intolerance is very common, the diet usually includes fermented foods that contain probiotics.

FERMENTED FOODS

Certain fermented foods contain high levels of probiotics or the health-promoting compounds they manufacture. Examples include sauerkraut, pickles, olives, wine, and dark beer. I'll walk readers through the options.

HOW MUCH DO I NEED?

The book will provide detailed information on daily requirements, plus a table presenting portion sizes and probiotic content of the foods listed in the chapter.

EXAMPLE: *Jolt Your Life! The Power of Intentional Change in a World That's Constantly Changing*

An outline from the proposal for *Jolt Your Life!* by Phil Cooke shows that an outline can be short yet do the job. Because editors saw sample chapters and

Phil had completed the manuscript, editors wouldn't be concerned about whether there was a book's worth of information in the outline. Rachelle Gardner at WordServe Literary Group sold the book to Thomas Nelson.

JOLT #13
CREATIVITY: THE REAL WONDER DRUG

> Creativity is a drug I cannot live without.
> —Cecil B. DeMille, director of *The Ten Commandments*

The critical need for creativity in our personal lives and its impact on change. The five reasons organizations lack creativity. The secrets to being more creative in our personal and business lives, and the keys to brainstorming. This chapter is a textbook on creative thinking that can help readers transform their thinking and see every aspect of their life as a compelling adventure.

HOT TIPS

- Establish goals for each chapter as well as your book
- What dramatic or inspirational impact do you want to achieve?
- How much humor, if any, do you want?
- How many anecdotes do you want to include?
- Write the outline your book needs. If your outlines are a half page or shorter, let them run one after the other. If they're longer, begin each outline on a new page.
- Outline every chapter, including the one you submit as a sample, so an editor can see how the chapters flow into one another and how an outline relates to a completed chapter.

MENTION JUICY CONTENT IN YOUR OUTLINE

If the salability of your book depends on revelations you are adding to the record, your outlines give you another chance to mention them. Weave your revelations into your outlines by writing *This chapter/The next part of the chapter reveals for the first time ...* Vary the wording.

When it comes to mentioning illustrations or other features, skip a line after each chapter description, type a header such as "Illustrations" or "Features," and then list them in the order they will appear. Include links you will add to the e-book edition.

EXAMPLE: *The Everyday Advocate:*
How to Stand Up for Your Autistic Child

Areva Martin's book blends memoir and advice. She followed each outline with boxed advice about how to discuss what the chapter covers.

CHAPTER 5
EMPOWERMENT CIRCLES

At the heart of my support system is my empowerment circle, a group of people who offer more than a shoulder to lean on. An empowerment circle is committed to providing guidance, encouragement, and challenges to its members. It is supportive, but also challenging, since empowered people have the ability to find solutions, make choices and then create the outcomes they desire.

The chapter discusses the steps for parents to take when creating a circle:

- Define the areas where they need the most help (driving to appointments, understanding medical terms, finding play dates, creating calm).

- List people who have the ability and resources to help (free time, a flexible schedule, a van, a willingness to listen, common sense).

- Invite everyone on the list to gather and discuss forming a mutual empowerment circle.

- Discuss the child's disability.

- Explain the type of help the parents need *and ways the parents can reciprocate.*

It's common for parents dealing with autism to feel alone and overwhelmed much of the time. This only increases the value of an empowerment circle. Not every parent will be able to find the right people easily. The chapter provides strategies to help identify, approach, test and cull the circle, drawing from a range of sources, from the PTA to the Internet, to experts and specialists they may not even know yet.

At its best, an empowerment circle can help minimize the emotional force of the blow when things go wrong and provide tangible assistance to avert—or prevent—a crisis. The chapter includes inspiring stories of lessons I've learned from my empowerment circles and the ways we've found to help each other that will motivate parents to create their own circle.

WHAT TO SAY ...

WHEN ASKING SOMEONE TO JOIN YOUR EMPOWERMENT CIRCLE

The people chosen to participate in an empowerment circle may be close friends or family, but the circle can extend further. Reciprocity and relevance are both important. An expert in autism who can also benefit from the circle might be invited, whether or not the parents know him. School administrators, caregivers and other specialists can also be included. Defining the intention of the circle helps clarify its value. Ways to introduce the concept include:

- "I'd like to invite you to join my empowerment circle. It is an alliance of people committed to actively supporting one another with help and advice."
- "You would be an ideal member of this group, because ... " [list the qualities that make you want to include them].
- "Would you be willing to meet with us next week to discuss the possibilities?"
- "I'd love to include you, but social friends are in a separate category. This group specifically exists to give us strength and empowerment in the challenges we face."

DOING YOURSELF A FAVOR: YOUR OUTLINE AS A GIFT

When you write your outline, you're doing yourself a favor. If you deliver your manuscript on time, and it lives up to what your proposal promises, your editor will have no reason to reject it.

If this is your first book, you will feel far more confident about tackling it once you've finished a chapter and have a clear vision of the rest of your book. Doing your outline will help you pick the best sample chapter to write.

How to Write a Book Proposal

Ace freelance editor Hal Zina Bennett, with whom I wrote *How to*
With a Collaborator, believes a well-written outline can make writing your
book "almost as easy as painting by the numbers."

Learning to write outlines is less painful than learning to ride a bicycle,
but it will last you as long. Like typing, the skill of outlining a book will help
you as long as you need it. Like the rest of your proposal, it's a test of your commitment to your book and a gift to the writer within you.

CHAPTER 26

Giving Your Outlines Structure and Heft

THE GOLDEN RULE FOR STRUCTURING YOUR OUTLINES

Make your outlines inviting and transparent.

If you summarize chapters, your outline will read like an article or short book, and editors will reject your proposal, thinking the idea doesn't have enough substance for a book. So you have to give each outline a structure that makes it read like an outline, not a summary. You will find these four approaches effective.

1. To help an editor grasp the essence of a chapter quickly, consider beginning each outline with a one-sentence overview of the chapter. Here are suggestions for doing this:

   - *This chapter covers ...*
   - *The goal (aim, purpose, object) of this chapter is to ...*
   - *This chapter has [or is divided into] X parts.* This alternative has the added virtue of telling the editor about the structure of the chapter. If you do this, you can write a sentence about each of the parts.

2. Use a number in the title, like *Ten Steps to ...*, or a time by which readers will gain the chapter's benefit. Your chapters can be part of the metaphor you use in the title of your book. As mentioned earlier, for *Guerrilla*

Marketing for Writers: 100 Weapons for Selling Your Work, we divided the book into one hundred short pieces. Each chapter title includes the number of weapons we cover. If you were going to write a book called *The House of Love*, your chapters could be the rooms in the house and what's in them.

You can divide chapters into parts, chunks, modules, steps, ways, or stages that are the organizing force of the chapter. But, unless your title indicates that your book is structured around numbers, using numbers for every chapter will make your book seem formulaic.

3. Conceptualize the information in your chapters in the form of an image, symbol, or metaphor that captures the essence of the chapter in a unifying, memorable way. Is it possible to visualize the material in your book as a shape like a circle, a triangle, or a pie? Could the information be compared to a jewel, plant, activity, machine, person, place, period, or event in history? Like an evocative title for a book, the right image can convey the tone and structure of a chapter.

My book on agents has separate chapters about a terrible day and a terrific day in the life of an agent. After beginning in the "morning" of each chapter, I made up a composite of the horrible and wonderful things that have befallen our agency over the years. Judging from the comments I get, those are the two most memorable chapters in the book. The search for the proper structure for your chapters and your book is another example of how reading comparable books will spark your creativity.

EXAMPLE: *Spiritual Pregnancy: 9 Months That Will Change Your Life Before You Give Birth*

Spirituality and childbirth, a timeless combination of subjects, helped Katharine Sands of the Sarah Jane Freymann Literary Agency sell *Spiritual Pregnancy*.

Endorsements from best-selling authors Deepak Chopra, Larry Dossey, and Dr. Andrew Weil made Katharine's job easier. Representing a promotable husband-and-wife team of parents who are OB/GYNs and coauthors of a previous prize-winning book on pregnancy made it more of a question of which lucky publisher was going to acquire the book. Here's a short but effective chapter outline from their proposal.

CHAPTER 5
THE MINDFUL MOTHER-TO-BE

Mindfulness is the process of understanding the body/mind/spirit connection and using basic physical and guided visualization exercises to expand that connection. Originally for stress reduction, these exercises have that benefit as well. Readers learn how to bond with their baby through gentle talk, counting fetal kicks, and other outer and inner ways of connecting mother and child.

Next come strategies for helping you write outlines for six kinds of books.

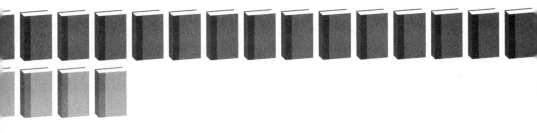

CHAPTER 27

No Time for Sophomores: Strategies for Outlining Six Kinds of Books

> **THE GOLDEN ROLE FOR GIVING YOUR BOOK A SOLID FOUNDATION**
>
> Create the structure that will serve your readers best.

In *Bird by Bird: Some Instructions on Writing and Life*, Anne Lamott recalls, "I started writing sophomoric articles for the college paper. Luckily, I was a sophomore." You can't use "being a sophomore" as an excuse for a shaky outline. Different kinds of books present different challenges. What follows is what you need to know for six kinds of books: how-tos, memoirs or biographies, interviews, exposés, humor, and anthologies. If you are writing something else, feel free to skip to the next chapter.

HOW-TO BOOKS

How-to books are staples in the book business. Publishers and book buyers welcome ideas that enable readers to lead better, richer lives. Successful how-to books offer a new idea or a new slant on an old idea that is backed up with promotion by an expert, celebrity, or promotable author.

With luck, a how-to book will combine a fresh, strong concept; an engaging voice; and the right timing. People want to know, but they're not always eager to learn. You need to entice them into wanting to learn by following your models and by

- using a down-to-earth, me-to-you tone. As in Lamott's *Bird by Bird*, the author has a distinctive, endearing, inspiring voice that keeps readers turning the pages.
- including jokes, quotes, cartoons, or anecdotes—both to create a rapport with readers and to help make the book as enjoyable to read as it is informative.
- giving readers something to do along the way to keep them involved and develop their ability
- explaining a skill in a clear step-by-step way that is reflected in the text and chapter titles.
- supplementing the text with illustrations, if needed, and presenting information in a visually appealing way instead of just endless blocks of copy.
- including links to video demonstrations and other information.

If you're writing an instructional book, such as an exercise book or a cookbook, begin each outline by describing the chapter's introductory remarks; also plan on including copy between exercises or recipes.

MEMOIRS AND BIOGRAPHIES

In *Another Life: A Memoir of Other People*, Michael Korda's excellent book about his four decades at Simon & Schuster and his other career as a bestselling author, he wrote that "[Jackie Susann] taught everybody in book publishing that what many people want to read more than anything else is a good story."

It's been said that memoirs are the novels of the twenty-first century. The success of *Angela's Ashes* by Frank McCourt, *Into the Wild* by John Krakauer, and *Longitude* by Dava Sobel helped unleash a continuing stream of memoirs, adventure travel books, and short, narrowly focused histories.

These books were bestsellers because they were compelling stories that enabled readers to live in other places, experience other people's lives, and learn something. They also enlarged the market for narrative nonfiction books.

Biographies present one temptation to avoid: summarizing a chapter instead of outlining it. *First, she did this, then she did this, and then she did this,* etc. Following are two outlines that avoid this; the first is written in first person for a memoir, and the second is written in third person for a biography.

However challenging doing the proposal for your memoir may be, take heart: The hardest part of writing your memoir may be surviving the research!

EXAMPLE: *The Scalpel and the Soul*

Allan Hamilton, who wrote a spiritual memoir, had an advantage in writing a solid outline—he had already completed the manuscript.

CHAPTER 3
THE DYING OF THE LIGHT

> The author recalls a phenomenon of euthanasia in his early veterinary work— an aura in the faces of dogs as they're put to sleep. In his third and fourth year of medical school, he sees a similar hue appearing around the faces of patients who are close to death. He's surprised to see this aura in his next-door neighbor who seems in good health. But a few days later, his neighbor is rushed to the hospital, and soon dies from lung cancer.
>
> Then the chapter describes how a near-death experience brings another patient on the hospital ward a renewed enthusiasm for a second chance. What worries the author, however, is the aura he sees in his face. Sure enough: Another heart attack comes, and it's fatal. The chapter ends with an emergency when the dead patient's wife collapses, almost dying because her pacemaker wire has suddenly broken in two. This incident leaves the author struggling over whether a physician should intervene or just bear witness.

Another chapter outline from this proposal is in Allan's proposal in Appendix D.

EXAMPLE: *The Mayor of Castro Street: The Life and Times of Harvey Milk*

The following outline is for the first chapter of Randy Shilts's proposal for *The Mayor of Castro Street*. Randy gave continuity to the chapters by including the time period of each chapter.

PART I
THE YEARS WITHOUT HOPE

CHAPTER ONE
THE MEN WITHOUT THEIR SHIRTS

Time: 1930–Korean War

The chapter opens with the story of how police round up a teenage Harvey Milk with other gay men cruising Central Park, marching them off to a paddy wagon for the crime of taking off their shirts in a gay section of Central Park. The police march the group through a family section of the park where shirtless men are left unmolested. For the first time, Milk realizes there's something wrong in society's treatment of gays.

This opening symbolizes Milk's life as a homosexual growing up decades before the phrase *gay rights* was ever used, and it also shows the social climate facing gays of that period. The chapter develops both of these themes. On the personal side, this segment outlines Milk's early family life on Long Island and his college years in Albany. Many of Milk's personality traits are evident during these years: his lust for the limelight, his stubborn dogmatism, his sense of humor, and, most significantly, his intense interest in politics.

Milk's ramblings in New York's gay milieu of the mid-forties and fifties offer an opportunity to capsulize the social and political status of gays at the time. The chapter also touches on the homosexual emancipation movement in Germany, which thrived well into the 1920s.

After telling about an experience of four-year-old Harvey Milk, for example, the narrative shifts to Germany in the same year when, on "The Night of the Long Knives," Hitler wiped out Germany's gay subculture. That marked the beginning of the dictator's attempts to exterminate homosexuals.

The gay genocide, coupled with the holocaust, exerts a powerful influence on Milk's thinking. Through such historical digressions, the first chapter introduces the book's four levels [described earlier in the proposal]. The chapter ends when Milk, at the apex of a budding career in the Navy, is booted out of the service because of his homosexuality.

Photos: Milk at four on a pony and in Navy uniform.

Coda: The book hit the *San Francisco Chronicle* best-seller list for the second time twenty-six years later in 2008 when the Oscar-winning movie *Milk* opened.

FOURTEEN TIPS ON WRITING A MEMOIR

Catherine Friend, author of *Hit by a Farm: How I Learned to Stop Worrying and Love the Barn*, gave these fourteen tips about writing a memoir at the San Francisco Writers Conference. You may find them helpful when writing your outline and sample chapter.

How to Write a Book Proposal

1. A memoir is a slice of life, not the whole thing. Don't share funny stories from your childhood or college days unless those stories directly relate to the slice you're writing about. Keep that slice as narrow as possible.

2. Make sure you tell *your* story, not your parents' or your brother's or your neighbor's. If these people have stories that fascinate you, and you're involved in the story, focus on how the events affected you. Tell the story using your life as the lens or filter.

3. Know your motivation. Why are you telling your story? To teach? Warn? Entertain? As therapy? If revenge is on the list, you might want to reconsider until you've cooled off.

4. Speaking of which, let your emotions age, like wine. If you're writing about something emotionally difficult, give yourself time to move beyond those emotions. If a memoir's narrator is incredibly angry or passionate on the page, then there's no room for me, as the reader, to experience those emotions. It sounds backwards, but the less emotional you are on the page, the deeper the emotions your readers will experience.

5. Don't start at the beginning. That's boring. Instead look for that defining moment, the one that told you your life was about to change. For me, that was the day I knelt behind a ram and squeezed his testicles. And don't get hung up on finding the perfect beginning, since that will likely be the last part of the book you write anyway. Just start somewhere.

6. Be willing to write about what went wrong. Sorry, but no one cares about the things that have gone right in your life. It's the mistakes and disasters that are interesting. I wrote not about my education or job successes, but about planting 200 grapevines upside down. When things go wrong, it creates tension.

7. You are the main character, so don't be perfect. Embrace your quirks and accept your flaws. This honesty will help you connect with readers. The fact that I'm grossed out by manure and don't like to work hard tells readers I have no business farming. If you let readers know you aren't

perfect, this creates tension. A memoir is just like a novel when it comes to tension—the more, the better.

8. How do you feel about yourself? If you think you're adorable and awesome, I don't want to read about you. If you despise yourself, I also don't want to read about you. Instead of self-love or self-loathing, aim for self-curiosity, or self-amusement. "Gosh, I wonder why I did that?" This can turn disasters like the upside-down grapevines into a compelling story.

9. Look for threads running through your story. Find two or three themes, and then make sure all your material connects to one of these threads. If you do this, you'll write a tight, cohesive memoir. Also, whenever two threads cross in a story, you'll create—once again—tension. Every time that farming interfered with my writing, talk about tension.

10. Put your story in context. What's happening in the world around you? Step outside yourself and consider family, community, state, nation. Yes, you're writing a memoir, but that doesn't mean it's all about you. The story of your car accident on August 12, 2001, may not include national events, but if you're writing about your car accident on September 12, 2001, you'd better step back and look at how this fits into bigger events.

11. Truth vs. Fact. Because memoir is creative nonfiction, it's meant to be shaped into a story. You don't always need to stick with an exact timeline, but you do need to stay truthful. If you find yourself saying, "But that's the way it happened," step back and see if you can reshape the truth into a story with a beginning, middle, and end. Do this not by making things up, but by looking at the event as a storyteller.

12. Speaking of which, break your material down into stories. Don't treat your slice of life as one big story. It's really many little ones, and approaching your memoir this way will make it more enjoyable for others to read. Just think about how you tell the story to a friend over pizza—you don't share every detail, you slow down at the good parts, and you end with the piece of the story that amazed you.

13. Memoir is based on memory, and memory is unreliable. So if you look to family or friends to validate your memories, don't be surprised if their memories are different than yours. This is your memoir, so you get to tell your version.

14. Relax and have fun. Don't take yourself or your story too seriously. Play around. Convert one story to a grocery list, another to a poem. Read lots of memoirs. Think outside the box. It may take a while, but you *will* find the best way to tell your story.

EXAMPLE: *Warped in Paris: Untangling the World at a French Tapestry Loom*

Here's how Lawrence Knowles's first-person outline describes the chapter without overusing the *I* word.

CHAPTER 8
IN SEARCH OF "TRUE TAPESTRY"

> At the beginning of the chapter, I overhear a furtive conversation between our two instructors, dismissing a newly finished commission as less than "true tapestry." Modern tapestry's struggles with its identity center on questions at the heart of my search for an antidote to the disembodiment of human experience in our technological society.
>
> Two weekend outings provide the chapter with a context for discussing these questions: to Angers, home of one of the masterpieces of medieval tapestry, the Angers Apocalypse, and the site of a museum devoted to France's leading twentieth-century designer, Jean Lurçat; and to Lausanne, Switzerland, to see an exhibit of contemporary tapestries.
>
> The pursuit of the meaning of true tapestry and its inherent, timeless values lead me to question the dichotomy between the tactile and the technological, and to doubt whether answers to today's problems in tapestry and beyond it can be found by pretending that we live in a simpler time and place.

INTERVIEW BOOKS

If you plan to write a history of Los Angeles, the information you need is available. If you outline it well, editors can assess the proposal easily. Books based on interviews, however, present these challenges.

- Even if you provide editors with a list of interview subjects, editors may not be able to gauge the value of future interviews.
- You can't prove you'll come away with a book's worth of publishable material.
- Predicting the length of your chapters may be more difficult.
- Asking everyone the same questions may yield repetitive answers.
- If a book has national scope, its examples should be from around the country. The Web may make meeting this challenge easier.

If, for example, you're profiling successful entrepreneurs, you can't just cover those in your area. Aim for as much diversity in location, background, type of product and service, experience, attitude, and lifestyle as you can in those you interview. Editors will expect the book to be comprehensive in presenting the range of the entrepreneurial experience. They'll want you to include people from major cities, which are also major book markets, and all regions of the country. Regional variations you encounter will add depth to your book.

You want to minimize your expenses for a proposal that might not sell, so interviews in your area, supplemented by telephone or online interviews, may suffice for the proposal. But indicate in your overview and outline that the manuscript will contain anecdotes from people around the country. A problem might arise later if your interviews don't yield the material you want, and you need more time or money to obtain additional interviews. Plan your research carefully and give yourself a cushion.

Interviewing as many people as you can in your initial research will enrich your proposal, help teach you how to overcome problems you encounter, and provide leads for other interviews. After published articles, the most convincing argument for publishing an interview book is offering a hefty portion—one-third to a half—of the manuscript.

Writers with interview articles to their credit may be attracted by the notion of doing a book of interviews, thinking, "Hey, I'll find twenty people who need publicity, do ten ten-page interviews, and I'll have a book." Well, editors aren't wild about collections of anything, including interviews, unless they meet one or more of the following four criteria:

- The interviews are wedded by a fresh, salable idea.

- The interviews are with celebrities or VIPs.
- The interviewer is famous.
- The author has a can't-miss promotion plan.

Editors are book people. For them, writing a book means taking an idea and developing it, structuring it, and using interview material to prove your points. Consider making your idea more like a book by building it around ideas you can use quotes from interviews to discuss. For example, instead of asking twenty movie stars to describe how they became famous, structure the book around the challenges they encountered such as training, getting a break, building a career, and coming to terms with fame. If you record interviews, you can put them on your website and include links to them.

HUMOR BOOKS

After Groucho Marx received a book from S.J. Perelman, Marx said to the humorist, "From the moment I picked up your book until I put it down, I was convulsed with laughter. Some day I intend reading it." Unless you have a track record like Perelman or experience as a stand-up comic, humor can be hard to sell with a proposal. Proving you can be funny for the length of a book, even a short one, is difficult. Therefore, if the book will be short, finish it. If you can't submit the whole manuscript, try to submit at least one third of it.

EXPOSÉS

A controversial book can sell if it

- is the right subject.
- has shocking revelations.
- is published at the right time.
- is written by an author who can publicize the book in a way that catches the attention of the media and the public.

Classics like *Silent Spring* by Rachel Carson, *The American Way of Death* by Jessica Mitford, *Unsafe at Any Speed* by Ralph Nader, *All the President's Men* by Bob Woodward and Carl Bernstein, *Fast Food Nation* by Eric Schlosser, the string of bestsellers about the Middle East since 9/11, and books about the financial meltdown have proven that exposés can sell.

But people don't like to get depressed, and they sure don't want to pay for the privilege. That's why, unless exposés are written by a promotable author and about a hot subject—Hollywood, politics, big business, or some other juicy subject with built-in national interest—exposés don't sell well.

If your book will bring bad news, consider being prescriptive as well as descriptive. People don't want to buy problems, they want to buy solutions. So if you can, develop a program for making the situation better. This will give your book a positive slant that may improve your title and your sales, and lead to more talks and publicity.

ANTHOLOGIES

The amazing success of the *Chicken Soup* series proves the commercial potential of anthologies blessed with the following:

- A great idea for a seemingly endless series of books that sell each other
- A system for test-marketing the stories to ensure they move readers and leave them craving more
- A huge potential readership
- Perpetual powerhouse promotion driven by the authors' zeal, creativity, and speaking ability
- A title strong enough to become a brand and generic enough to support a certain kind of story collection

And because most anthologies also don't have the strengths listed above, they don't fare well unless they are used in the classroom. Even the word *anthology* is deadly. Avoid the notion of a collection in the title if you can. If you're doing a treasury or celebration—less academic, more selling words—start with a strong concept and make sure the selections are worth including, that they hold up well against each other.

Make the case that the book will hold up over time. Try to make your selections flow naturally from one to the next. Splitting the book into parts and chapters and writing an introduction for each section—and perhaps each entry—helps ensure this. Include brief bios of your contributors before their entries, after their entries, or at the end of the sample text and the book.

Getting permissions can be time-consuming. Copyright holders may be abroad, may not respond to your inquiries, may charge you an exorbitant fee, or may refuse to quote a price until they know how your book will be published. Yet it's important your proposal include as accurate a round-figure cost estimate as you can obtain.

Two inducements for publishers to do anthologies are:

- They can usually be whatever length the market or your models suggest.
- If the first one works, there is often the potential for a series.

Next comes your sample chapter—the proof that you can write a book that will fulfill your publisher's expectations and yours.

CHAPTER 28

A Taste of the Feast:
A Q&A Session About Your Sample Chapter

> **THE GOLDEN RULE FOR WRITING YOUR SAMPLE CHAPTER**
>
> Blend style and content into a delectable slice of your book that leaves editors hungry for more.

I once saw a T-shirt that said, "Life is one audition after another." Your chapter is your audition for the role of author. If your overview is the sizzle, and your outline is the bones, your chapter is the steak—the meat of your proposal, a tasty sample of what's to come. It must be so substantial and enjoyable to read that editors will be convinced your book will be a movable feast.

Your writing must deliver what your introduction promises. The last part of your proposal is the only chance you have to strut your stuff, to prove you have the talent and craft to deliver what you promise. Your chapter must achieve the goals you set for it both in content and in its impact on readers. If it does, it will increase the value of your proposal by allaying editors' concerns about your ability to write the book.

An editor once said to us, "If it makes me cry, I'll buy it." Editors long to find the same things in books you do. A humor book must make them laugh; a dramatic or inspirational book must move them. How editors feel about your book when they finish your sample chapter will determine if they try to buy it and how much passion they bring to the challenge.

A Q&A ON WHAT TO SUBMIT

A cartoon by Edward Koren in *The New Yorker* shows a sedan speeding away from a bank robbery with the police in pursuit, and the driver reassures a bystander, "I'm only doing this to support my writing." If you're selling your first book, you will probably need to include a sample of your writing. The first decision you need to make is the number of chapters to prepare. This will depend on

- your knowledge of the subject.
- your track record.
- the time, information, and other resources at your disposal.
- how many sample chapters editors must see to become as excited as you want them to be.

Because you're working on spec on a proposal that may not sell, you want to minimize your time, effort, and expense. The answers to the eighteen questions in this chapter will help you understand how to prepare your chapter.

1. **Can I get away with not sending a chapter?** If you've already written an article or a book on the subject, your track record is strong enough, or, if your credentials are impeccable, you may not need a chapter. An outline submitted with previous work may suffice. You also may not need a sample if you've had several books published that attest to your ability to write the book you're proposing. A collection of blog posts may serve as a sample chapter, although you may want to improve them before submitting them.

   Teaching, running a professional practice, or being a journalist may also be enough to prove your credentials. But, as mentioned earlier, if you don't prepare a chapter, you should write a longer outline. If you must sell your book quickly because it's about a subject in the news, editors won't expect you to take the time to write a chapter.

2. **How many chapters should my book have?** As you string together the pieces of information that will become your book, they will fall into natural groupings that will become your chapters. Ten to twelve chapters are common for a 200- to 250-page manuscript. The longer your book,

the more chapters it will have. Take into consideration the trend toward shorter chapters and books, but adhere to the standard set by successful books on your subject.

3. **How long should my chapters be?** Serious books have longer chapters than books aimed at a mass audience. Your chapters are the building blocks of your book. Like the book itself, your chapters should not be one word longer than it takes to say what you want to say.

   There have been a string of bestsellers that are short and have short chapters. One of the reasons one of our books, Chérie Carter-Scott's *If Life Is a Game, These Are the Rules*, became a #1 *New York Times* bestseller is that her chapters averaged two pages each.

   Maintain a balance between making your chapters so thin that readers will ask, "How could he leave that out?" and so long that they say, "How much more is she going to pad this thing?" Similar books and your readers will set you straight.

HOT TIP

Do not repeat information in your chapter that you cover in outlines for other chapters. One goal of your outline is to enable editors to understand the context of your sample chapter. If you feel they need to know something from a previous chapter to understand your sample chapter, include a comment in brackets that alludes to what you covered earlier and, if you must, explain it concisely.

---

4. **How many chapters should I send an editor?** The answer depends on how long your chapters will be and the kind of book you're writing. Except for memoirs, editors expect to see about a tenth of a book. Here are three ways for you to judge what to send.

   - If your sample material reads like it's worth the advance you want for your book, you can sell most books with about 10 percent of the manuscript.

   - Editors don't need to read every exercise or recipe to know if you can write a how-to book, especially if you teach the subject.

   - If your book will be a series of chapters identical in structure and with the same kind of information, one chapter will suffice. If you were

How to Write a Book Proposal

going to write the guidebook to Europe's ten greatest cities, editors wouldn't get more jazzed by reading about a second city.

5. **How can I tell which is the best chapter to submit?** The only chapter to send is the one that best blends freshness and excitement. Let it come from the heart of the book and be a shining, representative sample of what is innovative and stimulating about your subject. Balance your passion for the subject and the time and effort you're willing to expend against what it will take to get editors so revved up about the book that they'll be outbidding each other to buy it.

   A cartoon by Jim Charlton in his collection *Books, Books, Book* shows a man standing at the counter of a bookstore about to buy a book. The clerk says to him, "You'll like this one, sir. It has a surprise ending in which the murderer turns out to be the detective." If the surprise ending is what will most entice editors, use it. But if you're not sure which chapter to use as a sample, preparing the outline will help you decide. Certain chapters usually stand out as being easier for you to write and more impressive for editors to read. Getting feedback on your proposal will convince you that you have chosen well.

6. **Is it okay to submit parts of different chapters?** Editors will want to see how a complete slice of your book reads, so make your sample material a complete segment or chapter, not part of one or more chapters.

   If you're doing an anthology, and you can get pieces of each part of your book but not a complete section, list the entries of your book as thoroughly as you can and then include one part of your book as complete as you can make it. Send at least 10 percent of the material from each section of your book.

7. **What if my book will have short chapters?** The shorter your chapters will be, the more of them editors will need to read.

8. **What if I haven't had anything published?** Your proposal will be all editors have to go on. The less experience you have as a writer or as an expert on the subject, the more chapters editors may need to be convinced that you can write your book. This will definitely be the case for a narrative book, the effectiveness of which depends on the writing.

Another circumstance that may require additional chapters is if your idea seems too ambitious in relation to your expertise or track record. Editors will want enough text to convince themselves and others that you are ready to tackle the project. As your in-house agent, whose job it is to stir up interest in your book, your editor needs that confidence to fight for your book.

If you were writing your first novel, most editors would expect to see the whole manuscript. Only a whole manuscript can prove you can develop character, plot, and setting for the length of a novel. If you're writing a nonfiction book that you'd like to have the impact of a novel—a dramatic story with mounting suspense about the solution of a crime or an inspirational book about someone heroically overcoming obstacles—an outline can't convey the emotional impact of your finished manuscript. If the emotional impact of your manuscript will be stronger if an editor reads the whole manuscript, be prepared to send it—or as much of it as you can.

The goals of your proposal are not to waste an editor's time and to use a minimum number of words to generate maximum excitement for your book. Therefore the criteria for deciding how much more than one chapter to send are:

- How much of the book are you willing and able to write before selling it?
- Will including additional chapters generate enough excitement to justify writing them?

9. **What if my book is divided into three parts?** If the three parts of your book are distinctive enough, and you think editors will need to see a sample of each, send them. They will read only far enough to reach a decision.

10. **What if my book is depressing?** If your subject is depressing, balance the bad news with humor or good news, if you can. Make at least the last chapter or last part of your book upbeat so editors will finish reading your proposal feeling positive about the subject, your proposal, and the prospect of working on it with you. Editors spend at least two years working on a book. They want to enjoy the time they spend working with an author. This is even more important with a book that doesn't

promise to become a bestseller. However, a book's literary or social value will overcome a depressing subject.

11. **Should I send the introduction?** Send the chapter that will most effectively sell your book. Many readers skip introductions to get into the meat of books. Your first chapter may not be representative of your book. Also, you introduced your book in your overview, so editors don't want to read that information again. In a how-to book, an introduction may not demonstrate how you will treat the instructional material that is the reason for your book.

12. **What if I've finished more of the book than I submit?** You will mention at the bottom of your table of contents that you have "completed a draft of X pages/the manuscript." If editors want to see more of it, they will ask.

13. **What if I have finished the manuscript?** Agents and editors are perpetually swamped and their submission guidelines indicate what to submit. They need just enough text to judge whether you can write the book. They and the other people in the house who review your proposal will read a short document faster than a long one. So even if you have more, don't send it unless an editor requests it or it's for one of the reasons mentioned above.

14. **If I'm submitting more than one chapter, do the chapters have to be in sequence?** Unless agent's and editors' guidelines indicate otherwise, your chapters don't have to be from the beginning of the book or in sequence, but make sure editors understand the context of the chapters you submit.

15. **What if my book has no chapters?** If your book doesn't break into chapters, an editor will still expect to see at least 10 percent of the manuscript.

16. **What if I'm doing an illustrated book?** Unless a large national audience already exists for your work, or your idea is extremely commercial, your book will need more than just illustrations. Make the project more substantial by writing the introduction for your book and providing captions and perhaps running text. Add enough text so browsers can't

finish it in a bookstore. Otherwise, unless they're giving the book as a gift or feel they must own it, they may not buy it.

Editors want captions to explain illustrations. They also want a compelling reason to go to the effort and expense of producing a picture book. As for the illustrations you include in the proposal, they should be gorgeous and represent the range of illustrations in your book.

17. **What if I want my book designed in a particular way?** If you have a vision of how you want your book to look, and you are able to design sample pages on your computer, or you can obtain the services of an experienced book designer, include a cover design and two facing spreads—four sample pages—as examples of the design you want for the book.

    These are only worth including if they are of professional quality. Even if you envision a book larger than 8½" × 11" (22cm × 28cm), make your sample pages the same size as the rest of your proposal. They will be easier to prepare, reproduce, submit, and read. Your publisher will have the final say on how your book is designed. If you present a cover design or suggest a format for your book, it must be with the understanding that if the salespeople say it won't fly, you will have to compromise or seek another publisher.

18. **How do you want editors to feel about your writing and your book when they finish reading your chapter?** Use the chapter that will most effectively make them feel that way.

Now you know what editors expect to see in proposals. Once you start doing it, the pieces will fall into place. When you commit to writing your proposal, your sense of anticipation about your book will grow as the project develops momentum and creates a life of its own.

But before you leap into action, the next chapter will explain why the best way to write your proposal may be to write your manuscript first!

PART VII:
ENSURING YOUR PROPOSAL
IS READY TO SUBMIT

CHAPTER 29

Making Your Proposal More Salable: The Benefits of Writing Your Manuscript First

If you can't or don't want to write your manuscript before writing your proposal, please skip to the next chapter.

Here I am with a book about proposals, and I'm about to suggest that you write your manuscript before your proposal. You're probably saying, "Geez, Larsen, make up your mind! Should I write the proposal or the manuscript?" That depends on you and your book.

Here's why 90 percent of nonfiction is sold with proposals:

- Writers need money to write the book.
- Writers don't want to risk writing the book and then find that they can't sell it.
- The book is on a subject in the news, so the writers want a commitment to publish the book before writing it.
- Agents make a living selling books, so they want to sell them as soon as they can.
- Editors prefer to receive proposals for most books. They're faster to read, and editors enjoy the creative satisfaction of helping writers shape their books. A complete manuscript may deprive them of that opportunity.
- Editors may be more excited by what they imagine the manuscript will be than what it actually is.

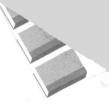

WHY WRITE YOUR MANUSCRIPT FIRST

Here are the benefits to writing your manuscript before writing your proposal:

- Picking the best sample chapter will be easier, even if you've just done a first draft.
- If editors want to see more of your manuscript than you include with your proposal, they can.
- You can blog or post parts of your manuscript online. (But save newsworthy revelations for when they'll do your book the most good.)
- If you give talks, you can test-market your information. (There's more on test-marketing in chapter twenty-one.)
- If you have ways to sell your book, online or off, you can prove it will sell.
- Your book may be worth more because you have removed the risk of whether you can or will write it.
- Your agent or publisher can start selling subsidiary rights, such as foreign rights, sooner.
- You'll receive all of your advance sooner. Advances are divided into at least two parts: half on signing and half on acceptance.
- Your book will be published sooner.
- You can get feedback on the manuscript.
- You can use your manuscript to obtain quotes and a foreword.
- You will prove you can write the book if your track record isn't impressive or your book is ambitious in scope.
- It will be easier to find promotional partners if you have a full manuscript.

If you can answer *yes* to the following questions, writing your manuscript before you write your proposal could be a great opportunity for you.

- Do you have the resources you need to write your book?
- Are you the only person who can write your book?
- Is your passion for writing your book, your faith in the quality and salability of it, and your ability to promote it great enough to risk writing a book that you may have to self-publish, if only to prove it will sell?

The next chapter shows why, when it comes to proposals, looks count.

CHAPTER 30

Making Your Work Look as Good as It Reads: Formatting Your Proposal

THE GOLDEN RULE FOR FORMATTING YOUR PROPOSAL

Double-space everything except your contact information.

Agents and editors know that how writers submit their proposals reflects how they write them. They can tell instantly how good a proposal will be from the way it looks. The appearance of your proposal will reflect the professionalism with which you are approaching editors, the subject, and your career. It reflects the effort you will devote to writing and promoting your book.

To ignite the enthusiasm you want from agents and editors, your proposal must look impeccable. Here is how to accomplish that.

YOUR TITLE PAGE

Type your title page and your table of contents in upper- and lowercase letters *on double-spaced pages.* Begin the numbering with the title page, but omit the number from page one. About four inches down the page, type and center the following.

A Proposal for
[title in italics in eighteen-point type]
[subtitle in italics in eighteen-point type]
by [yours truly]

Add your degree or your position and employer on the next line, if relevant: *Professor of Psychology, Stanford University.* If possible, skip a line and add either or both of the following lines.

Foreword by X

First in a Series of X Books

Near the bottom of the page, flush left, type the following single-spaced.

[your street address]
[city, state, zip code]
[day and evening phone numbers]
[website]
[blog]
[e-mail address]
[social network addresses]

An agent will add the agency's contact information to the title page or insert the agency's letterhead in front of your title page.

YOUR TABLE OF CONTENTS

After your title page comes the table of contents for your proposal. Besides showing an editor what's ahead, this page makes your proposal look carefully organized, like a miniature version of the book it aspires to be. It will also help editors find the parts of your proposal.

List the parts of the proposal flush left and then indent the sections of each part. (Sections will vary by proposal.) At the right margin, indicate the page on which each begins.

TABLE OF CONTENTS
OVERVIEW

Don't mention front matter such as a dedication, epigraph, or acknowledgments.

If you're submitting hard copy, add the following under the table of contents:

Enclosed separately in the folder:
The author's brochure
The author's articles, or articles about the author or subject
Supporting documents
Publicity material

If you're e-mailing your proposal, include links to this information.

> **HOT TIP**
>
> Editors will not expect you to design your book—they just want to be able to turn the pages as quickly as possible. We once received a proposal from someone who had gone hog wild with type fonts and had six different typefaces on one page. This made the page look like an amateur's attempt to dress up the proposal. Unless you have proven design skills or have access to them, keep your proposal simple in appearance like the samples in the book.

Writers are endlessly ingenious at finding wrong ways to submit their work. Here are tips for preparing, proofing, and submitting your proposal:

- Do double-space everything, including quotes and anecdotes, except for your contact information.

- Don't add extra spaces between paragraphs.

- Don't use different typefaces. Stick to standard fonts and sizes like Times New Roman, 12-point.

- Don't justify the right margin.

- Do use a header. Type your last name on the upper left margin of each page. Type the page number on the same line, flush right, as illustrated.

Larsen   11

- Do number pages consecutively—from one to the end of your proposal—not by section or chapter.

- Do type your proposal on one side of 8½" × 11" (22cm × 28cm) paper, if you're sending hard copy.

- Don't add graphic-design elements to the text unless you're a designer or using one and you're including spreads (sample pages of what you envision your book will look like). This is only for highly illustrated or designed books.

- Do proofread your proposal carefully and get eagle-eyed friends to check your work. You will spot different problems when you read your work on your computer, when you read it in hard copy, and when you hear it. Do all three.

- Run your index finger under each word as you read it aloud.

- Proofread your proposal from back to front so you can concentrate on the words and not be seduced into reading it.

- Submit hard copy without staples or any form of binding. A paper clip is acceptable, but it leaves an indentation.

- For a more professional look and greater protection if you need to resubmit a hard copy of the proposal, insert it in the right side of a double-pocket portfolio. You can use the left pocket for writing samples, illustrations, supporting documents, and your business card (if the left flap is scored). Put a self-adhesive label on the front of the folder with your title and name printed on it.

Every day every agent receives letters and proposals that don't follow these guidelines, so one simple way to make your proposal stand out is by using them.

CHAPTER 31

The Breakfast of Champions: Getting Feedback on Your Proposal

THE GOLDEN RULE FOR SHARING PROPOSALS
....

Do unto other writers proposals as you would have writers do unto yours.

I love criticism just as long as it's unqualified praise.

—Noël Coward

Jack Canfield and Mark Victor Hansen have a panel of forty readers who read every *Chicken Soup* story and grade it on a scale of one to ten. They use only the stories that score 9.5 and 10. Once you finish your proposal and query letter, it's time to bring in your own community of readers.

An editor once admitted, "An editor is someone who can talk about anything for five minutes and nothing for ten." Experts can give you advice that editors can't. But for everyone who reads it, your proposal will be a Rorschach test; they will spot only what they are able to see when they read it. Therefore the more people who review your work, the fewer problems it will have when you submit it.

MAKING YOUR WORK REJECTION-PROOF
WITH EIGHT KINDS OF READERS

By the time you've finished your proposal, you will need a respite. Author and editor Marty Asher believes in putting finished work under the bed for three months so you can look at it again with fresh eyes before submitting it. You may find yourself developing tunnel vision that impairs your ability to judge your work objectively. You may be so close to it you can't distinguish its faults from its virtues.

It's time to call on other readers. Create a community with eight kinds of readers who can advise you how to improve your work.

1. Friends and family: You need and deserve encouragement; let your friends and family give it to you. They will tell you they like it because they like you. What are friends and family for?

2. Writers: Tell writers you will be happy to review their proposals. This will give you experience critiquing prose and help you build a network of writers willing to return the favor.

3. A critique group: Join or start a critique group online or off—a group of writers that meets regularly to discuss its members' work will enable you to get feedback as you write. Working with more experienced writers than yourself will prove more productive than working with less experienced writers. Being able to give and receive constructive criticism is crucial. You may need to try more than one group until you find one that gives you what you need and whose members will benefit from your advice.

4. Potential buyers of your book: They may not be experts on writing or on the subject, but they know what they like. Would they buy your book if they found it in a bookstore? Try to enlist knowledgeable booksellers—who you also want to buy your book—to render an opinion at least on your idea, title, and promotion plan. (The better customer you are, the more likely they'll oblige.)

5. Well-read, objective readers: Even without knowing the subject, they can help with your writing.

6. Experts in your field: Approach people who know what you're writing about, including authors of competing titles. If you're presenting a controversial idea, find people who oppose it to go over your proposal to try to poke holes in it. You may not convert them, but you might earn their respect and avoid embarrassing yourself later.

7. A devil's advocate: Find a mentor who is the most valuable of all readers, the most critical critic, whose taste and judgment you respect, and in whose knowledge you have absolute confidence. A devil's advocate is a word wizard who can combine truth with charity, analyze the structure and development of your book, and spot every word, punctuation mark, idea, character, and incident that can be improved upon or removed.

8. A freelance editor: An optional possibility if you can't find the help you need. Find an editor who has worked on books, if possible like yours, that have been published by houses you want to publish your book. But even an editor is only one reader. The more readers you can enlist, the better.

If prospective editors don't have a website, ask for a list of published nonfiction books aimed at the general public for which they edited the proposals. Also, before you hire one, ask prospective editors if you may contact their clients or the agents who represent their clients. Freelance editors charge either a flat fee or an hourly rate that ranges from twenty-five dollars to more than two hundred dollars an hour.

Book doctors charge more than editors because, if necessary, they can doctor your manuscript—that is, rewrite it, not just show you what's wrong with it. So be clear about the help you need and your budget for it.

When you find an editor you want to work with, ask for an assessment of the proposal and an estimate of what it will cost to edit it and to check the revised version of it based on the editor's recommendations.

If your writing community doesn't lead you to the editor you need, check the Web and listings in *Literary Market Place*, *Writer's Market*, or the Resource Directory (Appendix A).

- Your work needs macroeditors and microeditors.

   - Macroeditors are right-brainers good with the big stuff like concept, titles and subtitles, structure, character, and story development

   - Microeditors are left-brainers who can spot every word, punctuation mark, sentence, and paragraph that need help

      Just as you can't look through both a telescope and microscope at the same time, your readers will usually be more adept at one skill than another. Find both kinds as well as readers who can do both kinds of editing.

- Think in rounds of editing. Don't assume that readers will give you feedback, you'll respond to it, and your proposal will be ready to submit. Get feedback on your revision.

WHAT YOU NEED TO KNOW

When you send your proposal (and later your manuscript) to be critiqued, include a note telling readers what you need feedback on. Being as specific as you can about the feedback you want will help your readers provide it. Ask them to

- give you feedback on your grammar, word use, punctuation, numbers, or repetition.
- rate the impact of each moving, humorous, or inspirational anecdote, scene, or chapter on a scale of 1 to 10.
- grade your proposal overall for content, impact, and enjoyment.
- tell you how your book affected their lives, if appropriate, which is valuable information you can use in talks, books, articles, blogs, and on your website.
- ask about questions the proposal raises but doesn't answer.

Instruct your reviewers to "spare the reader, not the writer." Write those words in large letters on every copy of the proposal or manuscript you share with your professional networks online or off.

Because people's reactions are subjective, receiving those reactions will prepare you for the range of responses to your book. You must trust your instincts. Sift through conflicting or confusing suggestions and follow only the advice that makes sense to you. Once you've sorted out the opinions of others and feel ready to return to your proposal with a fresh eye, revise it one more time. Then it's time to cut the literary umbilical cord and send your baby out into the real world.

HOT TIPS

- People love to see their name in print, so assure readers you will mention them on the acknowledgments page and give them an autographed copy of your book.

- If you're sending a hard copy of the proposal or want readers to print the proposal and mark it up, send as nice a pen with red ink as your budget allows.

- When you negotiate the sale of your book, ask your publisher if they will give you promotional copies you need for people who have given you feedback on your proposal and manuscript. These copies deserve to be considered part of the promotional copies you receive at no cost because the people you acknowledge will be salespeople who will show your book to people they know and display it prominently in their living room.

- See if you can get one or more of your readers to at least skim this book before reading your proposal so they can judge if you have provided editors what they need.

HOW TO BE A CHAMPION WRITER

No matter how successful they become, writers who are champs in their field will always consider feedback the breakfast of champions because they know it will enable them to have whatever they want for dinner.

Your book will be a pebble cast into a still body of water with no shore. It will continue to make ripples as long as readers, paper, and the Web help you keep it alive. The pleasure, enlightenment, or inspiration in your book will continue to affect readers, and they will express their gratitude for the experience—that alone is a compelling reason to put yourself in their service and write your books as well as you can. After your efforts to write and promote your work, it's the effect your book has on your readers that will determine its future.

The next part of the book will show you how to find the best publisher for your book.

PART VIII:
FINDING A HAPPY HOME
FOR YOUR BOOK

CHAPTER 32

Publishing on the Vertical Slope of Technology: Seeking the Right Publisher for You and Your Book

> ### THE GOLDEN RULE FOR GETTING YOUR BOOK PUBLISHED
> Choose the best option for you, based on your idea, your writing, the markets for your book, your platform, and your ability to reach potential readers.

Adair Lara wrote a little book called *You Know You're a Writer When ...* Here are three of her insights: You know you're a writer when ...

- You'll never forgive your parents for your happy childhood.
- You wonder which is a funnier word for a mineral, "feldspar" or "potash."
- There are three empty cereal bowls next to your computer—one for each of the day's meals.

And of course, you know you're a writer when you buy a copy of *You Know You're a Writer When ...*

You really know you're an author when you've transformed yourself from a writer with something to say into an author with something to sell. This section of the book is going to tell you how to find the right home for your book.

EIGHT OPTIONS FOR GETTING
YOUR BOOKS PUBLISHED

Your proposal is ready. Now what do you do? One reason now is the best time ever to be a writer is that you have more options for getting your book published. Here are eight of them.

1. You can self-publish your book by

    - photocopying your manuscript and selling it in a three-ring binder.

    - publishing it as a hardcover, a mass-market book, or a trade paperback using.

        - print-on-demand at no cost or for money.
        - print-quantity-needed for short runs
        - offset printing for longer runs.

    - publishing it online as a blog, articles, or an e-book.

2. You can collaborate with other writers in a co-op venture in which you share the production and marketing costs to create, for example, an anthology of your work.

3. You can pay for all the costs to publish your book to a vanity publisher or part of the costs to a subsidy publisher. Neither has credibility in the industry.

4. You can partner with a business or nonprofit that will support the writing and promotion of your book because it will further their cause.

5. You can publish it in other media such as software, podcast, audiobooks, or a calendar, or you can sell the rights to companies that do these products.

6. You can sell the rights to

    - an online or off-line trade or consumer periodical that will serialize your book.
    - a publisher for a flat fee, as a work-for-hire.
    - a small press, niche, or specialty publisher, or a regional publisher.
    - an academic or university press.

- a professional publisher that publishes books for a specific field.
- a midsize house.
- one of the "Six Sisters" (described in the next section).

7. You can work with a packager who provides publishers with finished files ready for the printer.

8. You can hire an agent.

THE SIX SISTERS

The New Yorker ran a cartoon by David Sipress that shows an executive standing in front of a room full of employees, and the executive says, "We're still the same great company we've always been, only we've ceased to exist." None of the big houses disappeared, but they face an uncertain future. Inertia keeps institutions, like individuals, from changing until changing is less painful than staying the same. Publishing is reinventing itself by making the transition from fifteenth-century to twenty-first-century technology, from the printing press to immediate worldwide downloads. The author-publisher-bookseller-reader paradigm is dead; technology has laid it to rest by transforming how books are written, edited, sold, marketed, and distributed.

Most American industries are controlled by fewer than ten corporations. The Six Sisters—multimedia, multinational conglomerates, most of whom are foreign-owned—dominate trade publishing. If you want to be published by a big house, here they are with a partial list of imprints.

1. Hachette Book Group, USA: A division of the French publishing conglomerate Lagardère, Hachette owns Little, Brown and Company and Grand Central Publishing, which has ten imprints.

2. HarperCollins Publishers: An American division of News Corporation that founder Rupert Murdoch imported from Australia, HarperCollins includes Harper, Harper Perennial, Harper Paperbacks, HarperOne, Avon, William Morrow, and Ecco.

3. Macmillan USA: A subsidiary of Germany's Holtzbrinck Publishing Group, Macmillan includes St. Martin's Press, Henry Holt, Picador, Tor,

Palgrave Macmillan, Bloomsbury USA/Walker & Company, and Farrar, Straus & Giroux.

4. Penguin Group (USA): A division of Pearson in Great Britain, Penguin Group includes Penguin, G.P. Putnam's Sons, Viking Press, Berkley Books, NAL, Plume, Grosset & Dunlap, Ace Books, Tarcher, Dutton Books, Penguin Press, Perigee Books, Riverhead, Gotham Books, DK Publishing, and Portfolio.

5. Random House: A division of Germany's Bertelsmann AG, Random House is the largest English-language publisher in the world. It has more than sixty imprints, including Random House Publishing Group, Knopf Doubleday Publishing Group, Ballantine Books, Crown, Three Rivers Press, Clarkson Potter, Pantheon Books, Nan A. Talese, Vintage, Anchor Books, Bantam, Dell, Delacorte, Broadway Books, Harmony Books, Villard Books, and Spiegel & Grau.

6. Simon & Schuster, a division of CBS, which includes Simon & Schuster, Pocket Books, Free Press, Scribner, Touchstone, Fireside, and Atria Books.

Collectively, their empires encompass movies, music, magazines, newspapers, television, and the Web. All of them have children's and spiritual/inspirational imprints and a speaker's bureau they own or partner with, and all their zip codes start with the number *100*.

THEIR MIDSIZE COUSINS

Midsize New York houses that contribute to the *Times* best-seller list include:

- Houghton Mifflin Harcourt
- Hyperion Books—part of Disney, so it has deep pockets
- W.W. Norton & Company
- Perseus Books Group—which has twelve imprints
- Rodale—headquartered in Emmaus, Pennsylvania
- John Wiley & Sons—across the Hudson in Hoboken
- Workman Publishing Company—which includes Algonquin Books

THE BLOCKBUSTER MENTALITY

Big houses need big books to help lead the rest of their three-lists-a-year into bookstores. More than 80 percent of books don't make money, and what you need more than a big publisher is success. It's better to be published by a small or midsize house and succeed than to be published by a big house and fail. But all books go through the publishing process—a personal, complex, slow-moving process that, at a big house, may take one and half to two years and involve more than one hundred people.

THE INVISIBLE BOOK CHAIN: AN OVERVIEW OF THE PUBLISHING PROCESS

The most powerful book chain in the world is invisible—it's all the people after you who become involved with your book. This outline of the publishing process will give you a sense of how complex and collaborative an enterprise publishing your book will be.

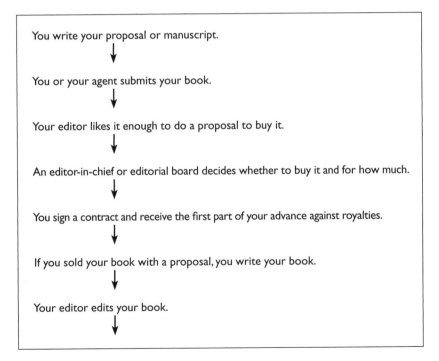

You write your proposal or manuscript.

↓

You or your agent submits your book.

↓

Your editor likes it enough to do a proposal to buy it.

↓

An editor-in-chief or editorial board decides whether to buy it and for how much.

↓

You sign a contract and receive the first part of your advance against royalties.

↓

If you sold your book with a proposal, you write your book.

↓

Your editor edits your book.

↓

You respond to your editor's suggestions.

↓

Your editor accepts your manuscript.

↓

You receive the second part of your advance.

↓

Your editor sends your book to the production department.

↓

The production department outsources the copyediting.

↓

You respond to your copyeditor's comments.

↓

The art department creates or outsources the interior design and the cover for a paperback or the hardcover jacket.

↓

In a series of launch meetings, your editor and the sales, marketing, publicity, and advertising departments

- position your book on one of your publisher's seasonal lists.
- create a trade and consumer-marketing strategy.
- choose the print, broadcast, and electronic trade and consumer media to carry out the strategy.
- prepare sales materials for sales conferences.

↓

Throughout the rest of the process, your agent and your publisher try to sell subsidiary rights.

↓

Your book and the plans for it are presented to the sales reps at a sales conference.

↓

Sales reps sell your book to on- and off-line bookstores, distributors, wholesalers, specialty stores, warehouse clubs, and 50,000 mass-market outlets.

↓

Your publisher sells your book to school, college, and public libraries.

↓

Your publisher's education department sells books with adoption potential.

↓

Your publisher's special-sales department sells books with premium and bulk-sales potential.

↓

The production department arranges for your book to be printed.

↓

Your publisher's warehouse receives books from the printer, ships orders, and later receives returns.

↓

Your publisher's advertising and publicity departments
- do prepublication promotion.
- send out review copies of your book with a news release or media kit.
- carry out their plans.

↓

Book reviewers review your book.

↓

Your publisher promotes your book for as long as sales justify it.

↓

You promote your book for as long as you want it to sell.

CHAPTER 33

Get Published or Self-Publish: Do You Need a Publisher?

Many writers have asked us, "If I have to do so much promotion, why do I need a publisher?" Good question. Self-published books become bestsellers. Anything is possible. However, publishers have more skill, experience, and resources than authors for carrying out the complex challenges of publishing books. Those challenges include:

- Having books edited, copyedited, designed, and produced
- Warehousing and shipping them
- Getting them into stores and keeping stores stocked
- Obtaining reviews
- Publicizing a book to trade and consumer print, broadcast, and electronic media
- Promoting books to schools, libraries, and consumers through catalogs, conventions, special offers, the Web, signings, and trade, consumer, and co-op advertising
- Selling subsidiary rights

Best-seller lists show that big houses accomplish this remarkable feat more often than other publishers. There were more than a million books published in 2009, most self-published, but *The New York Times* best-seller list included only about six hundred of them. This may not answer the question about whether you need a publisher, and it can't, because of three paradoxes.

1. Every book is a book, but every book is a unique combination of author, content, design, timing, price, promotion, distribution, sales, reviews, and responses from readers. What's best for you and your book depends on you, your book, your goals, and your ability to achieve them. This book will help clarify what's best for you, and you're welcome to call or write with questions.

2. Every author is an author, but every author is unique. Authors have their own combination of ability, passion, education, communities, income, goals, location, and accomplishments, as well as writing, speaking, media, work, and personal experience. This is also true of agents and editors.

3. Every publisher is a publisher, but every publisher is unique. They have their own staffs, locations, personalities, contracts, approaches to publishing, levels of passion, and commitments for a book—and more skill at doing some kinds of books than others.

This combination of unique elements makes every book a challenge that involves uncontrollable elements like timing and luck. Publishers draw on their experience to help them, but they're also improvising. Every book is a variation on a theme, and everyone wants to make beautiful music with it.

However, most of the time it's "triumph of hope over experience," as Samuel Johnson said about a second marriage. Fortunately, this book helps you understand what you need to know to have a happy, lasting, working marriage with your editor, your publisher, and your public. If your proposal gets publishers as pumped up about it as you want them to be, one lucky house will get behind it and be the ally you need to help ensure your book's success.

Next up: How to seduce editors into reading your proposal with your (e-) query letter.

CHAPTER 34

The Hook, the Book, and the Cook: Writing and Sending Your (E-)Query Letter

THE GOLDEN RULE FOR WRITING YOUR QUERY LETTER

Give editors the best reasons to say *yes* and no reasons to say *no*.

I'm collecting rejections on a city-by-city basis, and San Francisco has come up.

—From a query letter I once received

Like the other three parts of your proposal, every word of your query must convince editors to read the next word. Poor prose dooms query letters and proposals faster than anything else. It's been said that a query letter should be like a skirt: long enough to cover the subject but short enough to keep it interesting.

Your query letter doesn't have to be funny or imaginative, but it creates the first and perhaps only impression editors will have of you, so it must be impeccable. If your letter is poorly written, you've saved editors the trouble of reading your proposal. The prevailing wisdom: "If they can't write a letter, they couldn't write a book."

Limit your letter to one single-spaced page with indented paragraphs and a space between paragraphs.

How to Write a Book Proposal

THE HOOK, THE BOOK AND THE COOK

Agent Katharine Sands believes that the writing you do about your writing is as important as the writing itself. A query is a one-page, single-spaced letter with a space between three or four indented paragraphs, and without sounding self-serving—it describes the why, what, and who: the hook, the book, and the cook.

- **The hook:** Whatever will best justify publishing your book

  - (Optional) A selling quote about your book (or a previous book) from someone whose name will give it credibility and/or salability. The quote could also be about you.

  - (Optional) The reason you're writing the agent:

    - the name of someone who suggested you contact the agent
    - the book in which the author thanked the agent for selling that inspired you to write the letter
    - where you heard the agent speak
    - where you will hear the agent speak and hope to have the chance to discuss your book

  - Whatever will most excite agents about your book:

    - the opening paragraph
    - the most compelling fact or idea about your subject
    - a statistic about the interest of people or the media in the subject

- **The book:** The essence of your book:

  - A sentence with the title and the selling handle for the book, up to fifteen words that will convince booksellers to stock it. The models for it: one or two books, movies, or authors. "It's Harry Potter meets *Twilight*."

  - A one-sentence overview of your book, and, if appropriate, what it will do for your readers

  - The book's biggest markets

  - Its actual or estimated length

  - The length of your proposal and how many more pages of manuscript you have ready to send

- (Optional) The names of people who have agreed to give a foreword and cover quotes, if they're impressive
- (Optional) A link to illustrations, if they're important
- (Optional) Include the subjects or titles of the next two books, if you're proposing a series
- (Optional) Information about a self-published edition that will help sell it

- **The cook:** Why you're the right person to write the book
  - Your promotion plan: the four or five most effective things you will do to promote your book online and off, with numbers if they're impressive
  - Your platform: the most important things you have done and are doing to give yourself continuing visibility with potential readers, with numbers if they're impressive: your online activities, published work with links to it, and media and speaking experience with links to audio and video
  - (Optional) Your credentials; experience in your field; or years of research; prizes, contests, and awards in your field

Include anything else that will convince agents to ask to see your proposal.

MORE QUERY TIPS

- Don't send anything to more than one person at the same agency or publisher. Elizabeth and I receive enough submissions sent to both of us to convince me that some knave out there is suggesting writers do it. Duplication makes a bad impression and wastes writers' time and money.

- Don't send anything to a publishing house; send it to an editor. Big houses will return it unopened. Find the name of the right editor for your book and verify that the editor is still at the house. This is less important with agents, although you will create a more professional impression if you check to see which agent handles the kind of book you're writing and use the agent's name. Elizabeth handles fiction, but we receive fiction queries addressed to me.

- Once editors express interest in seeing your proposal, it is no longer unsolicited. Begin your cover letter with: *Many thanks for giving me the opportunity to send you my proposal for …*

- Find out how long it takes agents or editors to respond, make a note of the date by which you should have a response, and follow up by e-mail or phone if you don't receive a reply. Ask when you can expect to hear, and keep following up until you do, but be professional so you don't come across as a pest.

Someone once defined a manuscript as "something submitted in haste and returned at leisure." For the best treatment on the receiving end, submit your proposal properly. Agents and publishers do not assume responsibility for lost or damaged manuscripts, so if you're sending a hard copy, package your proposal carefully. Insert your proposal into a manila envelope or, for greater protection, a No. 5 mailing bag.

In *How to Write Short Stories*, Ring Lardner observes, "A good many young writers make the mistake of enclosing a stamped, self-addressed envelope, big enough for the manuscript to come back in. This is too much of a temptation to the editor." If you want your proposal back, enclose a stamped, self-addressed mailer big enough for it, or a prepaid return label from UPS or FedEx.

If you don't need the material back, include a No. 10 business-sized SASE or postcard to be sure to get a response. It may be cheaper to reprint your material than to pay for the return postage and perhaps receive an unusable proposal.

Agents and editors probably won't give you feedback on your work, but you are more likely to get it if you include an envelope. They have no obligation to respond or return submissions unless writers provide them with the means to do so.

HOT TIP

Assume agents and editors will reply only if they're interested or if writers include a SASE. But if you don't want your work returned, and you're willing to settle for hearing back from agents or editors only if they are interested in

Naturally, you want to be sure your proposal arrives—but don't call to find out! Agents and editors may not keep a log of submissions, and they hate wasting their time with *Did you get it?* calls. Instead, use UPS, spring for a return receipt at the post office, or clip a postcard to the front of your letter with your address filled in.

If you don't use a postcard, find out in advance from the agent or editor's website or directory listing how long the reading will take. A six- to eight-week turnaround is typical for established agents. Publishers vary in how quickly they process submissions, but they usually take longer than agents. Write or call if you don't hear back when the guidelines indicate you will.

Next come three ways to make your proposal more salable.

How to Write a Book Proposal

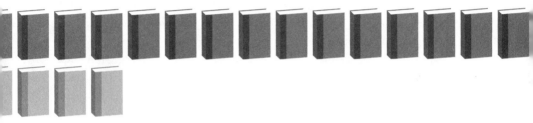

CHAPTER 35

The First Impression: Making Your Proposal Look Like It's Worth What You Want for It

THE GOLDEN RULE FOR SUBMITTING YOUR WORK

Make your proposal and how you submit it impeccable.

When an agent or editor asks you to e-mail your proposal, send it as one file in Word unless they indicate otherwise. E-mailing your proposal as a Word document is the easiest, fastest, most common way to do it. Keep in mind that the speed with which you e-mail your proposal may have no relationship to the amount of time it may take for a response. Agents and editors receive a lot of proposals, so regardless of how proposals arrive, it still takes time for agents and editors to get to them.

There are a few reasons you may need to send a hard copy.

- You're submitting a self-published book.
- An agent or editor prefers a printed version.
- Because of illustrations, the proposal may take too long for editors to download, or the illustrations won't look good enough.

If you're sending simultaneous submissions, which are generally accepted by agents and editors, you may have to send it electronically to some people and as hard copy to others.

BUILDING YOUR BOOK'S VALUE

Here are three ways you can increase the salability of your proposal: sample clips, illustrations, a surprise.

SAMPLE CLIPS

Outstanding samples of your published work demonstrate its acceptance by publications and their readers. Besides proving you're a professional, they show editors what you can do.

If you have recent clips that will impress an editor because of their quality, length, relevance, and range of subjects, or because of the periodicals in which they appeared, include links to up to six of them. When it's a magazine piece, include the cover of the magazine.

If you're sending hard copies of your proposal, only include copies of impressive articles about the subject of your book and links to other articles. Always send photocopies, not originals.

If you have an impressive story about yourself or rave reviews about a previous book, underline the key points and include links to them or copies of them.

Send clips or a published book only if they will help sell your proposal. Otherwise wait until an editor asks to see more. If you find stories on your subject in major periodicals, such as a cover story in *Newsweek*, that will make your proposal more salable, underline the relevant parts and include links or photocopies of the articles.

> **HOT TIP**
>
> Small or poorly produced periodicals, which may be where a writer's early work appears, will not impress editors. Use your judgment about what to include. When in doubt, leave it out unless your writing network advises otherwise.

ILLUSTRATIONS

Illustrations add to a book's salability, but they will also make a book more expensive for your publisher, book buyers, and perhaps you. If you will use illustrations that are critical to your book's content, include the illustrations for your sample chapter. It's best to integrate illustrations into the flow of the proposal (and digitally embedded if possible).

We once sold a book called *Raven: The Untold Story of the Rev. Jim Jones and His People* by Tim Reiterman; Reiterman was a reporter for *The San Francisco Examiner* and was wounded in Guyana. Tim didn't have to account for photographs, because his publisher knew he could obtain whatever pictures were needed. Tarcher successfully republished the book in 2008 for the thirtieth anniversary of Jonestown.

Whether your illustrations will be grouped together or spread throughout your book, let their impact on the book's content guide you in determining how much you have to show or include at the proposal stage, and whenever possible, ask how the editor prefers to review art.

Two Ways to Submit Your Illustrations

- If you can, scan slides, photographs, and artwork into your computer and digitally embed them in your text so you can submit your proposal electronically. This will also enable you to print as many copies as you need if you're submitting hard copies of your proposal. You can also scan additional artwork and text, and include a link to them in your proposal.
- Submit them in hard copy on request.

A SURPRISE

Consider including a happy surprise with your proposal to catch the attention of harried agents and editors. The ideal surprise

- relates to your book.
- is eye-catching.
- is imaginative.
- isn't expensive (so it doesn't seem like a bribe).
- may be humorous.
- grabs an editor's attention so effectively your proposal is read immediately.

An online surprise might be a link to information, a story, a video, or a free gift. If you're submitting a hard copy, a successful surprise lays flat, packs small, and plays big. Here are examples of surprises submitted with hard-copy proposals:

- An author who had written about *The Godfather* included a foot-long plastic fish wrapped in newspaper, which got our immediate attention.

- Less lucky was the woman who sent us an orange children's shoe with a letter that began *Now that I've got my foot in the door ...* We mentioned this to an agent friend, and she said she got the other shoe!

- AAR member Jillian Manus once submitted a proposal about assertiveness for women, and she enclosed a whip with a note saying *Submit to your editor.* The book sold quickly.

- Chocolate is always a safe bet (my partner, Elizabeth, assures me the iron helps her concentrate). But if your surprise is edible, it must be sealed.

The next chapter describes the joys of self-publishing.

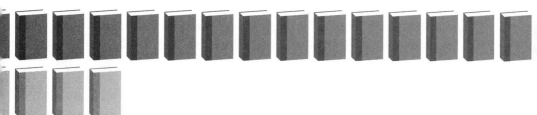

CHAPTER 36

DIY: The Joys of Self-Publishing

THE GOLDEN RULES FOR SELF-PUBLISHING YOUR BOOK

- Balance the desire for profit and control with the need to be responsible for the whole writing and publishing process.
- Do what you can do; find professionals to do what you can't.

It used to be said that if you publish your own book, you'll have a lot of books in your garage, so you'll work hard to sell them because you want to park your car. Thanks to technology, self-publishing your book no longer requires you to sacrifice your garage.

If you want to test-market your book before selling it to a publisher, you can make an all-out effort and create the book you've dreamed about. More than 500,000 writers do every year. Technology and the ease of self-publishing have made it a major trend. Self-publishing has advantages that can be summed up in three words: money, speed, and control.

- You have complete control over every aspect of your book: the title, content, editing, format (hardcover, trade paperback, or mass-market), size, length, cover, design, production, publication date, price, marketing, and selling and distribution.
- You control your book's film, foreign, and electronic rights.

- You make more money on every copy and on subsidiary rights.

Self-publishing is a venerable tradition in American letters. When self-publishing guru Dan Poynter gives workshops, he hands out a list of famous authors who have published their own work, including Walt Whitman, Henry David Thoreau, Edgar Allan Poe, and Mark Twain.

The One Minute Manager, What Color Is Your Parachute?, The Celestine Prophecy, The Christmas Box, The Shack, and *Rich Dad, Poor Dad* were all bestsellers, and they were all originally self-published books. AAR member Laurie Liss sold *The Christmas Box* for $4.2 million, a record sum for a self-published book, all the more remarkable because it included only North American hardcover rights!

If you have the luxury of writing your book before you sell it, and a way to sell copies, consider self-publishing it at least in manuscript form or as an e-book. If you're giving talks or classes, prove your book works. After you integrate feedback into your manuscript from your first readers, print a Special Limited Edition. Photocopy just enough double-spaced, one- or two-sided copies for each event and sell them in loose-leaf binder and ask for feedback. If you use one-sided pages, encourage readers to write on the blank side.

> **HOT TIP**
>
> Material in a loose-leaf binder has a greater perceived value than other forms of binding. One of our authors who taught classes sold what became a twenty-dollar trade paperback in a loose-leaf binder for forty-five dollars!

Even if you sell your book to a publisher, self-publishing it for your events will enable you to test-market it. You want people taking your book home and getting the benefit your title promises without your help. You want them telling you about their experience of reading your book and its effect on them. Then you want their responses and suggestions or, better yet, their marked-up copies.

The goal of your self-published edition, which you can also sell online, may be just to cover your costs, not to make a profit. Include a page about what kind of feedback you want at the beginning of the book. If you're selling a loose-leaf edition, keep adding changes before you reprint for each event, and keep reprinting until your audiences run out of suggestions. That's when

How to Write a Book Proposal

you're ready for the next step. If you sell your book to a publisher, agree on when you will stop selling your edition.

TAKING THE PLUNGE

If you generate enough publicity and sales through your efforts, publishers will be eager to buy the rights to publish your book. If your self-published book is professionally designed and edited, the publisher may be able to simply change the cover and the front matter, and print it as is. If you want to test-market a published version of your book before selling it to a publisher, you can make an all-out effort and create the book you've dreamed about.

One editor said to us, "If the author can sell two thousand copies a month for eight months, I want to see it." Other editors will not need as strong a track record. Another editor remarked that selling two thousand copies is the threshold for being taken seriously, but how long it takes to sell them is also a factor. If you test-market your book and sell enough copies, a publisher will buy it.

ON THE ROAD TO PROFITS

Gregory Godek drove around the country in his specially painted RV and sold more than one million copies of his self-published book *1,001 Ways to Be Romantic.* Greg said he spent 5 percent of his time writing his book and 95 percent of his time and $600,000 promoting it. One day he realized he wasn't a writer who promoted—he was a promoter who wrote. The book sold more than two million copies.

The Resource Directory (Appendix A) has suggestions to get you started in self-publishing. But if self-publishing isn't for you, you may want to join the tens of thousands of writers who sell their books to publishers every year. The following chapter will tell you how.

CHAPTER 37

Pushing the Envelope:
How to Sell Your Book Yourself

THE GOLDEN RULES FOR SELLING YOUR BOOK YOURSELF

- Research all potential publishers.
- Follow their submission guidelines.
- Get help with the contract.

If your book is good enough, anyone can sell it because any possible publisher will buy it. Writers sell more books than agents. Agents focus on the Six Sisters, the conglomerates that spend the most for books. But small, niche, academic, and university presses—even midsize and big houses—buy books from writers. The smaller the house, the more of its books they buy from writers. So, if your book won't interest agents, or you prefer not to use one, sell your book yourself. Here's how:

- Make sure your proposal or manuscript is ready to submit.
- Learn from the contacts and experiences of writers you know.
- Make a list of potential publishers by
  - visiting bookstores.
  - researching publishers in directories and on their websites. Check *Literary Market Place* and *Jeff Herman's Guide to Book Publishers, Editors,*

& Literary Agents, Check publishers of competing and comp
books. Contact authors in your field and authors published ᵥᵧ ...
you want to try.

- Prepare a list of editors by
  - reading acknowledgments in books.
  - asking editor-in-chiefs' assistants at prospective publishers who the right editor is for your book.
  - following up with calls to verify that editors are still there.

- E-mail (or snail mail with an SASE) a one-page query letter to as many editors as you wish simultaneously.
- Submit your work following publishers' guidelines in *Writer's Market* or on publishers' websites, letting them know if it's a multiple submission.
- Find out when you should expect a response and then follow up with publishers by phone, e-mail, and mail until you receive it.
- If editors want to make an offer, meet with them, if you can, to learn about
  - their vision for editing and publishing your book.
  - their books and their houses.
  - how they work, their personalities, and what your working marriage with them might be like.

- When you receive an offer, thank the editor, but don't discuss it. Tell the editor you'll get back to him or her, and use one of the following options to find help you.
  - Find an agent to negotiate the deal for you. The agent may be able to get you a better editor, publisher, and deal.
  - Get help from writers' organizations, including the Authors Guild, the National Writers Union, and the American Society of Journalists and Authors, that counsel members for free.
  - Find an agent or intellectual-property attorney who knows book contracts to help you negotiate the contract or review it on an hourly basis. Not getting help may cost more than what you pay for it.

- If other editors have your proposal, tell them you've gotten an offer and ask them to respond in two weeks. The editor who made the offer will expect to hear from you by then. If you use an agent, your agent may be willing to follow up with them. Small houses may have a take-it-or-leave-it policy about contracts or may not want to work with agents.

Once your proposal is accepted, allow up to two months for the contract to arrive and up to another two months for the advance. The larger the house, the more slowly paperwork moves through it.

- Celebrate! When the first part of your advance arrives, reward those who helped you and yourself.

If the prospect of selling your book doesn't tempt you, perhaps an agent can help you. The next chapter will tell you how.

CHAPTER 38

Meet the Matchmaker: How an Agent Can Help You

THE GOLDEN RULES FOR GETTING AND WORKING WITH AN AGENT

- Make sure your proposal is ready to submit.
- Be impeccably professional in contacting agents.
- Treat your relationship with your agent like a working marriage.

A writer sent his manuscript to a publisher, and when he didn't hear back, he wrote the publisher a letter: "Please respond immediately as I have other irons in the fire." Shortly after that, he received a note saying: "We have considered your manuscript and advise you to put it with the other irons."

This chapter will help you avoid rejections like that one. New writers approach agents without an understanding of agenting or publishing, so one of the fundamental services that agents perform for their clients is to transform them from writers with something to say into authors with something to sell. This literary alchemy changes writers from artists and craftspeople who can spin words into prose to authors who can spin prose into gold.

HOW AN AGENTS CAN HELP YOU

Here's how and why an agent can help you. An agent is

- a mediator between two realities: you and the marketplace.

- a scout who knows what publishers are looking for.

- a filter who sifts through thousands of submissions a year to discover prose with gold in it and then offers it to editors, who are grateful to agents for enabling them to do their jobs faster and more easily.

- a midwife who can provide editorial guidance and help you give birth to your idea, an essential part of making a book salable.

- a matchmaker who knows which editors and publishers to submit your book to and, just as important, which to avoid. An agent continues to send out a manuscript until it is sold or until the agent has tried all likely publishers. It's taken us as few as four phone calls and as long as ten years to sell a book.

- a negotiator. An Arab proverb says, "Trust in Allah, but tie your camel." In publishing, you tie your camel with a contract. When a publisher makes an offer for your book, your agent becomes a negotiator who hammers out the most favorable possible contract for your working marriage with your publisher.

  Publishers will offer an advance against royalties, usually based on their estimate of the first year's royalties. Large houses pay between $10,000 and $25,000 for most books, but they'll pay whatever agents or competing bidders convince them a book is worth.

  The contract between you and your publisher, which may be as long as thirty-six pages—and which you must understand, approve, and sign—enables your agent to act on your behalf and receive income earned through the contract. The agent deducts a 15 percent commission and forwards the rest to you.

  Your agent haggles about rights and money with your editor, so you can work harmoniously with your editor to make your books successful. An agent enables you to keep more subsidiary-rights income and receive

the income sooner than if your publisher handles the rights. Yᵣ
may appoint co-agents for film and foreign rights.

- a liaison and connector to the publishing world who helps you answer editorial, financial, production, and promotional questions that arise throughout the publication process.

- a bookkeeper who checks royalty statements and keeps track of the e-mail and paperwork a book generates.

- an advocate who helps solve problems, such as a late or rejected manuscript, a bad jacket design, or your editor leaving the house.

- a cheerleader for you and your books.

- a rainmaker who may be able to obtain assignments for you from editors or come up with ideas for you.

- a mentor who can advise you about your writing and your career.

- an oasis of encouragement in what may be a desert of rejection.

AGENT AS PAINKILLER

Some writers think people become agents for the same reason they become dentists: They like to inflict pain. Like editors, agents reject more than 95 percent of the submissions they see, but agents receive far more rejections than writers.

Consider these additional ways an agent can help you.

- Editors respond more quickly to submissions from agents than from writers because agented work is more likely to be publishable.

- As a continuing source of manuscripts, agents have more clout with editors than do writers.

- Editors may change jobs, and publishers may change hands at any time, so an agent may be the only stable element in your career.

- By absorbing rejections and by being a focal point for your business dealings, your agent frees you to write.

Writers who approach publishers without help are at greater risk of being taken advantage of. The selling of your book deserves the same level of care, skill, knowledge, passion, and experience you devote to writing it. An agent can't write your book as well as you can, but you can't sell it as well as an agent can. Even if you could do what an agent does, wouldn't you rather spend your time writing your books and helping them succeed?

NINE WAYS TO FIND THE AGENT YOU NEED

If you want your book published by a big house, and you don't have a track record, you may find it hard to get an agent. But this list of nine ways to find an agent proves it's easier than ever to find one.

1. Your writing community: The writers you know, online and off, will recommend agents. One way to get an agent's attention is if the first two words the agent sees or hears are the name of a client, editor, agent, author, teacher, or bookseller who suggested you contact the agent. Agents do consider the enthusiasm with which a recommendation is made. A note to the agent is more effective than someone just telling the writer to mention his or her name.

2. The Association of Authors' Representatives (AAR): The 450 agents in AAR are the best sources of experienced, reputable agents. Members are required to follow the AAR's code of ethics. The directories mentioned in item number five of this list indicate when an agent is a member, and you can look agents up at www.aaronline.org.

3. The Web: Blogs, Facebook, Twitter, Google. The sites in the Resource Directory (Appendix A) include agents' e-mail addresses and websites. PublishersMarketplace.com is an online news source and community for publishing insiders. If you become a member ($20/month), then you'll have access to a database of publishing deals made by agents and editors, as well as contact info for hundreds of publishing professionals.

4. Writers' organizations: Members of the writing organizations in the Resource Directory (Appendix A) will tell you about their agents.

5. Directories: Directories in the Resource Directory (Appendix A) vary in the kind and amount of information they provide. For the best results, check what several of them list about the same agency.

6. Literary events: Writing classes, readings, lectures, seminars, book signings, conferences, and book festivals present opportunities to meet and learn about agents and publishers. Conferences offer opportunities to meet agents.

7. Magazines: *Publishers Weekly, The Writer Magazine, Writer's Digest,* and *Poets & Writers* have articles by and about agents. If you don't want to splurge on a subscription to *Publishers Weekly*, read it at the library or online. The "Deals" column is a roundup of sales.

8. Books: Check the dedication and acknowledgment pages of books like yours. Grateful authors thank their editors and agents (always a good idea).

9. Your platform: Let agents or publishers find you—be visible online and off, get published, give talks, publicize your work and yourself. When your continuing national visibility is great enough, agents and editors will find you.

GETTING THE AGENT YOU NEED

In *Really Important Stuff My Kids Have Taught Me*, Cynthia L. Copeland wrote: " … [J]ust … keep banging until someone opens the door." It's the same with agents. Here are eight steps to getting the agent you need:

1. Find a salable idea.

2. Write a proposal or manuscript. The only time to contact agents is when you have something ready to sell.

3. Research potential agents online and off as the list above suggests.

4. Write an irresistible query letter.

5. Follow the submission guidelines of the agents you contact.

6. If the agent has a written agreement, read it to make sure you'll feel comfortable signing it, and feel free to ask the agent questions about it.

7. Meet interested agents to test the chemistry for your working marriage. Look at the challenge of finding and keeping an agent as creating and sustaining a marriage that has personal and professional aspects to it.

8. Choose the best agent for you, based on passion, personality, performance, and experience.

Then bask in the glow of satisfaction that an agent thinks enough of your book's potential and yours to represent you.

FOR LOVE AND MONEY: WHAT AGENTS CAN DO THAT YOU CAN'T

Like publishers, agents are motivated by love and money. They need big books to make big bucks. They also love to get excited about their books and authors. And they must do a good job on the first book if they expect to work on the next one.

If you have a salable book, you can sell it. Although writers sell more books than agents, an agent can help you in four ways you can't help yourself.

1. Agents understand editors' expectations, so when agents submit a proposal, it's stronger than you can make your proposal without help. Agents understand what will sell and how to present books to publishers. Editors have become agents, and agents have become editors. Most editors don't have the time they would like to edit; they have become in-house agents who sign up books and sing their praises all along the road to publication and past it.

   This has forced agents to become editors. Agents must make sure a proposal is ready before they submit it because editors can't buy books that will require more editing than they (or their assistant) can do. Also, an agent's reputation is on the line with every submission. If agents submit poor work, editors ignore them.

2. An agent is better able to get you the best editor and publisher for your book. There's a world of difference between a *yes* and the best possible *yes*.

3. An agent can understand contracts and negotiate better contract terms.

How to Write a Book Proposal

4. An agent can respond to the questions and problems that arise during the long publication process that you won't be able to answer for yourself. You can use your networks for advice, but whether you'll receive the same level of guidance is questionable. And it's unlikely you will be able to speak on your behalf as well as an agent will.

THE TOUGHER THE BUSINESS, THE MORE AGENTS NEED YOU

Finding new writers is one of the hardest parts of an agent's job, but it's also the best part. Agents want and need to discover new talent and hope they will be able to say *yes* every time they begin to read a proposal.

To make a living as agents, Elizabeth and I need to sell books to New York houses. But we're trapped in the publishing pyramid. At the apex of the pyramid are the 6 percent of writers that *Writer's Digest* estimates earn a living as writers and who have agents. At the bottom of the pyramid are the more than 90 percent of writers who aren't yet ready to sell their work to Big Apple publishers. Between them are the fewer than 5 percent of writers who are ready for a big or midsize house. But more than 1,200 agents are searching for these writers. You think you've got problems!

The tougher the business gets, the more urgently agents need writers. If you have a book that will interest large and midsize publishers, you will find an agent. As a writer, you are the most important person in the publishing business because you make it go. For more about agents and publishing, and to find out how to make yourself irresistible to agents and publishers, please see my book *How to Get a Literary Agent*.

If you want to cook up a successful book and enjoy it, turn the page.

CHAPTER 39

Recipes for a Successful Book and the Best Publishing Experience

A RECIPE FOR A SUCCESSFUL BOOK

What does your book need to succeed? Here are the ingredients for a successful book:

- A salable idea, craft, commitment, visibility, communities to help you, a knowledge of how publishing works, professionalism, and a commitment to writing, promotion, and building a career
- An irresistible proposal
- An agent who makes sure your proposal is 100 percent before publishers see it; obtains the best possible editor, publisher, and deal for you; and helps you throughout the publishing process
- A manuscript as close to perfect as you, your readers, and your editor can make it
- An effective title and cover
- The passion of all the links in the invisible book chain
- Large subsidiary-rights sales
- An effective promotional campaign by you and your publisher
- Rave reviews

- The right timing
- Word of mouth and mouse

All these ingredients must be seasoned and stirred with what every book needs: luck.

A RECIPE FOR THE BEST PUBLISHING EXPERIENCE

Whether you sell your book yourself or hire an agent, here's a recipe for having the best publishing experience for you and your book:

- Find an idea for a book you have the passion and commitment to write and promote.
- Know what your goals are for your book and be able to reach them through your efforts so that whatever your publisher does is gravy.
- Submit a rejection-proof proposal.
- Submit the manuscript you propose.
- Carry out your promotional plan.
- Meet the inevitable challenges.
- Deliver more than you promise.
- Be relentless but a pleasure to work with.
- Enjoy the process!

Whether writing is a means or an end for you, the following chapters will discuss how to use writing to create the future you want.

PART IX:
PLOTTING YOUR FUTURE

CHAPTER 40

Starting With the End in Mind:
Setting Your Personal and Professional Goals

THE GOLDEN RULE FOR SETTING YOUR GOALS
Create goals that keep you motivated and inspired.

ENVISIONING YOUR FUTURE

A maxim on Maui says, "The unaimed arrow never misses." That's okay if you're an unaimed arrow, but not if you want to be a successful author. In this case, you must hit the tiny bull's-eye of a small, distant target in a world with endless possibilities.

In *The 7 Habits of Highly Effective People,* Stephen Covey writes: "Begin with the end in mind." If you want to be successful, you must know your goals. The more clearly you see them, the more likely you are to achieve them. You can draw a portrait of yourself and your future on a blank piece of paper or your computer screen by summing up your personal and professional literary and financial goals, and how you will reach them.

Your answers will determine the kinds of books you write, how you write them, how many you write, and what you do to promote them and build your platform and your career. There are no wrong answers; make them whatever you want. The criteria for your answers are the following:

- Do your goals strike a realistic balance between writing for yourself and writing for the marketplace? If you want to earn a million dollars a year, and you want to write haiku, you've got a problem!
- Do the criteria motivate you to do everything you can to write and promote your books and to build your career?

Own your answers to these questions by starting them with the word *I*.

- Why do you want to write?
- In which literary forms do you want to write: nonfiction, poetry, novels, screenplays?
- In which media do you want to share your work—blogs, articles, talks, podcasts, audio, video, poetry, novels, nonfiction, screenplays?
- Which books are models for what you would like your books to be?
- Which authors are models for whom you would like to become?
- What do you want your books to communicate?
- What do you want your writing to achieve (a possible goal hook)?
- Which groups of readers do you most want to reach?
- How many books do you want to write each year?
- How many people do you want to read your blog and visit your website, and how many people do you want to connect with on social networks?
- Do you want to self-publish or be published by a publisher?
- Do you want to be published by a small, midsize, or large house?
- What advances would you like for your books?
- How much money do you want to earn a year from your writing?
- How many copies of your books do you want to sell every year?
- What position would you like to have as an author in your field?
- How many years will it take you to reach that position?
- How will you do it? (Sue Grafton advises writers to have a five-year plan.)
- How involved do you want to get with the writing process? Do you want to write your books yourself, work with an editor or collaborator, or hire a ghostwriter?
- How will you support your writing until it supports you?

Also consider your personal goals.

- How do you want to live?
- Where do you want to live?
- Do you want a family?
- How large do you want that family to be?
- What kind of a house do you want?
- What possessions do you want most?
- How many vacations do you want a year?
- How do you want to spend your vacations?
- How much income do you want when you retire?

Put your answers up where you write, and read them to keep you going. Change them whenever and however you wish. One way to verify your answers: Assume you've reached your goals. What's your life like?

Jack Canfield and Mark Victor Hansen believe in having giant goals. Their goal is to sell a billion books by 2020. Inventor Charles Franklin Kettering said, of the Wright brothers, that they "flew right through the smoke screen of impossibility." Writers who can't write as well as you and aren't as articulate or as good-looking as you are successful authors. If they can do it, so can you!

Life is indeed a journey, and you are both the traveler and the destination. As you approach the horizon of your possibilities, you will grow into them and become a more capable you. May your journey be filled with goals you reach and horizons that continue to recede as you advance into the best future you can imagine. Believe the words of Samuel Johnson: "Your aspirations are your possibilities."

Chapter twenty-one has suggestions for test-marketing your goals.

The following chapter offers building blocks for getting your book published.

CHAPTER 41

From Author to Authorpreneur: The Building Blocks for Growing From Small to Big

A lady was picking through the frozen turkeys at the grocery store, but she couldn't find one big enough for her family. She asked a stock boy, "Do these turkeys get any bigger?"

The stock boy replied, "No ma'am, they're dead."

If you're alive, you need to keep growing. The cost of living sure does, so you have to continue to be more productive to keep up with it. Václav Havel, author and former President of Czechoslovakia captures the right attitude for an author: "Vision is not enough; it must be combined with venture. It is not enough to stare up the steps; we must step up the stairs." Writers are like most agents and publishers—entrepreneurs running a business.

But beyond thinking of yourself as an entrepreneur, think of yourself as an *authorpreneur*. Here are sixteen ways to do it.

1. **Take responsibility for your book's success.** Publishers are responsible for lists of books and are limited in what they can do for any one of them and in how long they can help. Therefore you must think of yourself as copublisher and do as much as you can to make up for what your publisher can't do.

2. **Serve your readers.** Venture capitalist Brad Burnham says, "Customer service is the new marketing." Authors and publishers don't keep books

alive—readers do. In *What Would Google Do?*, Jeff Jarvis wrote: "Your customers are your ad agency." After writers, readers are the most important people in publishing. Serve them well enough, and they will spread the word.

British writer Wilfred Grenfell wrote: "The service we render to others is really the rent we pay for our room on this earth." Author and speaker Zig Ziglar created the Law of Reciprocity: "You can get everything in life you want if you will just help enough other people get what they want." Your readers want the same things out of life you do, so do whatever you can to serve your fans and maintain your relationships with them.

If your goal is to write books that lead to change, now is the best time to do it. Technology makes it easier for the right book to change the world. The world will never have too many writers devoted to putting their lives in the service of their ideas, their books, and their readers.

3. **Keep generating ideas and content.** The essence of being an authorpreneur is a continuing flow of ideas and content, short and long, for free and fees. Short work can lead to long work, free work to paid work. In addition to creating unexpected opportunities, your writing helps you build, serve, and maintain your communities.

4. **Practice niche craft.** Don't expect to build a career with a book. Your ideas create opportunities for talks, articles, books, publicity, building communities, and all the ways you can profit from them. Writing books on different subjects requires learning about new subjects and new fields and building new communities for each one. It's better to be a niche crafter: Find an idea for a series of related books you will be passionate about writing and promoting and then create a career out of it. Niche craft will enable you to build your brand and identity and create synergy between everything you do. It's the fastest, surest road to success.

5. **Honor your commitment to your career.** There's a cartoon showing a man and a woman on a couch talking. The man is saying: "Look, I'm not talking about a lifetime commitment. I'm talking about marriage." Becoming a successful authorpreneur will take a lifetime commitment.

Everything you do is an expression of your commitment to your goals. The fewer things there are that are more important to you than becoming a successful author, the more likely it is you'll become one.

6. **Come up with ways to build your business by serving your communities.** Rishad Tobaccowala of Publicis Groupe Media says, "Make money through the side door." In *The Author's Guide to Building an Online Platform* by Stephanie Chandler, Dan Kennedy—author of the *No B.S.* business series—reports that the deep connections his books make with readers make them better continuing customers for his other products and services than any other promotional strategy.

   But Dan uses promotion to drive readers into what he calls a *marketing funnel* that makes them customers for life. Many successful authors create a profit pyramid in which books are the base of their business, and may sell the most, but are the least profitable part of their enterprise. They use books to sell

   - other books, audiobooks, and e-books
   - CDs and DVDs
   - other products, such as workbooks
   - talks, (tele)seminars, webinars, and weekend and weeklong events
   - coaching, consulting, and training

   These authors create and control almost all of these products and services, which maximize their profits. They continue to build an e-mail list of fans who buy whatever they produce. If you're writing the kinds of books that lend themselves to this kind of brand extension, and you want to build a career, think of yourself as a multimedia, multinational conglomerate of one.

   Thoreau once said that it's not what you look at that counts, but what you see. What's important is not the problems you look at but the opportunities you see in them. Before the advent of technology, more millionaires were created during the Depression than any other period in our history.

7. **Do what you can to control your future.** You are at the mercy of luck—the unexpected—and you depend on the effort and goodwill of other

people and businesses. But do what you can to control your life instead of relinquishing control to others.

8. **Be pragmatic.** Business is sustained by the purity of profits—if there aren't any, businesses go under. They're forced to do what generates profit and abandon what doesn't. Psychologist Havelock Ellis said, "All the art of living lies in a fine mingling of letting go and holding on." So does your life; you will always be judging how to keep what you need, shedding what doesn't work and adapting to new circumstances.

9. **Welcome new technology.** The computer is the greatest tool writers have ever had for researching, writing and promoting their books, and building communities. In the past, technology advanced in stages. There was an advance in planes, trains, and automobiles, and then they would remain at that level until the next advance. But now we are on the vertical slope of technology. Driven by competition, new products and services, and the imperative for growth, advances in technology will continue to drive us at an accelerating rate toward a future no one can predict or control.

   This makes it imperative for you to do what your competitors are doing. Continue to improve your effectiveness by integrating new technology into your work and balancing the value of your efforts with the time they require.

10. **Embrace change.** As publishing reinvents itself, you need to track changes in the industry and the culture, understand how they affect you and your books, and take advantage of the opportunities that arise. Charles Darwin believed the smartest creatures aren't the ones who survive, nor the strongest, but rather the most adaptable. We are going to have to adapt more in this century than our species ever has.

   Although people still want and need the same kinds of information they always have, how they consume it affects how you write about and present it. You're going to need to adapt to challenges and opportunities created by technology, other media, and how they change the culture. The world's problems are complex and connected, their effects unpredictable. The human family, with writers at the forefront, can only solve them together. As Benjamin Franklin warned, we will either hang together, or we will hang separately.

11. **Make mistakes.** A.G. Lafley of Procter & Gamble says, "Being willing to make mistakes is the key to innovation." Mistakes are part of the learning process. Accept that you will make them, but console yourself by knowing that you will survive them and that your communities will help you avoid and fix them. As long as you learn from your mistakes, regard them as painful favors that enable you to grow. And follow Groucho Marx's advice: "Learn from the mistakes of others. You can never live long enough to make them all yourself."

12. **Overcome obstacles.** Obstacles test commitment—the greater your goals, and the greater the obstacles in your path, the sweeter your success. You can't have achievements without challenges any more than you can have courage without fear; obstacles are the hills you climb to get where you want to go. Prevent problems by minimizing risk, but look at problems as opportunities to do something different and better, and be resourceful at solving them.

13. **Express your gratitude.** The people who help you deserve an expression of gratitude commensurate with the value of their assistance. The criterion for whether your responses are effective is how recipients feel about continuing to help you.

14. **Be a lifelong learner.** The British statesman Benjamin Disraeli one said, "The most successful people in life are generally those who have the best information." Make learning about writing, marketing, publishing, your field, and working smarter a perpetual endeavor. If you want to keep earning, you've got to keep learning. At the same time, know what you can do and find help for the rest. This will require friends who will help you for free, as well as paid professionals.

15. **Be creative in everything you do.** There's a T-shirt that says: *I hate it when my cat thinks outside of a box.* Today, you not only have to think outside of the box, you have to think outside of the room the box is in. Your ability to be creative separates you from everyone else on the

planet—it's what you alone can bring to everything you do. Being creative is like working a muscle: The more you stretch, the more creative you become.

Hundreds of thousands of authors have books and websites. Using your creativity to do what you do differently and better is one way for you to cut through the static of other books and authors.

16. **Grow yourself.** Hunter S. Thompson said, "I hate to advocate drugs, alcohol, violence, or insanity to anyone, but they've always worked for me." Finding what works for you as your life evolves is a continuing process of experimentation. You are the most important element in your success, so continue to nurture your skills, your body, your intellect, your passion, and your spirit. To fulfill your potential, you must continue to seek challenges that enable you to grow.

This advice will help your personal as well as your professional life, so I hope you can use it. The book ends with the promise of spring.

CHAPTER 42

Spring Is Coming:
The Prologue

We are the people we have been waiting for.
—THE MOTTO OF THE MIT VEHICLE DESIGN SUMMIT

I hope this book is the prologue to a career that enables you to reach your goals. This book can change your life. If you have a salable idea, prepare a proposal, sell it, and write your book. You will no longer be just a writer with an idea—once your book is published, you'll be an author with a book to your credit.

You will have increased your writing and promotional skills, your understanding of publishing, and the value of your communities. These strengths will make you more valuable to your publisher because you will be a better writer and more able to make your future books successful.

A PARTING PROMISE

Success doesn't come in *cans*, it comes in *wills*: the will to do whatever it takes to get where you want to go. I promise you can accomplish far more than whatever you think you can. More people in more places than ever want what only you can bring to the world, so plant yourself in the biggest pot you can. Spring is coming.

You are a verb, and the verb is *becoming*. Ernest Hemingway once said the act of becoming is the more enjoyable part of success. I wish you a long, rewarding life of becoming an ever more successful author! As actress Sarah Bernhardt said, "It is by spending oneself that one becomes rich."

THANK YOU!

Huge thanks for spending your most valuable asset, your time, with the book and for any suggestions you may have to improve it. Please call me at (415) 673-0939 or e-mail me at larsenpoma@aol.com if you have questions.

Onward!

Resource Directory
Website annotations by Lindsey Clemons

One reason now is the best time to be a writer is the astonishing amount of help there is available online. Only the Web could hope to corral and update all the resources for all writers online and off, an entrepreneurial opportunity waiting to be seized.

Because of space limitations, the following extremely selective, tip-of-the-iceberg list can only point you in the right direction, as will Google. Sites often have "About" or "FAQ" links. They may offer blogs and newsletters. Some sites are listed twice. Wikipedia has an introduction to whatever you want to know about.

The following sources were most helpful in compiling this information.

- David Marshall and Bonnie Kaufman at Berrett-Koehler Publishers

- *The Author's Guide to Building an Online Platform* by Stephanie Chandler

- *Plug Your Book! Online Book Marketing for Authors* by Steve Weber

- *Red Hot Internet Publicity* by Penny C. Sansevieri

Ask your communities about products and services before committing a significant amount time or money to them. Learn from what successful authors in your field are doing. Happy tapping!

Advertising

www.google.com/adwords: Pay per click. allows users to create text, image, and video ads to display in Google search results and/or on the Google Network.

http://searchmarketing.yahoo.com: Pay per click. allows users to create text ads that are displayed in Yahoo search results.

Affiliate Programs

www.amazon.com: Enables users to earn a commission on all sales generated by the link.

www.clickbank.com: Allows users to sell, promote, and buy products on an online retail outlet.

www.indiebound.org: Provides links to independent bookstore websites for book purchases to support local retailers.

Article Syndication

www.amazines.com: Provides writers with the capability to search and submit articles in many categories.

www.authorconnection.com: Allows writers to submit articles for editors to discover.

Author Communities

www.librarything.com: Allows authors to create their own page, showcase books to potentially interested readers, personally connect with readers, and promote readings and talks. Members can also catalog their books, receive book suggestions, and participate in groups and posted discussions.

www.redroom.com: Provides authors with an online home page, professional coaching and editing services, and a place to discuss and buy books.

www.shewrites.com: An online community for women writers to create a profile, build a network, share news, upload content, get expert advice, and read and submit to the She Writes blog.

Best-Seller Lists

www.amazon.com: Includes over 100 categories and subcategories, and books "most gifted" and "most wished for" on Amazon. Updated hourly.

www.nytimes.com: Reflects sales from both bookstores (roughly 4,000) and wholesalers (50,000). Updated weekly.

www.usatoday.com: Ranks 150 titles weekly in all formats. Updated weekly.

Blog Aggregator

www.bloglines.com: Allows users to select and merge news feeds and blogs onto one home page. Free.

Blog Directories

www.blogcatalog.com: Allows members to access the blog directory, search and organize their favorite blogs, receive the latest news from all over the world, and participate in discussions. Free.

www.bloggernity.com: Lists over thirty categories of blogs in its directory. Free.

www.blogpulse.com: A blog search engine that discovers trends in blogs, calculates statistics, tracks conversations, and identifies and analyzes top-rated blogs. Free.

Blog Platforms

www.blogger.com: Allows users to customize and publish a blog, host a website for free, and connect with a Google account.

www.tumblr.com: Allows users to post videos, music, links, photos, and text messages to a customized blog, and promotes its easy access and simple interface.

www.wordpress.com: Allows users to create a customized blog using free or paid features, tracks blog stats, and lets multiple authors contribute to one blog.

Blog Promotions

www.kping.com: Notifies (or pings) blog tracking sites of newly published material from the Web.

www.pingomatic.com: Updates different search engines when a blog has been updated.

Blog Syndication

www.blogburst.com: Advertises users' blogs on major online publishers and media destinations.

Blog-to-E-mail Services

www.feedblitz.com: Monitors, converts, and delivers blogs, RSS feeds and Web URLs to subscribers' e-mail in-boxes.

www.google.com/reader: Stores new posts and news from user selected blogs and websites in one place, allows users to share favorite items with friends, helps find new content that will interest users.

Book Clubs

www.bookmovement.com: Introduces new titles to members, allows member clubs to create and connect through a customized web page, offers reading guides and schedule updates for each selected book. Free.

Buzz Generators

www.digg.com: Allows community members to submit news, video, and images to the website and rate (digg) submissions posted by other members.

www.gather.com: Gives members the opportunity to voice their opinions, advice, and expertise on daily news, and offers payment for popular contributed content.

www.mixx.com: Delivers web content that is hand selected by each user and allows users to post and rate content.

Document Sharing

www.edocr.com: Publishes and distributes a member's or an organization's public documents.

www.google.com/documents: Allows users to upload documents, access documents from any computer or smart phone, and share documents to increase productivity.

www.scribd.com: Converts members' files (including PDF and Power-Point) into a web document and connects interested readers.

E-Book Publishers

www.scribd.com: The largest social publishing site.

www.smashwords.com: An e-book publisher and distribution platform that gives e-book authors and publishers the power to control the sampling, marketing, and price of their work.

www.blurb.com: Like Scribd, Blurb publishes short work as well as books.

Editorial Services

www.bookdocs.com: Provides manuscript evaluations, developmental and line editing, consultation on book proposals and conceptual development, and ghostwriting and collaboration.

www.editcetera.com: Offers coaching and ghostwriting, crafting of book proposal and sample chapters, developmental editing of a first draft, and line editing of a late draft, and for authors interested in self-publishing, help with book design, production editing, and/or proof-reading.

www.editorsforum.org: The Bay Area Editors' Forum has more than 300 members.

www.the-efa.org: Editorial Freelancers Association gives clients instant access to EFA members (editors, writers, proofreaders, translators, etc.) through free job postings.

Expert Listings for Journalists

www.helpareporter.com: Connects reporters and sources in an online social network.

https://profnet.prnewswire.com: Connects reporters to expert sources through a database of profiles.

Forums and Message Boards

www.allexperts.com: Provides message boards on multiple categories where members' questions can be answered by expert volunteers.

www.bulletinboards.com: Allows members to create their own message boards that are free of outside advertizing.

www.wordcrossing.com: Gives members the option of designing custom message boards, forums, or chat rooms to add to their websites.

Groups

www.authornation.com: A free online community designed specifically for authors, writers, poets and readers.

www.ning.com: Allows members to create their own social network or group.

www.pub-forum.net: Dedicated to creating an open discussion of any and all issues affecting publishers.

Intellectual-Property Attorneys (IPA)

www.calawyersforthearts.org: California Lawyers for the Arts bridging the gap between the art and legal communities by providing a referral system for artists of all sorts to find a lawyer.

www.law-arts.org: Lawyers for the Creative Arts gives artists of all media the opportunity to apply for free legal services.

www.vlany.com: Volunteer Lawyers for the Arts provides educational and legal services, advocacy and mediation to the arts community. Pro bono services are available for low-income artists and nonprofit arts organizations.

Writers' organizations have IPAs.

Literary Agents

www.aar-online.com: Association of Authors' Representatives lists information about agents who have applied and qualified by meeting specific professional standards and subscribing to a Canon of Ethics.

www.agentquery.com: A free searchable database of over nine hundred reputable literary agents.

www.blog.nathanbransford.com: Offers news, advice, and contests for writers and links to other blogging agents and editors in the blog roll.

www.guidetoliteraryagents.com/blog: Posts interviews and articles from writers and agents, links to other agents' and editors' blogs, and links to www.writersmarket.com.

Marketing

www.amarketingexpert.com: Penny Sansevieri offers classes, publicity services, and a free newsletter.

www.authorbuzz.com: Puts authors directly in touch with readers, booksellers, and librarians and partners with online publications like DearReader.com and Shelf Awareness.

www.bookmarket.com: Lists book publishing statistics, free marketing advice, book promotion advice, Internet marketing resources, author resources, publishers resources, free downloads, and a subscription for John Kremer's Book Marketing Tip of the Week.

www.judycullins.com: Writing and marketing advice and classes.

www.parapublishing.com: Offers information on writing books, producing books, running a business, marketing and distribution, audio and video clips of Dan Poynter's speaking engagements, and a free newsletter.

Dan Poynter's Self-Publishing Manual Vol. 2 has a list of reading and writing communities on which you can post a cover, blurb, and link without cost, although registration may be required.

Your publisher may have downloadable information about online promotion.

Media Lists

www.gebbieinc.com: Offers paid access to annual all-in-one media directories in both print and electronic versions.

www.medialistsonline.com: Gives users the opportunity to create their own customized media contact list.

Newsletters

www.constantcontact.com: Helps create and distribute newsletters using e-mail marketing, online survey, and event-marketing tools.

www.icontact.com: Helps create and send e-mails and newsletters using e-mail marketing software (that can also be used on smart phones).

Photo Sharing

www.flickr.com: Organizes photos and videos and allows members to share them through various forms of online and printed mediums.

www.photobucket.com: Uploads, shares, links, and finds photos, videos and graphics for free. Users can host their own images and video sand share them on social networking sites.

www.shutterfly.com: Uploads photos and makes them available for publishing on personal websites, photo books, cards and stationary, prints and posters, and calendars.

Podcast Directories

www.itunes.com: Gives users access to search and download podcasts by subject and popularity. Users can also submit to make and publish their own podcasts.

www.librivox.org: Provides free podcasts of audiobooks in the public domain.

www.podcastalley.com: A directory listed by genre. Members can submit podcasts.

Podcasting

www.audioacrobat.com: Records, publishes, streams, uploads, and downloads audio and video podcasts. Audio podcasts can be recorded and managed over the phone.

www.howtomakepodcasts.com: Offers advice and tutorials.

www.yaktivate.com: Offers seventy-four podcasting channels in its international directory and a marketing strategy.

Press-Release Distribution

www.businesswire.com: Helps users send press releases and digital multimedia to local, international, and vertical markets.

www.clickpress.com: Allows users to search and submit news and press releases. Free.

www.free-press-release.com: Helps members customize, manage, and distribute press releases. Free.

www.marketwire.com: Helps members distribute professional press releases, manage media contacts, and add multimedia to their communication.

www.pressmethod.com: Distributes submitted press releases to e-mail subscriptions and news and search engines. Free.

www.prnewswire.com: Uses its multichannel distribution network, audience intelligence, and targeting services to help connect to the media and consumers.

Print-on-Demand Publishing and Services

www.authorsolutions.com: Lets authors self-publish through the AuthorHouse, iUniverse, Trafford, Xlibris, and Wordclay brands.

www.createspace.com: Amazon helps authors design book, manages manufacturing and shipping, and makes books available through multiple channels.

www.lightningsource.com: Benefits small publishers with printing and distribution.

www.lulu.com: Gives authors the opportunity to publish their work while still keeping editorial and copyright control.

Self-Publishing

www.blurb.com: Publishes, shares, promotes, and sells books designed by authors.

www.ibpa-online.com: Provides education, training, resources and support for the publishing community and holds an annual event called the Publishing University.

www.parapublishing.com: Offers tips and expert advice on self-publishing including everything from book design and typesetting to distribution.

www.spannet.org: Small Publishers Association of North America is a community of authors and publishers working to learn and teach writing, marketing, and production.

Speaking

www.nsaspeaker.org: National Speakers Association provides resources and education to its members, offers a free online directory of speakers, and helps emerging speakers get started through the NSA's Academy for Professional Speakers.

www.speakermatch.com: Allows organizations to post an open call for speakers and presents emerging speakers to event organizers.

www.speakernetnews.com: A free weekly online newsletter that is sent out to professional speakers, consultants, trainers, and authors, featuring: Tips on sales, marketing, PR, requests for advice, want ads, and services and products that benefit speakers.

Teleseminars

www.freeconference.com: Allows members to hold conference calls with up to 150 participants, record conferences, schedule and manage conferences online, and includes many other features.

www.freeconferencecall.com: Gives members a free teleconference line that can be accessed at all times and can include up to ninety-six participants for an unlimited number of free six-hour calls.

Writers' Organizations

www.asja.org: The American Society of Journalists and Authors is a community of independent nonfiction writers.

www.associationofwriters.com: The International Association of Writers promotes, educates, and connects published and unpublished writers.

www.authorsguild.com: The Authors Guild gives authors free book contract reviews from a legal staff, potential discounted health benefits, and low-cost website services.

www.nwu.org: The National Writers Union is a labor union that represents freelance writers.

www.wnba-books.org: A community of publishing people with chapters around the country.

www.literarymarketplace.com, www.writersmarket.com, www.readersread.com, and www.dmoz.org/arts/writers_resources/organizations list other writers' organizations.

Writing Advice

www.absolutewrite.com: Provides information for writers at all levels.

www.writersdigest.com: Provides information, resources, and a community for writers through articles, tips, prompts, and nine blogs.

www.writersweekly.com: Provides books, articles, warnings, markets, and a forum to writers in an e-zine.

Writing Events and Listings

www.ibpa-online.com: Independent Book Publishers Association lists links to upcoming book fairs and events put on by regional affiliates of the American Booksellers Association.

www.shawguides.com: Lists upcoming writers conferences, writing workshops, and writing retreats.

BOOKS

On Marketing

Author 101 Bestselling Book Publicity: The Insider's Guide to Promoting Your Book—and Yourself, Rick Frishman and Robyn Freedman Spizman, with Mark Steisel

The Author's Guide to Building an Online Platform: Leveraging the Internet to Sell More Books, Stephanie Chandler

Book Marketing From A–Z, edited by Francine Silverman

Ezine Marketing Magic: How to Start Your Own Successful Newsletter or Ezine, Terry Whalin (free e-book at www.terrylinks.com/rwnews)

From Entrepreneur to Infopreneur: Make Money With Books, eBooks, and Information Products, Stephanie Chandler

Get Known Before the Book Deal: Use Your Personal Strengths to Grow an Author Platform, Christina Katz

Get Slightly Famous: Become a Celebrity in Your Field and Attract More Business With Less Effort, 2nd Edition, Steven Van Yoder

Guerrilla Marketing for Writers: 100 No-Cost, Low-Cost Weapons for Selling Your Work, Jay Conrad Levinson, Rick Frishman, Michael Larsen, and David L. Hancock

Jumpstart Your Publishing Dreams: Insider Secrets to Skyrocket Your Success, W. Terry Whalin

1001 Ways to Market Your Books: For Authors and Publishers, John Kremer

Red Hot Internet Publicity: An Insider's Guide to Marketing Your Book on the Internet, Penny C. Sansevieri

Sell Your Book on Amazon: Top-Secret Tips Guaranteed to Increase Sales for Print-On-Demand and Self-Publishing Writers, Brent Sampson

Smashwords Book Marketing Guide, Mark Coker (free e-book at www.smashwords.com)

Talk Radio Wants You: An Intimate Guide to 700 Shows and How to Get Invited, Francine Silverman

The Yearbook of Experts, Authorities & Spokespersons: An Encyclopedia of Sources, Mitchell P. Davis

On Publishing

Be Your Own Literary Agent: The Ultimate Insider's Guide to Getting Published, Martin P. Levin

The Complete Idiot's Guide to Getting Published, Sheree Bykofsky and Jennifer Basye Sander

Dan Poynter's Self-Publishing Manual: How to Write, Print and Sell Your Own Book, Dan Poynter

Dan Poynter's Self-Publishing Manual Vol 2: How to Write, Print, and Sell Your Own Book Employing the Latest Technologies and the Newest Techniques, Dan Poynter

Guide to Literary Agents (annual guide), edited by Chuck Sambuchino

How to Be Your Own Literary Agent: An Insider's Guide to Getting Your Book Published, Richard Curtis

How to Get a Literary Agent, Michael Larsen

How to Publish a Book & Sell a Million Copies, Ted Nicholas

Jeff Herman's Guide to Book Publishers, Editors, and Literary Agents 2011, Jeff Herman

Kirsch's Handbook of Publishing Law, Jonathan Kirsch

Literary Market Place (annual directory)

Making the List: A Cultural History of the American Bestseller 1900–1999, Michael Korda

Making the Perfect Pitch: How to Catch a Literary Agent's Eye, edited by Katharine Sands

Publish Your Nonfiction Book: Strategies for Learning the Industry, Selling Your Book, and Building a Successful Career, Sharlene Martin and Anthony Flacco

Speak and Grow Rich, Dottie Walters and Lilly Walters

Straight Talk from the Editor, 18 Keys to a Rejection-Proof Submission, W. Terry Whalin (free e-book at www.straighttalkeditor.com)

Twitter Revolution: How Social Media and Mobile Marketing Is Changing the Way We Do Business and Market Online, Deborah Micek and Warren Whitlock

TwittFaced: Your Toolkit for Understanding & Maximizing Social Media, Jacob Morgan and Josh Peters

What Would Google Do?, Jeff Jarvis

Writer's Market (annual guide)

On Writing

Bird by Bird: Some Instructions on Writing and Life, Anne Lamott

Book Proposals That Sell: 21 Secrets to Speed Your Success, W. Terry Whalin (free e-book at www.bookproposals.ws)

Bulletproof Book Proposals, Pam Brodowsky and Eric Neuhaus

The Elements of Style, William Strunk Jr. and E.B. White

Ghostwriters From the Inside Out: How to Find and Hire the Perfect Ghostwriter, Michael Rasmussen and Jason Tarasi

How to Write With a Collaborator, Hal Zina Bennett, with Michael Larsen

Nonfiction Book Proposals Anybody Can Write: How to Get a Contract and Advance Before Writing Your Book, Elizabeth Lyon

On Writing Well, William Zinsser

Write a Book Without Lifting a Finger: How to Hire a Ghostwriter Even If You're on a Shoestring Budget, Mahesh Grossman

Write the Perfect Book Proposal: 10 That Sold and Why, Jeff Herman and Deborah Levine Herman

APPENDIX B

Bringing in a Media Whiz: Why Hire a Publicist?

When it works, publicity is cost-effective. But no matter how big a publisher's commitment to a book, publicity and its effect on sales isn't guaranteed. Lack of control over publicity creates four uncertainties that haunt authors and publicists.

1. Getting publicity
2. When a show or story may run
3. How effective the author and the publicity are
4. Whether the publicity affects sales

However, if you can, hire a publicist. Freelance publicists are more accountable and more motivated than staff publicists to produce results as a way to

- justify their fees.
- maintain their reputations.
- do a good job so you'll hire them for future books.
- earn recommendations to other authors.

Like other industries, publishing has a network of organizations, events, and trade and consumer media. You need a publicist who has the creativity to come up with an irresistible media hook and the experience and contacts to use it. You also want someone you'll enjoy working with.

Ideally, the publicist has publicized books on your subject for publishers that you want to buy your book. Check with a publicist's clients about his or her results, reliability, and personality before hiring one.

If you approach large publicity firms, the people you talk to may not be the ones you'll work with, so be sure to meet whoever that is. Request written proposals from publicists who balance cost, effectiveness, and creativity. If you can, find a publicist whose name will impress publishers. Naming anyone will make the idea real; naming someone publishers are aware of will make you look more professional because you know what it takes to get the job done right.

If online promotion is the most important part of your campaign, you need a publicist with proven effectiveness. Your communities, your staff publicist, including authors of books like yours, may be able to recommend publicists. You may need different publicists for a tour, online promotion, and radio call-in shows.

Another way a publicist may be willing to help you: advising you about your promotion plan. A publicist should be able to help you strike a balance between online and off-line promotion, depending on your strengths as a promoter and the kind of book you're writing.

Once your book is sold, your publisher may make suggestions for other ways to spend your time and money. Your publisher may also be able to help you with part of your plan so you're able to do other things.

Marketing Your Book With Other People's Money: The Quest for Partners to Help You Promote Your Book

---

THE GOLDEN RULE FOR CREATING PARTNERSHIPS

Forge win-win strategic alliances by convincing your potential partners that your book will add to their visibility, their bottom line, their image, their prestige, or all four.

You probably know bank robber Willie Sutton's famous answer when asked why he robbed banks: "Because that's where the money is." Want to do one thing to ensure the sale and the success of your book? Finding a promotional partner to invest in your book, an optional element for your promotion plan, will enable you to leapfrog over the lack of a platform or a weak promotion plan. The right promotional partner will make any publisher want to acquire your book because a partner will go a long way to making your book failproof.

Publilcist Rick Frishman is a coauthor of *Guerrilla Marketing for Writers*. According to Rick, everyone's favorite radio station is WIFM: What's In It For Me? Publishers can't spend enough money to promote most of their books, but corporations and nonprofit associations and foundations can and will help promote your book if you can show them what's in it for them.

If an organization, or even a wealthy, passionate individual, can benefit enough from being associated with you and your book, you will be able to partner for profit with OPM—other people's money. You supply the content power and person power; they supply the platform and the money power.

MACROCASH FROM MICROSOFT

Because of the value of the *Guerrilla Marketing* brand, Microsoft's small-business website hired Jay Conrad Levinson to write a book about how to use technology to market a small business. A new chapter appeared on the site every month. Two months after the last chapter appeared, Addison-Wesley published *Guerrilla Marketing With Technology: Unleashing the Full Potential of Your Small Business*. This is an excellent example of what Jay calls fusion marketing—the e-book promoted the traditional book, and Jay got paid twice for writing it!

HOW A BUSINESS OR ORGANIZATION CAN HELP YOU

You can use your proposal to find a business or nonprofit that will benefit from being associated with you. If you do, get a written commitment. With luck and tenacity, you will be able to write that your promotion plan will "integrate the support of [name of organization], which will promote the book in the following ways... ."

How can an organization help you? The organization can

- give you a grant to write the book.
- buy books to sell or give away.
- create a publicity and advertising campaign based on your book and show you and your book in its ads.
- include your book when consumers purchase its products or services.
- have its publicist set up a national tour for you.
- arrange for you to speak while you travel, perhaps for the organization's chapters or branches.
- include in its in-house newsletter and on its website an article about you and an excerpt or serialization of your book.
- add a link to your website from its website.
- put its name on the book's cover, if it will help your book's credibility.

- have the head of the organization give a quote or write a foreword for your book.
- open the doors to its communities.

Besides being associated with a book that makes an organization look good, what's in it for a partner that supports you?

- If the partner buys enough books, your publisher will be happy to customize the cover and text. Bringing your partner's written commitment for a big bulk or premium sale when you sell your proposal will assure the sale of your book since your partner will help underwrite the publisher's first printing and will promote your book.

- If your partner will bear the costs, your publisher will include in the book a blow-in, postage-paid reply card readers can use to request information, a free sample, or a special offer. (A blow-in card is a card that's literally blown into the book rather than inserted by hand or machine. Budget permitting, you can use a blow-in card to make a special offer to your readers.)

- Your partner can use one or perhaps more blank pages in the front or back of the book as they wish.

This is just a starter set of ideas. You, your partner, and your publisher are limited only by your imaginations.

PICKING A PARTNER

Seek a partner with whom you will enjoy collaborating. Be sure you and your readers will feel comfortable with the partner's products, services, or beliefs. Avoid a partner who could undercut your credibility.

Let's suppose you're writing a book about how to stop smoking. Who are likely partners for you to approach? You could try

- Kaiser or Blue Cross
- the American Medical Association
- health or life insurance companies
- manufacturers of products people use to wean themselves from nicotine
- a hospital chain

- a medical school.
- organizations people join to kick the habit.

On the other hand, even if a cigarette maker were willing to help you (don't hold your breath), accepting its help would damage your credibility.

Fusion marketing is a tremendously powerful idea, but it will be valuable to publishers only if you can convince the partner to make its commitments in writing and make the e-mail or letter the last page of your proposal.

Such a partnership may or may not be a possibility for your book. Even if it is, you can't assume it will happen easily or quickly, especially if you haven't yet written your book. You're more likely to make a partnership happen

- after you sell your proposal.
- when you have a manuscript.
- when you have an accepted manuscript.
- when you have a finished book to show.
- after your book succeeds.

If these things haven't happened yet, don't let that keep you from trying. You will be publicizing your book and getting feedback that can help make your book better, perhaps more enticing to potential partners, so your next attempt will be more effective. You will also plant seeds that may one day bear fruit.

HOT TIPS

- You can have as many noncompeting partners as you want.
- You may be able to accelerate the process of partnering by taking it as far as it can go online before you meet with anyone. You can determine the contact person, e-mail a query that includes a link to your proposal, and answer the contact's questions. Travel expenses may become a factor, so don't mention meeting with an organization if you don't have the means to do it.
- Ask your communities to help you find and make contacts with potential partners.

If your name and credentials won't impress potential partners, try to find a successful author, opinion maker, or group who will vouch for your character and credibility by writing a letter you can include at the end of your proposal—and quote in your initial letter.

You know you're making progress if an organization tells you to come back when you have your manuscript or your book. This enables you to tell editors that an organization has seen your proposal and expressed interest in your book. That's better than nothing, but only barely because it's impossible to predict whether the interest will blossom into a partnership. *Guerrilla Marketing for Writers* has more information on promotional partners.

Four Sample Proposals

Here are four proposals that begin with a list of the reasons we were able to sell them. The proposals are single-spaced, but you should double-space your proposal. The pages aren't numbered, but there are page breaks between pages.

You'll find the following proposals.

- *The Scalpel and the Soul: Encounters with Surgery, the Supernatural, and the Healing Power of Hope* by Allan J. Hamilton

- *The Only Leadership Book You'll Ever Need: How to Build Organizations Where Employees Love to Come to Work* by Peter Stark and Jane Flaherty

- *2048: Humanity's Agreement to Live Together* by Kirk Boyd

- *Zen Mind, Zen Horse: The Spiritual Principles That Horses Bring to Life*

PROPOSAL I:
THE SCALPEL AND THE SOUL:
ENCOUNTERS WITH SURGERY, THE SUPERNATURAL,
AND THE HEALING POWER OF HOPE

Why This Book Sold

This moving, life-changing book had so much going for it.

- The triumphant story of a man who began as a janitor and became a Harvard-trained neurosurgeon and a technical adviser to the hit series *Grey's Anatomy*
- Remarkable stories about Allan's experiences
- A strong promotion plan with a matching promotion budget
- Allan's proven ability to speak
- A foreword by best-selling author Andrew Weil
- Its appeal to large readerships of people personally or professionally interested in two subjects of enduring interest: health and spirituality
- The promise of future books
- A draft of the manuscript, which means Allan knew what the chapters contained and how long they were. He didn't have to be as concerned as other writers about aiming for one line of outline for every page of manuscript. Because Allan had a manuscript, he wrote about the book in the present tense.

Note the slight title change. Tarcher published *The Scalpel and the Soul*, and, in 2009, it won a Silver Nautilus Award.

Michael Larsen-Elizabeth Pomada Literary Agents
Helping Writers Launch Careers Since 1972
1029 Jones Street / San Francisco, California 94109
T: 415-673-0939
larsenpoma@aol.com / www.larsen-pomada.com

A Proposal for
The Soul & the Scalpel:
Surgery as a Path to Spiritual Transformation for Physicians and Patients
Includes Life-Saving Advice Based on the
Author's Thirty Years of Experience
By Allan J. Hamilton, MD, FACS
Professor of Neurosurgery &
Clinical Professor of Radiation Oncology & Psychology
University of Arizona, Tucson, AZ
Foreword by Andrew Weil, MD

X Y Road

Tucson, AZ 857

Tel: (520)

Fax: (520)

E-mail: ranchobosque@mac.com

www.allanhamilton.com

──────────────**PAGE BREAK**──────────────

Table of Contents

Overview

──────────────**PAGE BREAK**──────────────

EDITOR'S NOTE
....

- Start the overview 4" from the top of the page.

- This is an outstanding example of hooking editors.

Overview

- A young burn victim remains in a coma until a ghost appears.
- A doctor discovers he can predict when a patient will die.
- A physician needs the help of a Navajo shaman to exorcise the spirit of his dead patient.
- A group of residents must decide if they can secretly let a convicted child murderer die on the operating table.
- A patient has a premonition he's going to die but his surgeon promises to prove him wrong.

How to Write a Book Proposal

These events happened, and I was involved in them. Each left me with an unforgettable, haunting lesson. Although I am a Harvard-trained brain surgeon, nothing prepared me for the spiritual challenges I faced caring for patients nor the pitfalls in which I failed them.

Based on thirty years of experience, *The Soul and the Scalpel: Surgery as a Path to Spiritual Transformation for Physicians and Patients* will tell the stories of these remarkable patients and share their moral and spiritual lessons.

For physicians, these supernatural inklings and intrusions are disturbing. Doctors can't be candid with colleagues or patients because they're trained to disregard the inexplicable and unbelievable. They're taught to discount the elusive, evanescent powers of the soul. Superstition, omens, and divine spirits smack of madness. Doctors are supposed to practice medicine not voodoo.

But patients have the same experiences. Life-threatening illness or surgery frequently brings dormant spirituality to life. The soul often needs more intensive care than the body. *The Soul & the Scalpel*:

- Explores how premonition, superstition, hope, and faith not only become factors in how patients feel but change outcomes
- Validates the spiritual manifestations physicians see every day
- Empowers patients to voice their spiritual needs when they seek medical help
- Addresses the mysterious, attractive powers the soul exerts during life-threatening events

The book can help save the lives of people facing surgery or suffering from a major illness. It will also help healthcare professionals to save lives.

The Book's Structure

The first part of the book is eighteen stories. They start with the author's first job as a janitor and culminate in experiences drawn from his position as Chief of

Neurosurgery and Chairman of the Department of Surgery at the University of Arizona. He made mistakes, and he pulls no punches in describing them.

The book addresses ten spiritual or emotional crises that may occur during surgery and hospitalization:

- Removing patients' hope
- A premonition of death
- Near-death experience
- Divine intervention
- Scientific and clinical biases of physicians
- The impact of religious belief
- Physicians' fear of mortality
- Statistical lies and cancer survival
- How alternative medicine goes mainstream
- Failing to see God's purposes

The second part of the book is advice, extracted from the stories, to help patients and physicians achieve the best possible outcomes from surgery. The suggestions will help patients through the medical crises and the spiritual doubts that can arise during recovery.

The advice covers topics such as:

- Why the best doctor is one who is dumb and safe
- How patients can make sure they're not victims of a medical error
- When to fire a doctor
- When *not* to consent to surgery
- How to avoid *ghost surgery*—surgery being done by someone other than their surgeon while patients are under anesthesia
- How to get good food—even in a hospital
- The guidelines will also help doctors address the emotional issues and spiritual catastrophes their patients may encounter. It will explain:
  - Why physicians should try to spot omens or premonitions
  - Why it's better to see patients in the evening than first thing in the morning
  - How intuition can lead to the correct diagnosis
  - Why doctors should never give casual, free medical advice

- The three things that make every patient smile
- Why doctors should never run to an emergency

The manuscript contains 95,000 words in twenty chapters. The final manuscript will also include a five-page resource directory and an index.

Andrew Weil and the author have known each other and worked together for fifteen years. Andrew has read drafts of the manuscript, and he will write the foreword.

EDITOR'S NOTE

The commitment by one of the top best-selling authors in the field gives the book immediate credibility. Allan's section on markets is long but proves he knows the markets for the book well.

Markets

The book will attract three large groups of readers:

- Individuals and their families confronting a serious illness or surgery
- Healthcare professionals
- Readers interested in spirituality, alternative medicine, and mind-body connections

In March 2005, *USA Today* had a cover story on evolving trends among books that became bestsellers in the preceding decade. By far, the most popular category between 1994 and 2004 was books about spirituality and religion.

The second largest group constituted self-help books, especially those focusing on health improvements aimed at the aging baby boomers (like Andrew Weil's books or Bill Phillips's *Body for Life*). *Soul* will appeal to these top two groups, combining advice relating to major surgery or illness while guiding readers through the spiritual issues affecting their well-being.

Thirty-five percent of Americans will confront major illness or surgery in the next five years. Everyone in such a crisis needs help. In 2005, the American Hospital Association reported almost forty million admissions to our hospitals.

According to Solucient Leadership Institute data, an astounding five million patients went into intensive care last year, which suggests that their illnesses were life threatening. The book will help potential patients, be a get-well gift for individuals in recovery, and serve as an inspirational book for families confronting a loved one's illness or death. As of 2005, the National Center for Health Statistics reports that over 1.3 million people a year facing terminal illness are enrolled in hospice or home healthcare.

Few groups of patients touch the heart more directly than those diagnosed with malignant brain tumors. The book discusses cases involving patients with brain tumors—the author's subspecialty. There are 25,000–30,000 new cases of malignant brain tumors diagnosed a year, and the number is climbing. *Soul* will appeal to these patients. The author hopes that the book will help relieve anxieties and empower patients to harness their spiritual and emotional resources when they confront health crises.

The book assists healthcare professionals to become more comfortable in anticipating and responding to spiritual questions. There is a trend towards developing curricula in medical schools that address spiritual issues. According to a 2004 report from Yale University in the *Journal of the American Medical Association*, from 1994 to 2004, the number of medical schools offering courses in spirituality rose from seventeen (13%) to eighty-four (66%).

The National Center for Health Workforce Analysis reported that in 2001, enrollments in allopathic (traditional, evidence-based) medicine were 66,000 with an additional 200,000 in the nursing field.

Osteopaths, podiatrists, dentists, and other health professionals are also looking for leadership from the medical professions. There is therefore a large and growing pool of healthcare workers who will be motivated to read about the spiritual issues they will encounter.

The book will have adoption potential in spiritually oriented curricula in medical schools. Interest in the manuscript has been expressed by professionals around the country who lead courses on Spirituality and Medicine such as:

- Joseph Alpert, MD, University of Arizona
- Stephen Kliemer, D.Min, Oregon Health Sciences Center
- Rev. James Evinger, University of Rochester School of Medicine

Readers' interest in the mind-body connection is at an all-time high. This stems from a profound interest in religious and spiritual issues as baby boomers face serious illness and death. They want emphasis on both allopathic and alternative medicine. The National Institutes of Health revealed that 62 percent of individuals reported using alternative medicine or prayer in the previous twelve months. The book reinforces and encourages individuals to incorporate their spiritual practices and beliefs into traditional medical care.

The book also appeals to doctors and patients because it contains valuable information and insights for helping them. *Soul* validates their desire to connect to powers beyond their own, to call on the divine and supernatural forces to rally around them and help sustain them.

The book enables family members of someone who's either a patient or a healthcare worker to help those they love when they confront challenges. They will understand what their loved ones face and how best to support them.

Bookstores

Just as *The Purpose Driven Life* has sold so well in trade and Christian bookstores, *Soul* will also sell in both kinds of stores. The book's stories are inspirational with respect to faith in God and the scientific proof of the existence of the soul and life after death.

According to the Christian Booksellers Association, Christian-oriented medical books have sold well in both kinds of stores including:

- Dr. Joe Vander Veer: *A Surgeon's Devotions*
- Dr. G. Scott Morris: *Relief for the Body, Renewal for the Soul: A Doctor's True Stories of Healing and Hope*
- Margaret Carroll Lamkin: *My Flesh and My Heart May Fail: Life on the Edge of Open Heart Surgery*

Community cancer centers sponsor patient-support groups, and this book will inspire discussion of spirituality among cancer patients and the growing number of survivors. There are more than 650 cancer hospitals and treatment centers to which the author is highly motivated to speak. The promotion plan discusses this.

Subsidiary Rights

The male lead in *Grey's Anatomy* is a neurosurgeon. Executive Producer Linda Klein has expressed interest in seeing stories in the book.

3 Lbs., a series starring Stanley Tucci as one of two neurosurgeons who are the lead characters, premiered on CBS in last November. One character is an older, methodical surgeon while the younger one is more personal and compassionate. *Soul* contains eighteen stories about neurosurgery, adapting them for either series is a possibility.

Other shows with a spiritual bent such as *The Medium* and *Ghost Whisperer* may also be interested.

The book will also have potential for foreign-rights sales and the One Spirit Book club.

Spin-offs

The author will write five follow-up books:

[A list of titles and information about them followed. I've only included the last book, which is on a different but related subject and which Allan decided to write next.]

The author is also a well-known horse trainer and has completed a 90,000-word manuscript on a unique method of applying both ancient Chinese (chi) and Japanese (Zen) philosophies to the art of horsemanship, tentatively entitled: *Zen, Chi and the Art of Horsemanship*. It's a training book but contains stories, philosophical discussions, and spiritual insights drawn from the world of horse training that will interest riders and non-riders.

The Author's Platform

During the last ten years, the author has given more than three hundred presentations and earned an average of $XX,000. Many of these have been professional and academic appearances related to the author's research and expertise, but have also included speeches for the public with up to two hundred in attendance at such venues as the San Francisco Museum of Modern Art, the New Orleans aquarium, and an outdoor address in an amphitheater in Puerto Rico.

Many of these were sponsored by Fortune 500 pharmaceutical and medical equipment manufacturers such as [list].

The author is consistently ranked among the top tenth percentile of speakers in terms of audience feedback and evaluations. He will launch a mailing campaign to land himself back on corporate speaking circuits, aiming for inspirational talks for conventions and sales meetings. In addition, there has been an increasing acceptance in standard medical venues for talks on spirituality. ("Spirituality and the Neurosurgeon," at the 2006 Western Neurosurgical Society in Seattle, had the largest audience of the three-day conference).

Dr. Hamilton has appeared on National Public Radio, CNN's *Anderson Cooper 360°*, and The Discovery Channel on a wide variety of topics. He has earned a reputation as a speaker who can discuss sophisticated topics in a way that the public enjoys.

Allan has written more than forty scientific peer-reviewed articles and a dozen medical textbook chapters, a monograph on treating brain tumors, and he has also published five articles for the public on his experiences as a physician.

He and his family host three conferences a year to help empower cancer patients and survivors to increase their spiritual awareness for a better recovery and quality of life.

EDITOR'S NOTE

Tarcher didn't match the promotion budget but was conscientious in promoting the book. Allan gave talks around the country and more than one hundred media interviews Tarcher arranged for him.

Promotion

To promote the book the author will:

- Match your out-of-pocket promotion budget up to $X0,000 on signing to carry out the plan
- Do a media tour of the top ten markets and signings the staff publicist arranges on publication
- Hire a publicist. The author has already contacted [mentions three publicists]. He will meet with them and discuss this decision with you. The publicist will do a television satellite tour, promote speaking engagements, and coordinate bookstore events as well as obtain interviews.
- Have a staff member arrange three talks a day in tour cities
- Continue to speak during the year of publication at six annual meetings or conventions and do two other talks in the convention cities

- Continue to travel to six conventions a year and use this business-related travel to obtain other speaking and bookselling opportunities
- Continue to give one or two additional talks a month and sell books or arrange to have them sold
- Sell X,000 copies the year of publication
- Send 650 promotional copies of book to:
    - 350 directors of the top community cancer centers offering to speak
    - 100 leaders in the area of Spirituality and Medicine, and academic, philanthropic, religious, hospice, and hospital chaplaincy organizations
    - 100 directors of a curriculum on Spirituality and Medicine with an offer to speak, do a teleconference, and a Q&A session if they adopt the book
    - 50 chairpersons of conferences on the subject of Spirituality and Medicine
    - 50 columnists and commentators with expertise in both medicine and spirituality
- Establish a website with ordering capabilities, booking information, the speaking schedule, a monthly newsletter, the media kit, and a Q&A forum
- Use a full-time administrator to mail X,000 brochures about the book, the website, and ordering information to hospital chaplains, hospital-based social workers, and mental-health workers to encourage group and class adoptions
- Offer a visit or call-in Q&A to book clubs with twelve or more members
- Start a virtual reading club with scheduled teleconferences for discussion. Encourage members to send inspiring stories for posting on the site

Celebrity Contacts/Endorsements

The author will ask the following people for quotes: [list of ten impressive people in media, medicine, and government]

Competing and Complementary Books

Books with overlapping themes include:

- Zhi Gang Sha: *Soul Mind Body Medicine: A Complete Soul Healing System for Optimum Health* (New World Library, 2006. 364 pages). Includes mind-body spiritual methods outlined for one hundred ailments. New Age-oriented how-to. Not anecdotal or by a physician.

- Bernie S. Siegel, M.D.: *Love, Medicine, & Miracles: Lessons Learned About Self-Healing From a Surgeon's Experience with Exceptional Patients*, HarperCollins, 1998, 226 pages). A bestseller that talks about the power of love in surgical practice. Offers cancer-related anecdotes that are more emotionally than spiritually oriented.

- Larry Dossey, M.D.: *Reinventing Medicine: Beyond Mind-Body to a New Era of Healing*, (HarperCollins, 1999, 230 pages). Reviews experiences of non-locality in healing like praying for someone across the country. Does not include personal patient stories or experiences relating to the supernatural.

- G. Scott Morris: *Relief for the Body, Renewal for the Soul: A Doctor's True Stories of Healing and Hope* (Paraclete Press, 2001, 140 pages). Stories from a minister-physician working with inner-city poor in Memphis. Christian orientation. No professional or academic tension between the high-tech world of surgery and spirituality.

- Katrina Firlik: *Another Day in the Frontal Lobe: A Brain Surgeon Exposes Life on the Inside* (Random House, 2006, 264 pages). Describes author's experiences as the first woman resident in the neurosurgical residency program at the University of Pittsburgh. Coming-of-age story focused only on first five years of training and aspects of neurosurgery in the future. Does not aim at mind-brain conundrums in neurosurgery and is not inspirational.

Soul is the first memoir that covers a whole surgical career and focuses on the spiritual surprises and challenges involved in the journey. The book allows readers to share in the spectrum of surgical experiences from beginning medical school to the insights of a chairman of a surgery department.

While there are books that allow readers to experience the coming of age in medical school or surgical residency, none enables readers to become privy to the pitfalls and failings that physicians, struggling with the arrogance of science, the greed for money, or the appetite for power, endure. This book is unique because it takes readers from the seduction of surgical initiation to the humbling revelations of spirituality.

The book allows readers to judge the impact of manifestations of the super-natural: ghosts, taboos, omens, intuition, premonition, prayer, religious faith, and finally, the author's reflections about coming into contact with the soul. The book is a journey into the realm of spiritual transformation where science and spirit meet.

EDITOR'S NOTE

Any editor would be impressed with the recognition Allan had received and would appreciate the humorous, self-deprecating final sentence, especially coming from a doctor.

About the Author

Allan Hamilton never envisioned becoming one of the top brain surgeons in the country. He began his college career wanting to be a painter and landed his first job as a janitor. He is a board-certified, Harvard-trained brain surgeon and a tenured Professor of Neurosurgery who has Clinical professorships in the Departments of Radiation Oncology and Psychology at the University of Arizona Health Sciences in Tucson. Allan also served as the Chief of Neurosurgery and then as the Chairman of the Department of Surgery.

He has received more than two dozen honors and awards including:

- Being voted by peers as "One of the Best Doctors in America" for seven consecutive years
- The Bernard Cosman Award, the highest honor in the United States, for innovation in neurosurgery
- Being the only American neurosurgeon awarded the Lars Leksell Award, the highest international award for innovation for discovering and developing the field of extra-cranial radiosurgery
- Being recognized as "One of the Outstanding Intellectuals of the 21st Century"
- The Robert G. Ojemann Award from the Upjohn Company for Out-standing Educator in Neurosurgery
- Arizona Dean's Teaching Scholar Award for Teaching

Dr. Hamilton has been a proponent of re-establishing what he terms "intimacy as the heart of modern medicine" and has criticized the escalating rate of errors in healthcare.

He is a Professor of Neurosurgery and a Director of a medical think tank—the Arizona Simulation Technology and Education Center—which serves seven clinical departments developing innovative educational and simulation scenarios to improve surgical technique, enhance medical care, and reduce mistakes committed by physicians, nurses, and emergency-response personnel.

At his ranch outside of Tucson, the author raises rare Lipizzaner horses, descendants of the legendary Spanish Riding School in Vienna. Because of his janitorial skills, he's still quite fond of mucking out the stalls in his barn.

————————————PAGE BREAK————————————

The Outline
List of Chapters

──────────PAGE BREAK──────────

Chapter 17
The Luck of the Draw

The chapter compares the treatment of two patients with malignant, aggressive brain tumors who are unlikely to survive. The first part of the chapter is about a hard-drinking, chain-smoking man who endures the usual litany of surgical, radiation, and chemotherapy treatments while his brain tumor advances relentlessly. He is admitted to hospice care and awaits the end. After six months, he flunks out of hospice because he's not dying. Seven years later, his tumor appears to have stopped dead in its tracks for no reason that science can explain.

The second part of the chapter is about a patient who is a clean-shaven, hard-working engineering student at the university. His tumor is removed, he undergoes treatments, and his scans remain tumor free. He goes on to finish a Ph.D. in engineering, marry, and raise a family.

The chapter ends with the author concluding that statistics have limited ability to predict the future. Both patients defy all odds of how and when they should die. They take remarkably different paths but find a cure for a cureless disease.

PROPOSAL 2:
THE ONLY LEADERSHIP BOOK YOU'LL EVER NEED:
HOW TO BUILD ORGANIZATIONS
WHERE EMPLOYEES LOVE TO COME TO WORK

Why This Book Sold

Because of the authors' track record, visibility, incentive to promote the book, and test-marketing, it was failproof. Peter Stark and Jane Flaherty

- had successfully self-published the book because it delivers on what it promises, so publishers received the book and a hard copy of the proposal.

- have a strong promotion plan. Even a publisher who wouldn't match their promotion budget would know the author would promote the book because it would help build their business.

- aimed at a market with more than 25 million potential readers and class adopotions.

- do one hundred presentations a year.

- are committed to buying a four-figure quantity of books for four years.

- are both promoting the book.

- garnered positive media attention for their edition and won the Indie Book Award for the best business book.

- had written eight books, including one that sold very well.

- showed the book didn't face much competition.

- brought more than twenty years of experience as consultants to the book.

- based the book on research with more than 250 companies and more than 100,000 employees.

- listed two spin-off books.

EDITOR'S NOTE

For editors, having a quote from a top business author on the title page is a good sign.

Career Press changed the title to somewhat match the authors' previous book: *The Only Negotiating Guide You'll Ever Need.*

"To succeed in business, treat your employees well and they will treat your customers well.

Peter Stark and Jane Flaherty get it! Read this book and keep your people *engaged!*"

–Ken Blanchard, coauthor of *The One Minute Manager*®
and *Leading at a Higher Level*

A Proposal for
Engaged!
How Leaders Build Organizations
Where Employees Love to Come to Work
by Peter Barron Stark and Jane Flaherty

Peter Barron Stark Companies
11417 W. Bernardo Ct.
San Diego, CA 92127
Telephone:
Cell:
Fax:
peter@pbsconsulting.com
www.pbsconsulting.com

———————————PAGE BREAK———————————

Table of Contents

———————————PAGE BREAK———————————

EDITOR'S NOTE

During the recession, making the case for the book was easy, especially with the list of the book's special features. But Peter and Jane also showed its value for when the recession was over.

Overview

Industries are laying people off and not replacing them, and they are combining positions. Businesses are asking their workforce to do more with less, so workers who are still employed carry a huge burden.

The key to keeping employees excited about coming to work, focused on their job, and optimistic about tomorrow is engagement. Communicating how much the business values its workers is crucial for maintaining maximum commitment. Keeping employees engaged and growing in their jobs is essential for preventing the shortage of workers that the authors predict when the economy turns around.

EDITOR'S NOTE
....

Your book will probably be published two years after you have the idea for it. Editors want you to look ahead so your book will be salable long after publication. Peter and Jane made the book relevant after the economy improves.

Engaged! How Leaders Build Organizations Where Employees Love to Come to Work is the first book on leadership and workplace excellence that provides executives, managers and supervisors with the Ten Keys to Workplace Excellence and seventy-six strategies they can use immediately. *Engaged!* is based on twenty years of research with more than 250 organizations representing more than 100,000 employees. It's a comprehensive resource for every business professional who wants to create an environment that is a great place for employees to work.

The seventy-six strategies apply the concepts in the first six chapters and show how the authors' clients build great organizations. They have memorable, humorous titles and help ensure that readers are equipped to create great places to work.

The book's goal is to be a must-read for leaders who are focused on the future. These leaders understand they cannot reach their full potential without the commitment and loyalty of their employees. They appreciate the value of creating an environment that will put them in touch with those responsible for their success.

Whether their team walks on water, or employees are barely keeping their heads above it, managers will discover what their employees think, and how to apply that understanding to create workplace excellence.

Engaged! will have enduring value because readers will want to refer again and again to the Ten Keys and the seventy-six strategies. The authors had *Engaged!* professionally edited. The book is 58,000 words and includes an introduction and seven chapters.

Since its publication in March, *Engaged!* has sold more than X,000 copies and has been featured by *Forbes.com, Reuters, IndustryWeek* and *Incentive.* TheStreet.com and Geezeo.com listed the book as one of the leading and must-read books for 2009 on management, sales and marketing. *Engaged!* was the winner of the 2009 Indie Book Award in the business category.

Special Features

Engaged! is a handbook of proven information that:

- Provides a framework that will enable organizations to rise above any competitor
- Tells leaders how to engage a workforce so it brings its best to the workplace every day
- Offers insights managers need about the thoughts employees have toward their jobs, organizations, supervisors, and management managers
- Reveals the secrets of great organizations and what their leaders do differently
- Examines the hard data for guiding leaders' efforts and building higher levels of excellence
- Delineates the ten differences between the best-of-the-best organizations—those that employees rate in the top 25 percent—and the rest
- Identifies the roadblocks to engagement and describe what leaders can do single-handedly to make a difference, even in the most difficult situations
- Outlines the need and the opportunity to create an exceptional workplace
- Presents the compelling case for engaged employees/workplace excellence and why organizations want to be *the* employer of choice
- Describes the ten keys used by best-of-the-best organizations to create employee engagement
- Enables managers to understand the six priceless outcomes organizations can expect when they achieve workplace excellence
- Shows the steps leaders need to take to create excellence in their area of influence
- Allows readers to assess their own skills as leaders

- Shows that salaries have little influence on whether employees decide to stay or leave organizations
- Discusses the eleven stupid things leaders do and offers twelve steps for recovering from them

> **EDITOR'S NOTE**
>
> The book's timeless, bottom-line benefit—to such a large, potential group of readers who will take the book as a tax deduction or have their company buy it for them—made the decision to acquire the book easier.

Markets

With more than 25 million leadership professionals in the United States alone, there are strong markets for the book in the business world, especially with executives, managers, and supervisors whose organizations conduct employee opinion surveys.

Another market is the X,000 leaders the authors work with a year. Of this group, approximately 25 percent take part in an Employee Opinion Survey at their organization. These managers will receive a copy of the book the first year they do a survey.

Engaged! can be sold in business-to-business catalogs and business-supply stores.

The book will have textbook potential for university leadership courses and corporate in-house training programs. The authors will have a teacher's guide for these uses on their website.

Potential subsidiary-rights sales include foreign rights, first and second serial rights, an audio book, and action cards.

Spin-offs

The authors will write two books that will help sell *Engaged!*: [list]

> **EDITOR'S NOTE**
>
> The authors' experience and visibility, and their use of the book in their work, were more incentives for the publisher.

The Authors' Platforms
Peter and Jane's Books

How One Leader Can Make a Difference: The Only Guide to Employee Opinion Surveys You'll Ever Need, (Bentley Press, 2007, self-published)

The Only Negotiating Guide You'll Ever Need: 101 Ways to Win Every Time in Any Situation, (Broadway Books, 2003)

Lifetime Leadership—Leaving Your Legacy (Bentley Press, 2001, self-published)

The Competent Leader (HRD Press, 1999)

The Manager's Pocket Guide to Leadership Skills (HRD Press, 1999)

The Confident Leader (HRD Press, 1995)

It's Negotiable (Jossey-Bass, Pfeiffer, 1994, OP)

Peter Barron Stark and Jane Flaherty are internationally acclaimed speakers with more than twenty years of experience as researchers, managers, and executive coaches. They consult with organizations and train leaders in the United States and abroad. They present more than one hundred days a year to more than XX,000 people on topics including workplace excellence, leadership, customer service and negotiation.

The authors' website, www.employeeopinionsurveys.com, is one of the top three sites on the Web for employee opinion surveys.

For the negotiating book, Peter and Jane did more than forty radio shows and ten TV shows, including CNN and Bloomberg.

Peter Barron Stark

Peter is president of the Peter Barron Stark Companies. He conducts employee opinion surveys and trains executives, managers and supervisors in the art of leadership. He holds the prestigious designations of Accredited Speaker from Toastmasters International and Certified Speaking Professional from the National Speakers Association. These awards make him one of the most sought-after professional speakers on leadership.

Peter has been featured in *Forbes, Newsweek,* the *New York Times, Selling Power,* the *San Diego Business Journal, San Diego Daily Transcript, Credit Union Management, The Street, American Way, Entrepreneur, Boston Globe, Chicago Tribune, Credit Union Times, Communication Briefings, Association of Legal Administrators, Independent Business, Home Office Computing* and *Training.*

He also writes and publishes two newsletters, *The Quest for Workplace Excellence* and *The Master Negotiator,* delivered to more than X,000 corporate partners and business professionals. For ten years, Peter taught negotiation and leadership at San Diego State University.

Jane Flaherty

Jane is a senior consultant and trainer for Peter Barron Stark Companies. She has twenty-five years of experience designing and delivering training programs. She has trained 50,000 managers and employees in the areas of leadership, motivation, communication and negotiation. She specializes in using leadership skills to resolve conflict, improve communication, and strengthen relationships and teamwork.

Client List

Peter and Jane partner with organizations around the world, including: [two-column list of clients fill the page]

EDITOR'S NOTE

Career Press didn't match the authors' budget, but the authors were committed to promoting the book because it promotes their business.

Promotion

To promote the book, Peter and Jane will:

- Match your consumer, out-of-pocket promotion budget up to $X0,000 on signing to carry out the plan
- Hire a publicist to contact the on- and off-line media to supplement the efforts of their staff publicist
- Buy X,000 copies a year for four years and continue to buy them after that

- Partner with X and other successful authors such as X and X to do an e-mail blast to more than 300,000 people, offering bonus materials if people buy the book on pub date
- Send 250 promotional copies to their largest corporate clients, including [list of companies in paragraph form], encouraging them to buy books for employees, and will supply the promotional copies that the publisher cannot
- Promote the book in their e-mail newsletters, *Peter Stark's Leadership Quote, The Quest for Workplace Excellence* and *The Master Negotiator,* which have more than X,X00 subscribers
- Hire an online marketer to ensure that employeeopinionsurveys.com and peterstark.com are highly ranked on Google in the leadership and workplace excellence categories
- Offer excerpts for their clients' newsletters, which will be very receptive to them
- Build a website for the book featuring highlights, downloads, reader reviews and ancillary products
- Use YouTube and social networking to create buzz for the book
- Blog about the book at peterstark.com
- Offer a money-back guarantee

Competing Books

Recent titles focus on what makes a great company but none relates the behavior of managers to the success of organizations. The following books try to uncover why some organizations are more successful than others but none includes a practical approach for managers:

- Lee. J. Colan, Ph.D., *Engaging the Hearts and Minds of All Your Employees*, McGraw-Hill, 2008. Provides practical tools to engage employees and ignite the fire of "Passionate Performance." Uses well-known examples such as Nordstrom, Southwest Airlines, the 80/20 rule and SMART goals.
- Julie Gebauer and Don Lowman, *Closing the Engagement Gap*, Penguin Group, 2008. Research-based work describes five keys to unlock employees' potential and cites Towers Perrins' Global Workforce Study to identify the ten top items that drive employee engagement. Has good

examples but doesn't inspire or challenge readers to take action to create an engaged workforce.

- Sarah Cook, *The Essential Guide to Employee Engagement*, Kogan Page, 2008. A textbook-like work that explains the benefits of an engaged workforce related to customer satisfaction and profitability. Doesn't provide advice on what to do to create a work environment that attracts and retains employees.

PROPOSAL 3:
2048: HUMANITY'S AGREEMENT TO LIVE TOGETHER

Why This Book Sold

This is the most ambitious book we've ever represented. Dr. John Kirk Boyd, Esq. has giant goals, but beyond having a clear vision of what needs to be done and how to do it, he proves he has the ability, visibility, credibility, and support system to make it happen. Kirk's determination helped convince Berrett-Koehler to take a leap of faith, which was rewarded when *2048* spent four weeks on the *San Francisco Chronicle* best-seller list.

His overview is longer than most, but he has a lot to say. He brings to the book

- the right idea at the right time.
- a platform that shows he can give the book the visibility it needs.
- an irresistible promotion plan.
- the support of a major university, an organization, an advisory board, and an international community.
- superb academic and professional credentials.
- backlist sales potential.
- two spin-off titles.
- professionally done cover art that BK used for the book. (The word *written* was ommitted from the final title.)
- the patience to wait until he had all the pieces in place to make the book as successful as he wanted it to be.

A Proposal for
2048

Humanity's Written Agreement to Live Together
By Dr. John Kirk Boyd, Esq.
The First of Three Books

Dr. John Kirk Boyd, Esq.
Executive Director, 2048 Project
University of California, Berkeley
353 Boalt Hall, School of Law
Berkeley, CA 94720
XXX-XXX-XXXX
kboyd@law.berkeley.edu
www.2048.berkeley.edu

──────────────PAGE BREAK──────────────

TABLE OF CONTENTS

After years of war or before a pending calamity such as global warming, people, businesses, and nations often take steps to advance human rights. *2048: Humanity's Written Agreement to Live Together* will be the first book to combine:

- the importance of human rights
- the historic struggles for rights
- the evolution of human-rights documents
- the story of the most important social movement of the century: creating an agreement for humanity to live together in peace and prosperity based on rights and the rule of law

- The premise of the book is that many of the problems humanity faces— war, poverty, and environmental destruction—are the by-product of a flawed international social order.

- The 2048 Project is part of an evolutionary process for humanity to come to an agreement. Over the centuries, statements, documents, and leaders have advanced the process.

- In his State of the Union speech in 1941, President Franklin Roosevelt distilled the process into four freedoms. He said that if we want to live in peace and prosperity, every person in every country must have freedom of speech, freedom of religion, freedom from want, and freedom from fear. When all people have the first three, we share the fourth. 2048 will explain how Roosevelt's plan—with one addition, freedom from degradation for the environment—is part of the agreement.

————————————PAGE BREAK————————————

EDITOR'S NOTE

Editors are idealists. They would all be sympathetic to Kirk's idea, but they are still forced to prove a book's commercial value to the editorial board.

Overview

After years of war or before a pending calamity such as global warming, people, businesses, and nations often take steps to advance human rights. *2048: Humanity's Written Agreement to Live Together* will be the first book to combine:

- the importance of human rights
- the historic struggles for rights
- the evolution of human-rights documents

- the story of the most important social movement of the century: creating an agreement for humanity to live together in peace and prosperity based on rights and the rule of law

The premise of the book is that many of the problems humanity faces—war, poverty, and environmental destruction—are the by-product of a flawed international social order.

In 1948, all countries signed the Universal Declaration of Human Rights (UDHR), an agreement that promised a new social order for an era of peace and prosperity. However, it remains unenforceable in court. The goal of *2048* is to help make the rights in the Declaration enforceable by 2048, the 100th anniversary of the Universal Declaration.

The 2048 Project is based at the University of California, Berkeley, School of Law. The author and his colleagues launched it to enable the public and people in academia, business, and government around the world to collaborate on the agreement. Through its programs and website, the 2048 Project provides education, research materials, a forum for posting documents, and a setting for international conferences.

The book will describe how the project is creating this framework through an international human-rights movement. The book will add a fresh perspective to the dialogue along with a university-supported program that makes it easy for readers to participate. The author will do everything he can to make the book and the project help each other succeed.

EDITOR'S NOTE

Putting the quest for the agreement into historical context is important: Just as the suffering of World War II led to the Universal Declaration of Human Rights, our present problems are leading to the 2048 agreement.

An Historical Perspective

The 2048 Project is part of an evolutionary process for humanity to come to an agreement. Over the centuries, statements, documents, and leaders have advanced the process.

In his State of the Union speech in 1941, President Franklin Roosevelt distilled the process into four freedoms. He said that if we want to live in peace and prosperity, every person in every country must have freedom of speech, freedom of religion, freedom from want, and freedom from fear. When all people have the first three, we share the fourth. 2048 will explain how Roosevelt's plan—with one addition, freedom from degradation for the environment—is part of the agreement.

The 2048 Project is also part of the legacy of Eleanor Roosevelt and her work at the United Nations on the Universal Declaration of Human Rights, which included the four freedoms. The story of how she and other world leaders drafted the declaration is exciting, full of colorful characters and Cold War intrigue. Eleanor's story will inspire readers to act.

In 1953, the European Convention on Human Rights also mentioned the Four Freedoms and took the first steps to enforce the Universal Declaration. The European Convention is now enforceable in forty-six countries with the right to appeal to the Court of Human Rights in France with judges from all of these countries. The success of the European Convention has enabled countries that have been at war with one another for centuries to live together in peace.

Now it is time for what has worked for the European community to benefit the rest of the world. The 2048 Project will design an International Convention on Human Rights based on the European Convention and the decisions of the Court of Human Rights.

The manuscript will be 226 pages in fourteen chapters with back matter and will have nineteen photos and illustrations. The back matter will include endnotes, a timeline of human rights documents, an appendix with the text of the Universal Declaration, and a resource directory of magazines, events, websites, and organizations.

The endnotes will include sources that will interest teachers, scholars, librarians, and other professionals in human rights, law, philosophy, and political science.

The manuscript is more than half finished, and the author will deliver it six months after receiving the advance.

EDITOR'S NOTE

Kirk did a fine job of describing the markets for the book without numbers, except for the one that does the job.

Markets

A Google search for *human rights* yields *562 million links*. Students, multinational corporations and nonprofits, conservatives and progressives, and people of all religious faiths around the world are collaborating on the agreement. Book sales will reflect the interest in the subject and the diversity of the contributors:

- **Businesses and nonprofits:** *2048* will be at the heart of the concern about globalization because it is about how to make capitalism an economic model. The project will establish a baseline of enforceable rights for businesses similar to the baseline developed after Upton Sinclair wrote *The Jungle*, his classic about the meatpacking industry.

  Business leaders know that transnational regulation is coming and that a mandatory transnational framework is needed because it creates a level playing field. As a co-keynote speaker during the launch of the project at the law school, Robert Haas, Chairman Emeritus of the apparel company Levi Strauss, called for an "international framework for enforceable human rights." Levi's and other businesses have an economic incentive to support the project, so *2048* will have markets in both the business and nonprofit sectors because it provides a plan for helping them.

- **People personally or professionally interested in contemporary issues:** President-Elect Obama has already been addressing rights in his book *The Audacity of Hope* and with his cabinet appointments. He elevated the Ambassador to the United Nations to the cabinet. The author has met Obama and discussed the project with him. The Berkeley law school Dean, Christopher Edley, taught Obama at Harvard and was an active advisor on his campaign. Dean Edley participated in the launch event for *2048* at the law school. He is well positioned to incorporate the project into the administration.

- **Schools:** The book will be an easy read for students as well as adults and will be well suited for high school and university courses. There are more than 900 million students around the world between the ages of fifteen and twenty-five, and 100 million new students a year. In America alone, there are more than 40 million.

They need to learn about the history of human-rights documents, because the text of the Universal Declaration obligates the countries that signed it—including the United States—to teach about the document. Many countries and states, including California, have passed laws requiring every high-school curriculum to teach human rights. *2048* will meet this demand.

Professors at universities and law schools throughout the United States and abroad who know about the project will assign the book. The author teaches human rights at U.C. and will assign the book.

2048 will also be part of an existing curriculum. The curriculum is available to high school and university teachers on the *2048* website, and is part of the annual international celebration of human rights on December 10 for International Human Rights Day.

In addition to cities such as San Francisco, where the Supervisors and the Mayor passed a resolution supporting the project, Dr. Boyd spoke at an event at the Geneva Conference Center in 2008, and the center is already booked for Human Rights Day in 2009, the third consecutive year.

2048 is also poised to ride the growing wave of departments teaching international rights and global studies, burgeoning fields with enrollments increasing each year. The field of human rights is growing today like the field of environmental law did twenty years ago. The trend will continue.

- School, college, and public libraries will buy the book.

EDITOR'S NOTE

The following books are so well known that just their titles suffice.

Complementary Books

- *An Inconvenient Truth*, Al Gore
- *Lies and the Lying Liars Who Tell Them*, Al Franken
- *Stupid White Men*, Michael Moore
- *1984*, George Orwell

- *The Rights of Man* or *What Are We Fighting For?*, H.G. Wells
- *Rights of Man*, Thomas Paine
- *Of the Social Contract*, Jean-Jacques Rousseau

2048 focuses on timely issues like these books and aspires to be as readable. *1984* became synonymous with the dangers of a police state. Published in 1950, its sales continued to grow as 1984 approached and afterward. So it will be for *2048*. As time passes and participation continues to grow, the logo [the cover art] and the cover will be more recognizable but will symbolize a positive future.

The Author's Platform

The author is the Executive Director of the 2048 Project, a project within the Institute for Global Challenges and the Law at the University of California, Berkeley, School of Law. His position enables him to keep the book in the public eye and accomplish the mission of the book and project:

- Kirk gives more than twenty talks a year at universities, conferences, and nonprofit organizations, as well as at events planned by students, peace groups, and service organizations such as Rotary International.
- He has made more than seventy-five presentations internationally at conferences, lectures, discussion panels, and media events, including radio and television.
- The author has appeared before the Commission on Human Rights and the Human Rights Council for seven of the last eight years, and spoken in Norway, Spain, Russia, Brazil, Serbia, and India.
- The Project is organizing regional and international conferences with the participation of academic, government, and business leaders. The first international conference was held in 2008 and was the first of several international celebrations commemorating the sixtieth anniversary of the Universal Declaration.
- The next international conference will be February 2010 and will be held in Dubai. The Project has been awarded a $200,000 grant by the Dubai Human Rights Association to commission one hundred papers from top scholars, business leaders, and government representatives to revise the Arab Charter on Human Rights and to consider the fit

of the Arab Charter within an International Convention on Human Rights. The papers will be presented at the conference and the author will edit them into a book.

- The law school has launched the project as a "sustained research project." The university has a multiyear commitment to dedicate faculty, student, and financial resources to the project. It's designed to continue for the next forty years, so there will be continuing opportunities for the author to sell the book in the United States and abroad.
- The project is a membership organization. As a premium, new members receive *2048* and a quarterly e-newsletter that will encourage them to forward it to as many people as they can.
- Kirk has more than twenty-one years of teaching and practice. He has built an extensive network including the networks of the codirectors, an advisory board, and drafters, many of whom are renowned in their field and have extensive contacts that they will use to promote the book. The advisory board is a group of scholars, judges, lawyers, and professional people who participate in strategic planning, fundraising, and supervising the drafting of documents. The Board has seventeen members, including a Nobel Laureate.

Here is how the author is building his visibility in 2009: [list of ten significant events]

- The author is also an active member of Rotary International and will continue speaking to Rotary clubs in the United States and abroad.
- The author will mail one hundred copies of the manuscript to authors, politicians, businesspeople, media people, and professors. The cover letter will refer to the recipients' work and explain how their work complements the work of the 2048 Project. The letter will also request that recipients comment on the manuscript. This will create a buzz about the book before publication.

EDITOR'S NOTE

Only a tiny percentage of authors can bring to a plan what Kirk does, but few authors have goals as great as his. The challenge is to align your plan with your goals.

Promotion

To promote the book, the author will:

- Provide a $25,000 promotion budget, which the author asks the publisher to match
- Do talks and media appearances in thirty major markets during the three months after publication and for five years as part of his job. Among the places he will speak are:
  - annually to the United Nations Human Rights Council, Geneva
  - bi-annual conferences at the School of Law and other locations
  - annual World Social Forum and regional meetings at designated locations
  - annual World Economic Forum in Davos, Switzerland
  - five annual State, National, and International Bar Association meetings
  - plenary session every three years for the World Federation of United Nations Associations
- Purchase 5,000 hardcover copies of the book and 10,000 copies of the paperback edition
- Send the hardcovers to:
  - 2,000 teachers, educational, political, and business leaders
  - 500 authors, actors, media hosts, musicians who can incorporate the book's ideas into their work
  - 200 copies to drafters and other supporters
  - 200 copies to individuals and foundations that can help fund the project and *2048*
  - 100 trade and media publications
  - 2,000 members of the project for their membership fee
  - Send the first 2,000 trade paperback copies to additional educators, media people, and participants in the project and to those who justify following up with
  - Distribute 5,000 to people and organizations that become members
  - Distribute the remainder domestically and internationally to bolster participation in the project and lay the groundwork for the next two books

- Purchase 1,000 paperback copies a year for three years to distribute to new members and others
- Use the 2048 Project website for pre- and post-publication sales
- Prepare a press kit for use online and in hard copy
- Send press kits to one hundred media outlets, talk shows, magazines, newspapers, bloggers, and websites interested in stories about *2048*, avoiding duplication of your efforts
- Use the services of two marketing experts to help promote the book
- Blog and use YouTube and Facebook

The book, the website, and the newsletter will note that profits from the book and book sales will go to the project, an incentive for individuals and organizations to buy it for themselves and to give to others.

Spin-offs

The next two books will be:

- *2048: The 1% Solution.* How 1% of humanity, directing 1% of nonprofit resources, can convince world leaders to invest 1% of their GNP on people's needs. Partly written. Completion: 2010.
- *2048: Plan for Humanity.* A compilation of stories that explains the thinking behind the wording of regional conventions and the International Convention by contributors from high-school students to television talk-show hosts and Nobel laureates who have used *2048*. Completion: 2012.

EDITOR'S NOTE
Some of the following information is part of John's platform but is just as impressive in his bio.

About the Author

Dr. John Kirk Boyd:

- Earned three law degrees, including a doctorate, from U.C. Berkeley, Boalt Hall, School of Law

- Was trained as a trial lawyer by one of the top trial attorneys in the United States, Jim Brosnahan, of Morrison & Foerster, San Francisco
- Used this training both at Morrison & Foerster, and as a founding partner of his own law firm, Boyd, Huffman, Williams & Urla, to win large civil-rights and human-rights cases in state and federal courts
- Has argued at every level of court, including the Supreme Court
- Has a wealth of experience in practice and the academic world that gives him insights that few people have into a plan that will work in the courts of all countries. This experience gives him credibility to promote the book in a variety of venues.
- Has worked for state and federal judges and has been on numerous boards and committees, including a committee of judges and lawyers drafting model rules for the federal judiciary, and a working group drafting the Bill of Rights for the Russian Constitution for which he spent three months in Moscow
- Has been an advisor to Constitutional Courts, such as the Supreme Court in Armenia, where he taught Constitutional Law at American University
- Teaches International Human Rights, Civil Rights, International Law, Free Speech, and Constitutional Law at U.C. He enjoys teaching and speaking, and students consistently give him extremely high teaching evaluations.

---------------PAGE BREAK---------------

The Outline
List of Chapters

—————————PAGE BREAK—————————

Part Three

First Steps to 2048

Chapter 9

Regional Agreements Exist

"It works."

—René Cassin, winner of the Nobel Peace Prize for his work in drafting the European Convention

The chapter develops the idea that the agreement is part of an evolutionary process. The beginning of the chapter asserts that the five freedoms (discussed in previous chapters) are not wishful thinking but fundamental principles of law that were embedded in regional human-rights documents.

Then it explains how the European Convention on Human Rights was created to take the first steps toward the enforcement of the Four Freedoms in European courts. Next the chapter discusses how René Cassin (photo), a war hero, lawyer, Jewish leader, and colleague of Eleanor Roosevelt (photo), brought citizens of many countries together to draft the Convention. The last part of the chapter describes its ratification and how well it has worked.

PROPOSAL 4:
ZEN MIND, ZEN HORSE:
THE SPIRITUAL PRINCIPLES THAT HORSES BRING TO LIFE

Why This Book Sold

Allan J. Hamilton, MD wrote the proposal for *The Scalpel and the Soul* that began this section. He also brings a great combination of strengths to this how-to book, including the following:

- A new idea on an old subject
- His experience as a trainer and speaker
- His platform and promotion plan
- His understanding of the markets for the book and how to reach them
- A finished manuscript
- The success of *Scalpel*

Worth noting: *Zen* didn't sell because of the success of *Scalpel*. There is an overlap because of the spirituality in both books, but Allan was once again a new author in a new, comparatively tiny field, writing another kind of book that had to sell on its own merits—as well as on Allan's. Storey Publishing bought *Zen* because of the proposal and because of what Allan brought to the book. Pam Art, the president of Storey, visited Allan's ranch, which helped strengthen the relationship. Note the change in title.

A Proposal for
Zen and the Art of Horse Training:
How Taking a Walk With Your Horse Can Transform the Rest of Your Life
By Allan J. Hamilton, MD
Professor of Neurosurgery, Radiation Oncology, Psychology, &
Computer & Electrical Engineering at The University of Arizona
Owner and Horse Trainer, Rancho Bosque, Tucson, AZ
Author of *The Scalpel and the Soul:*
Encounters With Surgery, the Supernatural, and the Healing Power of Hope—
Winner of a Silver Nautilus Award

Rancho Bosque, LLC
X Y Road

Tucson, AZ 857XX
Phone: (520) XXX-XXXX
Fax: (520) XXX-XXXX
info@ranchobosque.com
www.ranchobosque.com

————————————PAGE BREAK————————————

Table of Contents

————————————PAGE BREAK————————————

EDITOR'S NOTE

Editors love books that offer new wine in a new bottle, a new idea conceptualized in a fresh way. *Zen* has a proven new East-meets-West approach to training horses that transforms the trainer.

Overview

We have evolved into the super-predator species of our planet. *Homo sapiens* has accomplished this feat over several hundred thousand years by relying on dramatic expansions in brain capacity and, in particular, on an ever-increasing specialization of language, tool-making, and cognitive abilities—all functions derived from our dominant, left cerebral hemisphere.

But we have paid a price for this: Our left-brain dominance required the creation of an ego—a separate identity that has cut us off from the music of the universe. Instead, we hear a single voice—the *I* from within with its endless monologue of thoughts echoing inside our heads.

Fortunately, we are blessed with a right hemisphere too. In most of us, it has been largely neglected and many of its functions have been allowed to atrophy. The right side is without speech, without a voice, so it is hard for us to focus on it. But it is also the seat of our higher intuitive, emotional, and holistic functions.

While the left brain developed an exclusive strategy, the right brain has sought to remain inclusive. As individuals, we are dominated by the egocentric perspective of the left-sided *me* and have less access to the alternative, spiritual communion offered by our right-sided *we*. The right side has an innate drive to experience a common connection and unity with all life around us. There is a path to spiritual fulfillment, but we must reawaken our right brains to find it.

While humans honed left-sided hemispheric function, another species developed a right-brain approach. As quintessential prey animals, horses evolved over 50 million years to feel inclusive and protected within the shared identity of their herds. They developed little use for vocalization since it made them more vulnerable to predators. They refined a unique method for enhancing the energy characteristics of their body language to converse efficiently and silently with each other. Horses learned to transmit this energy masterfully through gaze, stance, and gesture and thus became the high priests of emotive, non-verbal, right-brain function.

The universe crackles with vital, purposeful, life-giving energy called *chi*. Based on more than twenty years of experience training scores of horses, *Zen and the Art of Training Horses: How Taking Your Horse for a Walk Can Transform the Rest of Your Life* will be the first book to provide an easy-to-follow program for learning how to master that energy with horses. Any novice can do the techniques, and the book provides a guaranteed approach to raising mindful awareness.

The manuscript is 76,000 words. The author envisions the book as an 8½" × 11" hardcover, illustrated with photos and figures. The author will add a two-page bibliography and an index. He will obtain permissions for illustrations not in the public domain.

People can only know chi by relying on the abilities of the right brain. Chi depends on emotional and intuitive intelligence rather than one that is cognitive or verbal. Consider this: When doing meditation, practitioners close their eyes, focus on their breathing, and repeatedly bring their random, distracting thoughts back to breathing. Why does this spiritual practice follow these steps? Because all of them are aimed at silencing the left hemisphere, so the right brain can allow the mindful connection to occur.

By using the safe, simple groundwork exercises in *Zen*, readers open up neural pathways in the right hemisphere to sense and communicate in energy rather than words.

Gradually, readers develop the innate but dormant capacity to tap into chi and summon it at will. By using the techniques in a systematic way, readers see through their horse's responses how to assemble, focus, and direct chi harmoniously and to use it in their lives. There is no easier way to tap into the power of chi than to work with horses.

Zen is Monty Roberts meets Eckhart Tolle. It's a spiritual guide that introduces an original, innovative system of natural horsemanship. It is filled with new principles and techniques. The exercises teach readers to quiet their inner voice and reinforce the spiritual inclinations of the nonverbal right side of their brain.

Zen is also a book about spiritual practices and techniques drawn from diverse cultures and belief systems. From the science of behavioral psychology to the symbolism of Native American ceremony, from the wisdom of Zen monks to the musings of Texas cowboys, readers gain insight into working with horses from the perspective of time-honored spiritual principles.

When our intention emerges as clear, quiet, penetrating energy, even if only for a fraction of a second, a horse gives us immediate physical feedback. This gives us a way to visualize and hone the nascent spiritual abilities. As those skills grow, we acquire profound spiritual insight and power.

EDITOR'S NOTE

When you have something new to offer, call attention to it.

Special Features

The book's special features include:

- A *new learning model* using the concept of a round pen and a Native American hoop, assigning each cardinal directions and colors as a spiritual training principle:
  - North (black)—empathy
  - East (white)—affirmation

- South (yellow)—intention
- West (red)—pressure and release

Associated with each direction are the four components of awareness:

- the soul: consciousness, awareness, beliefs, and morality
- the mind: reason, analysis, learning, and strategic vision
- the body: discipline, willpower, exercise, and mortality
- the heart: emotion, passion, commitment, and altruism

- A *new, four-step learning paradigm*—the ARDP ladder: Ask, Request, Demand, and Promise
  - The *4 C's of Leadership:* Command, Compassion, Control, and Communication
  - *Original tables* explaining/comparing right and left cerebral hemispheres functions and prey vs. predator characteristics

The manuscript has stories about his experiences:

The first chapter opens with the author's disappearance on his first ride on a horse on his first night at sleep-away camp. The misadventure saved him from one of the most shattering public humiliations of his life. This was the first of many times that a horse transformed his life.

The book then explains why horses appeal to the emotional, intuitive functions located in the right cerebral hemisphere. The foundation of spirituality lies in the right brain because it yearns for a communal identity rather than an individual one. Readers discover the effortless connection between intention and result, between thought and deed. There are stories about:

- How inner-city gang members learn to train wild horses
- Saving a horse found at a slaughterhouse tied up with a bridle made out of barbed wire
- How a horse saves the author's life in a blizzard
- The author being bucked off his horse and breaking his back
- A frightened, wild horse that will die if the author can't give it medical attention
- The author's daughter slipping off her pony with her foot helplessly hung up in the stirrup

- How the author's grandfather's horse was shot out from under him in one of the last cavalry charges of World War I

The book proceeds through the fundamental tasks, including: selecting a horse, grooming, cleaning hooves, leading, teaching a horse to stop, backing up, backing up in a circle, circling on the hindquarters, teaching a horse not to spook, preparing a horse for the farrier and veterinarian, trailering, saddling a horse for the first time, jumping over obstacles, and getting a horse to come to you.

The book illustrates the right-brained and spiritual lessons in the sequence of training tasks, such as:

- Awakening the right brain
- Having the impeccable intention of a fence post
- Experiencing bubbles of awareness
- Learning the four directions of the round pen
- Knowing the 4 Cs of being *otancan* (Sioux term for leader)
- Understanding the paradox of prey vs. predator and left vs. right hemisphere
- Discovering the science of how people learn from reward and how horses learn from release
- Learning the chi of focus and ARDP paradigm
- Developing infinite patience and taking baby steps
- Living in the moment
- Experiencing and using the physical properties of chi
- Facing one's fears
- Searching for success rather than finding failure
- Deepening purity of purpose and integrity of action
- Turning problems upside down to find the answers
- Learning why horses accept us when we are willing to be ourselves

EDITOR'S NOTE

Allan zeros in on the primary market for the book, which is small. Therefore, a large house (for instance, Tarcher, the imprint at Penguin that published *Scalpel* but doesn't do horse books) won't be interested. But Allan does prove that potential readers can and do buy such books, and he shows where to reach them.

Markets

The primary audience for the book is women interested in horses and their training.

- Nearly 4 percent of American households own horses, 4,500,000 horse owners.
- Although the most widely known trainers tend be men, more than 80 percent of the horse market is women.
- Women operate 65 percent of all horse farms.
- According to the USA Equestrian Federation, the median income for horse-owning households is $80,000 to $135,000, and the majority of those owners are female, average age: 39.
- *Equestrian* magazine identifies its readers as being 85 percent women, 66 percent with college degrees, with an average income of $185,000, and spending more than $16,000 per year in equine-related purchases.
- TheHorse.com is a leading website for equine health-care consumers and identifies its audience profile as 87 percent female, with an average income of $70,000, with more than 70 percent having purchased or researched books and/or videos online.

Women outnumber men nearly five to one as:

- Buyers of horse training clinics and seminars, equine-related products and training materials
- Participants in equine-assisted therapy (EAT) and learning (EAL) experiences

Specialty Stores and Outlets

The market is both rural and urban. The countryside dotted with feed stores, and every major city has equestrian and riding-supply stores, both of which carry books. Tucson offers an example of the density of horse-related outlets. The area has a population of more than 500,000 people, and a Google search for "equine supplies" yields almost 700 results.

The Internet has become one of the main resources for purchasing horse books, with such dedicated websites as booksonhorses.com, horsebooks online.com, horsekeeping.com, and horsebooks.com.

Subsidiary Rights

Horseback riding is immensely popular in Europe, Japan, Australia, and New Zealand. Translation sales are likely from Europe, because of its emphasis on groundwork training, and Asia, because of its spiritual practices. The Middle East has a long tradition of literature, both lyric and mystical, about horses, which is a vibrant part of Muslim culture.

Sounds True, a company specializing in the production of popular, spiritually oriented CDs (including authors such as Thomas Merton, Eckhart Tolle, Carolyn Myss, and others) has expressed interest in the book.

The author will produce an instructional DVD.

The Author's Platform

The author has given training and equine-assisted learning clinics around the United States and Europe for more than a decade to hundreds of individuals—from Fortune 500 CEOs to drug addicts, from leaders in government to victims of domestic violence.

The techniques have been tested with every kind of horse, from docile ranch horses to wild mustangs, from thoroughbreds hot off the track to plough horses, and they have always worked. Allan and his wife raise and train Lipizzaner horses, a rare breed of horses with a 450-year lineage that perform at the famous Spanish Riding School in Vienna.

Allan is the author of *The Scalpel and the Soul: Encounters With Surgery, the Supernatural, and the Healing Power of Hope*—Tarcher, 2008; trade paperback, April, 2009—which won a Silver Nautilus Award.

For *Scalpel*, the author:

- Did more than one hundred radio interviews
- Did a dozen TV interviews
- Did X talks. Many of the presentations were to spiritually oriented audiences, and audience members expressed interest in this book.
- Had X magazine articles published
- Built a listserv of more than X,000 readers who receive the author's newsletter and are notified about appearances and interviews
- Set up a monthly article with Boomer Living, a subscriber-based newsletter that focuses on well-being

Allan has also:

- Given more than three hundred public presentations and speeches to lay and professional audiences and is widely sought as a motivational speaker

- Been featured in more than a dozen magazines, including *Western Horseman, Equus,* and *Horse & Rider*
- Had his work televised on *Arizona Illustrated* and the Discovery Channel
- Developed the largest equine-assisted therapy program in the United States to assist youth at risk from the juvenile justice system. More than 300 staff and 4,000 children have gone through it.
- Spoken by invitation at the Irish National Racing Academy and Education Center, and to the Irish Parliament about equine-assisted therapy and learning to help rescue thoroughbred racehorses

    Recent interviews and appearances are available at the author's Website, www.allanhamilton.com. Many of the presentations were to spiritually oriented audiences, and audience members have expressed interest in this book.

EDITOR'S NOTE

Allan's plan shows he knows what he must do to make the book succeed; his platform and experience with *Scalpel* prove he can do it. I sent the proposal to large, small, and midsize houses. And even though small, niche, or midsize houses won't match Allan's budget, his budget is still an expression of his commitment to the book. Editors will understand that the book is a labor of love that Allan wants to be part of his legacy, and that he will promote it.

Promotion

To promote the book, the author will:

- Match the publisher's out-of-pocket consumer promotion budget up to $X0,000 on signing to carry out the campaign
- Hire X for a year to publicize the book in print, broadcast, and electronic media
- Tour the following seven cities: New York, Chicago, Dallas, Denver, Seattle, San Francisco, and Los Angeles
- Sell books at the ten clinics in the United States and Europe he gives a year
- Speak at the six largest equine venues and sell the book: [list]
- Add two equine topics to his listings with four speaker bureaus. The author is recognized as the originator of equine training methods to

promote awareness of nonverbal communication, and his training methods and programs have been adopted in six American universities. He is already receiving invitations to discuss the book's ideas.

- Start an e-newsletter based on the book
- Have his webmaster build a dedicated website once the title is chosen
- Do a blog
- Continue to build an e-mail list

Obtaining a Foreword

The author will approach Monty Roberts to write the foreword. Monty is the best-known living horseman in the world. He is the model for the main character played by Robert Redford in the movie *The Horse Whisperer*, based on the novel by Nicholas Evans. He is the author of *The Man Who Listens to Horses: The Story of a Real-Life Horse Whisperer; Horse Sense for People; From My Hands to Yours: Lessons From a Lifetime of Training Championship Horses*, and *Shy Boy: The Horse That Came In From the Wild*.

The author has visited Monty and his wife Pat at their Flag Is Up Farms in Solvang, California, and have attended two of his seminars. He is one of the most generous, forthright individuals the author has ever met. The author believes Monty will endorse the book after he has read it because it reinforces his original concepts regarding nonverbal communication among horses. The book pays homage to Monty's contributions six times.

Endorsements

The author will try to secure quotes from the following people, some of whom he knows: [list of seventeen well-known horse experts, authors, and movie people]

EDITOR'S NOTE

In retrospect, it's amusing that the publisher of the only competing book bought Allan's book. But then, who would be better able to judge its value? It also testifies to the importance of being able to assess competing books objectively.

A Competing Book

Cherry Hill, *How to Think Like a Horse: The Essential Handbook for Understanding Why Horses Do What They Do* (Storey Publishing, 2006). Reviews the horse's five senses, temperament, and behavioral responses, explains the benefits of understanding how horses think, and relates this to training. Doesn't explain the biological basis for the horse's behaviors, nor does it concentrate on human neurobiological issues, spirituality, or provide a hands-on approach with exercises.

Complementary Books

The top five books on horses on Amazon.com are:

- *Equus* by Tim Flach
- *How to Think Like a Horse: The Essential Handbook for Understanding Why Horses Do What They Do* by Cherry Hill
- *Chosen by a Horse* by Susan Richards
- *The Soul of a Horse: Life Lessons From the Herd* by Joe Camp
- *What Your Horse Wants You to Know: What Horses' "Bad" Behavior Means, and How to Correct It* by Gincy Self Bucklin

These titles suggest how motivated potential readers of *Zen* are to understand how horses think and what they can teach us.

——————————PAGE BREAK——————————

About the Author

Zen came out of both the author's profession as a brain surgeon and his avocation as a horse trainer. As a neurosurgeon, Allan Hamilton, M.D., FACS, can speak about cerebral hemispheric function, development of language, and the ability of the right hemispheric functions to enhance spiritual awareness. As a horse trainer for twenty years, he can discuss the principles of manipulating chi as an integral part of the groundwork training of horses and the spiritual lessons and insights they provide.

Allan graduated from Harvard Medical School and completed his surgical internship and neurosurgical training at the Massachusetts General Hospital in Boston. In 1990, he joined the neurosurgical faculty at the University of Arizona. In 1995, he became the Chief of Neurosurgery and in 1997 became the youngest Chairman of the Department of Surgery ever.

During this time, the author was recognized for his research into the design and application of computerized guidance systems in neurosurgery and new methods for systemic administration of chemotherapy. Among the honors and awards the author received are:

- The Bernard J. Cosman Award by the American Society for Stereotactic and Functional Neurosurgery
- The Lars Leksell Prize from the European Society of Neurosurgery for pioneering innovation in the field of neurosurgery. He is the only American to receive this award.
- Selection by his peers as "One of America's Best Doctors" for the last twelve consecutive years
- Professorships in Neurosurgery, Radiation Oncology, Psychology, and Electrical and Computer Engineering

The author has:
- Written more than twenty textbook chapters and more than fifty peer-reviewed medical articles
- Served as medical script consultant to the TV series *Grey's Anatomy* and occasionally consults the spin-off series, *Private Practice*
- Has been featured in articles in the *Journal of Alternative and Complementary Therapy*, and the *British Medical Journal*

─────────────PAGE BREAK─────────────

EDITOR'S NOTE

Allan had already written another book, taught horse techniques for more than a decade, and finished the horse manuscript, so he just wrote an annotated list of chapters. The sample chapters proved Allan could write the book. The how-to chapter showed how he would integrate illustrations, which he would pay for, and gave a sense of how many illustrations the book would have.

The Outline

Introduction: Half Chi, Half DNA

Chapter 1: Days of Thunder
Tells the story of how at age eleven, without knowing how to ride, the author disappeared on horseback on his first night at sleepaway camp, the first of many transformational experiences with horses and an adventure that saved him from what might have been a shattering public humiliation.

Chapter 2: The Two Sides of Me
- Presents a theory about why the verbal, fluent, left hemisphere of the human brain separates us from the world.
- Describes how this creates our individual identity, while the right side, which longs to tell us about the potential for unity with the universe, remains mute.

Chapter 3: Chi and Equus
Introduces the concepts of chi, yin and yang, vital energy, and the evolution of equine nonverbal communication.

Chapter 4: Grooming: Part I
Describes grooming and the opportunities for self-discovery.

Chapter 5: Searching for Chi

- Explains how readers can demonstrate chi for themselves.
- Shows how the brain concentrates chi, focuses attention, and translates chi into action.

Chapter 6: Grooming: Part II
Reviews how to care for a horse's health and appearance and how that translates into the sense of service and devotion.

Chapter 7: The Magic Dog
- Offers Native American folklore about horses.

- Describes the key concepts of the sacred Round Pen, the Four Cardinal Directions, and their links to the four key values of empathy, learning, intention, and wisdom.
- Introduces the four Cs, the qualities every horse looks for in its leader: Command, Compassion, Control, and Communication.

Chapter 8: Natural Horsemanship: A Hemispheric History
Covers the evolution of horsemanship from ancient times to now, showing its roots in the European tradition of dressage and the Mexican tradition of the cowboy, the *vaquero*.

Chapter 9: Prey, Predator, and the Psychology of Learning
- Compares the similarities between right/left cerebral hemisphere function and prey/predator qualities.
- Introduces the key concepts of training and learning.

Chapter 10: Patience
Tells the story of a gelding who refused to climb into a trailer and then violently attacked his caretakers. As his owners were preparing to shoot him, the author showed up and promised the couple he could get the horse into a trailer if he was given a year to coach the reluctant horse.

Chapter 11: Leading the Way
- Provides a hierarchical approach to training—Ask, Request, Demand, and Promise—and applies it to leading a horse.
- Gives instructions in steps that are used throughout the book. They reinforce the need for us to clear our mind of agendas and clarify our intentions. Includes the story of how the author put his own needs before the needs of my horse and how this led to a terrible accident in front of the press.

Chapter 12: Now and the Ocean Liner
- Describes the difficulty of focusing on the present and shows why working with a horse teaches us to dwell in the here and now.
- Explains how to recognize and practice being present and how to contain ourselves in the moment. Intention becomes inherently self-fulfilling and virtually effortless.

Chapter 13: Tiny Bubbles of Chi

- Describes how trainers can summon, move, and direct chi around a horse to get it to move forward, backward, and in a circle, which leads to a new level of skill in manipulating chi.
- Compares a prey animal to a predator in energy conservation and how that can be used to effortlessly bring a horse back into proper leading position.
- Tells the story of the author's grandfather as a cavalry officer during World War I and his profound partnership with horses, and the tragedy of losing horses on the battlefield.

Chapter 14: Picking Up the Pace
- Demonstrates more about the properties of chi. Shows how to use these qualities to ask a horse to walk and jog alongside.
- Discusses the elasticity of chi and how to harness it at different gaits.
- Explains the need to become a source of abundant praise, to reward the behaviors we seek rather than punish the ones we don't.

Chapter 15: Whoa! and Quit It!
- Describes how to use chi to train the horse to stop, change directions, lead over poles, and walk on a platform.
- Shows how to let the horse's prey nature transform trainers, helping them to leave their predatory nature behind and think and feel like a horse.
- Includes a personal story about a dangerous spook when a horse suddenly encounters a blue heron standing in the middle of a bridle path.

Chapter 16: Sending Out and Backing Up
- Teaches how to focus chi through training aids such as a wand or lariat.
- Explains how to channel intense chi or completely drain it out at will, which illustrates the ability to energize a situation or drain its intensity.
- Expands on how to enhance the energetic quality of chi, even to potentially dangerous levels.

Chapter 17: The Farrier and the Vet
- Describes using the principles of baby steps and chi techniques to get a horse prepared for visits from the veterinarian and the farrier, and how to defuse tense situations.
- Discusses parallels with visits to the hospital.

- Includes a story about a dangerous horse that came to understand mercy and how that changed the lives of the horse and the author.

Chapter 18: Side Passing and Jumping
Shows how to use elegant levels of chi to teach a horse to:
- side pass
- jump
- move in a figure-of-eight
- harness powerful concentrations of chi before launching over a jump
- evoke a ballet-like finesse when horses and handlers learn how to weave in and out of barrels

Chapter 19: Come to Me
Tells how to create an island of peace and tranquillity in which the horse will want to join the trainer.

Chapter 20: From Sack to Saddle
- Demonstrates using the sacking process to prepare a horse to cinch and saddle safely.
- Tells about a woman whose horse had struck out at her after refusing to let her bridle it and how the author learned why and cured the problem with molasses.
- Describes the author going on a trail ride with his daughter when her saddle slipped under her pony's belly. The frightened pony was ready to bolt when the author noticed his daughter's foot stuck in the stirrup and the horse's hooves next to her head.

Chapter 21: A Leg Up
- Builds on the sacking out process to the conclusion of saddling and riding a horse. Shows the moment of transformation in the relationship between predator and prey. All the groundwork in the book has led to this point, and this is where the book pauses, before developing the issues of riding.
- Discusses the purity of purpose that comes from dwelling on the ground, eyeball to eyeball, with a horse, and why it takes 1,000 hours to go beyond being a novice rider.

Chapter 22: Stopping and Spooking

- Demonstrates using chi to teach a horse to stop.
- Differentiates between casual and emergency stops.
- Explains spooking safely in place.
- Describes losing our predatory nature to approach fear and panic from an empathetic, patient perspective.
- Shows how teaching a horse to face its fears helps us learn to face our own.

Chapter 23: Trailering

Tackles a difficult problem by taking a Zen-like approach. Instead of being intent on getting the horse into the trailer, it advises focusing on asking the horse to *leave* the trailer. The chapter uses this example to suggest that readers can often tackle life's problems by turning them upside down.

Chapter 24: A Word About Gender and Buying Horses
- Analyzes how to overcome biases.
- Shows how prejudices against stallions can turn them into rogue horses.
- Tells the story of a stallion whose intractable will led to him being tied up in a slaughterhouse with a bridle made of barbed wire and how this horse was physically and emotionally rehabilitated.

Epilogue
- Why owners and trainers owe horses a spiritual debt that can never be repaid.
- Why humans lie and horses never do.
- How we waste a huge amount of energy by maintaining a role for others.
- What horses can teach us about self-acceptance and about our connection with nature.

Appendix

Offers ten exercises readers can do with horses to expand their spiritual awareness

Sample Chapters
- Introduction
- Chapter 11: Leading the Way

Chapter 11 includes examples of figures and photos to show how the author will use illustrations.

ABOUT THE AUTHOR

Michael Larsen worked for Bantam, William Morrow and Pyramid (now part of Berkeley). He and his wife, Elizabeth Pomada, started Larsen-Pomada Literary Agents in San Francisco in 1972. They are founding members of the Association of Authors' Representatives and have sold books to more than one hundred publishers.

Mike is eager to find adult nonfiction of interest to big and midsize houses. Elizabeth handles adult fiction, narrative nonfiction, and books for women. Their colleague, Laurie McLean, represents genre fiction and middle-grade and young-adult books.

Mike wrote *How to Get a Literary Agent*. With Jay Conrad Levinson, Rick Frishman, and David Hancock, he is co-author of the second edition of *Guerrilla Marketing for Writers: 100 No-Cost, Low-Cost Weapons for Selling Your Work*.

He also wrote *The Worry Bead Book: A Guide to the World's Oldest and Simplest Way to Beat Stress* and *How to Write With a Collaborator* with Hal Zina Bennett. In 1972, Michael and Elizabeth created the media directory *California Publicity Outlets*.

They also coauthored the six books in the *Painted Ladies* series: *Painted Ladies: San Francisco's Resplendent Victorians, Daughters of Painted Ladies: America's Resplendent Victorians* (chosen by *Publishers Weekly* as one of the best books of 1987), *The Painted Ladies Guide to Victorian California, How to Create Your Own Painted Lady: A Comprehensive Guide to Beautifying Your Victorian Home, The Painted Ladies Revisited: San Francisco's Resplendent Victorians Inside and Out,* and *America's Painted Ladies: The Ultimate Celebration of Our Victorians*.

Mike and Elizabeth give talks on writing, agenting, proposals, and publishing for groups and conferences.

Mike also started Larsen Literary Consulting for nonfiction writers. He consults with writers about their books, proposals, and careers. He and Elizabeth are codirectors of the San Francisco Writers Conference, which takes place on Presidents' Day weekend in February (www.sfwriters.org).

You can reach the agency at www.larsenpomada.com, (415) 673-0939, or at 1029 Jones St., San Francisco, California 94109.

Index